Active Learning in the Digital Age Classroom

Active Learning in the Digital Age Classroom

Ann Heide   Dale Henderson

Contributing Author
Lisa Neale

HEINEMANN
Portsmouth, NH

Published in the United States by
Heinemann
A division of Reed Elsevier Inc.
361 Hanover Street
Portsmouth, NH 03801–3912
www.heinemann.com
Offices and agents throughout the world

© 2001 Trifolium Books Inc.
Published by Arrangement with Trifolium Books Inc., Toronto, Canada
(First Edition published under the title The Technological Classroom: A Blueprint for Success, ©1994 Trifolium Books Inc.)

Special Note: This resource has been reviewed for bias and stereotyping.

Library of Congress Cataloging-in-Publication Data

Heide, Ann, 1948–
Active learning in the digital age classroom / Ann Heide and Dale Henderson.
    p.cm.
Rev. ed. of: The technological classroom. ©1994.
Includes bibliographical references and index.
ISBN 0-325-00392-0
1. Computer-assisted instruction. 2. Internet in education. 3. Active Learning.
I. Henderson, Dale, 1948– II. Title.

LB1028.5 .H355 1994
371.33'4—dc21   2001039405

Project Editor: Wendy Thomas
Indexer: Wendy Scavuzzo
Design, layout, graphics: Beth Crane, Heidy Lawrance Associates
Cartoons and artwork: Larry Stewart, James Fairbairn
Project coordinator: Jim Rogerson
Production coordinator: Heidy Lawrance Associates
Cover design: Fizzz Design Inc.

    05   04   03   02   01   1   2   3   4   5

Printed and bound in Canada

This book's text stock contains more than 50% recycled paper.

The activities recommended in this book have been tested and are safe when carried out as suggested. The publishers can accept no responsibility for any damage caused or sustained by use or misuse of ideas or materials mentioned in this book.

Permissions:
The authors and publisher would like to thank the following for granting permission for use of their material: Apple Canada (Figs. 4-10, 4-11, 4-26, 4-31, 4-32, 9-2, 9-9), Screen shots reprinted by permission from Apple Canada, Inc.; Corel Corporation Limited (Figs. 4-8, 4-17, 4-18, 4-27, 4-28), Screen shots from WordPerfect 9, Quattro Pro 9 are Copyright 1999 Corel Corporation Limited, reprinted by permission. Screen shots from CorelDRAW 8 are Copyright 1997 Corel Corporation Limited, reprinted by permission; NECTAR (Figs. 4-3, 7-4, 7-5, 7-7); Ottawa-Carleton Catholic School Board (Fig. 7-1); Eastern Ontario Catholic Curriculum Cooperative (EOCCC) (Figs. 7-3, 7-6, 7-11, 7-12). Ontario Curriculum Planner (Fig. 9-1), ©Queen's Printer for Ontario, 2001. Reproduced with permission.

TABLE OF CONTENTS

Using the *Active Learning in the Digital Age Classroom* Web site

The *Active Learning in the Digital Age Classroom* Web site, located at **www.heinemann.com**, is designed to complement and enhance your reading. Wherever you see **www** in this book, you will know that there are one or more Web links on the *Active Learning in the Digital Age Classroom* Web site that relate to the topic about which you are reading. For ease of reference, these are organized by **chapter**. This Web site also contains a **photo gallery** which offers a range of images, showing Information and Communication Technologies (ICT) at work in the classroom.

You may wish to visit the Web site following your reading of each chapter in *Active Learning in the Digital Age Classroom*, or may prefer to have your computer nearby to enable you to refer to sites and photos of interest as you get to the **www** in the text. We have not included a **Glossary of Technical Terms** in this book because there are many excellent glossaries available on-line. We encourage you to access one of these on-line glossaries by following the links found at the *Active Learning in the Digital Age Classroom* Web site.

As we all know, Web site addresses change often. The *Active Learning in the Digital Age Classroom* Web site enables us to provide Web links which are current, up-to-date and accurate. While we have retained some Web site addresses which we think are likely to remain stable in the book itself, the majority of the recommended Web links are included in the *Active Learning in the Digital Age Classroom* Web site. These will be reviewed and updated regularly to include the latest available Web-based resources on the use of ICT in education.

Acknowledgments

We offer our sincere thanks to all those who have contributed to the development of this project.
- Jim Rogerson for encouraging us to write this book and keeping us on track;
- Dawn Vincent for efficiently handling the comings and goings of paper, e-mail and Web site files;
- Wendy Thomas for her attention to detail and expert advice;
- Larry Stewart, artist, and Paul Telfer, photographer, for work that stands the test of time;
- Ann Marie Hill, Ph.D. (Queen's University), Douglas McDougall, Ph.D. (University of Toronto), Cheryl Prokopanko (Manitoba Education & Training), and David B. Zandvliet, Ph.D. (Simon Fraser University) for their insightful and valuable feedback on this project at manuscript stage;
- Our many colleagues at home and around the world, who not only do amazing work with ICT in their schools and classrooms but also share their discoveries and stories;
- The teacher candidates at the University of Ottawa who inspired, challenged and contributed their excellent work and ideas to this endeavor.

Ann Heide and Dale Henderson

INTRODUCTION

A hum of activity fills the room. In one corner, students are gathered around a TV, engrossed in a video about the rain forest. Nearby, two partners are using a video camera to produce a news broadcast about a local environmental issue. At a bank of computers against the wall, pairs of students are obviously deeply involved in their tasks. A closer look reveals that each team is doing something different: setting up a simulated ecosystem on a remote island, using a graphics program to design an emission-free car, writing a poem about the environment, building a database of endangered species, researching the causes of acid rain using an encyclopedia stored on CD-ROM, and assembling a multimedia presentation related to the environmental theme. It's hard to find the teacher at first, but there she is, working with another small group of students who are involved in researching information on the Internet. Once they are settled, she moves on to check the progress of the two other students who are building a water filter in a different area of the classroom.

The scene we have described above is what you might see if you peeked into today's digital age classroom, where engaged learners are engrossed in active learning using information and communication technology. Active learning isn't a new idea. It goes back at least as far as Socrates and was a major emphasis among progressive educators such as John Dewey early in the 1900s. Active learning involves putting our students in dynamic situations in which they read, view, listen, think deeply, and communicate. Active learning places significant responsibility for learning in the hands of the learners themselves. Active learning in the digital age classroom involves harnessing the power of information and communication technology to enable and enhance active learning.

This brief glance into the digital age classroom may raise more questions than it answers. We hope this book will provide the answers to *your* questions about using information and communication technology for active learning in the classroom. In it, we examine the theoretical and practical issues surrounding today's technology-integrated classroom. It is based on our experience in designing and implementing technology-integrated curriculum. A number of assumptions underlie the philosophy we present in this book.

- The term *technology* in this book refers primarily to information and communication technology (ICT); however, we also include references to older electronic equipment (such as TVs, VCRs) still useful as educational technologies.
- Each kind of technology has specific strengths that need to be recognized and capitalized on.
- ICT and educational technologies should be viewed as tools to assist in the acquisition of knowledge and development of skills rather than as an end in itself.
- ICT and educational technologies can improve student learning, particularly in the areas of accessing information, problem solving, and communicating, and they can assist in preparing students for the labor force.
- The use of ICT and educational technologies must be integrated into the curriculum and day-to-day experiences of the student and teacher.
- For significant change to occur and continue, educators should understand the change process involved in transforming to a technology-integrated classroom and be provided with ongoing support throughout this process.

Whenever we as teachers undertake a change in curriculum delivery or in teaching methods and styles, it is not a decision we take lightly. Being aware that the progress of our students is at stake, we can be reluctant to proceed until all our questions are answered. We feel the need to be sure the transition will be smooth and that every student will benefit. So it is that this book addresses the many practical issues that accompany the use of information and communication technology in the classroom. Our goal is to include topics about which we are most frequently asked.

- How do I get started?
- What equipment do I need?
- Where will I put this equipment?
- How can I arrange my classroom to facilitate student use of the technology?
- Are there safety factors that I should consider?
- How do I set up and control workstations?
- How do I teach students to use the hardware and software?
- How can I ensure that my students take proper care of the equipment?
- How can ICT and educational technologies make my classroom more student-centered?
- How can ICT and educational technologies help me to individualize my program?

- Where do outcomes-based learning and cooperative learning fit in?
- What about assessment and evaluation in this setting?
- What should I say to parents?
- In what ways can ICT and educational technologies assist students with special needs?
- Should I change the way in which my timetable is organized?
- How can I arrange equal accessibility to the technology for all students in my class?
- What is the role of the teacher in this environment?
- In what ways can ICT and educational technologies make me more efficient in my job?
- How can I get others involved?

Because we believe that good classroom practices derive from carefully researched theories, we provide practical strategies based on both research and experience. We hope you will use some of the ideas in this book to develop your own philosophy and unique, personal approach to the integration of ICT, educational technologies, and learning. We cannot provide a resource to suit the needs of all grades in all subject areas, but we can provide a sample of possibilities based on things that have worked for others and for us. The practical suggestions are intended to be motivators and thought-provoking starting points you can adapt and modify to suit your own situation, your needs, and your students' needs. Whether you are new to ICT and educational technologies, simply interested in change, or reconsidering the current use of ICT and educational technologies in your classroom, we hope our ideas are helpful. Above all else, we hope that the addition of ICT and educational technologies to your classroom will be an exciting and enriching experience for you and your students!

WHY INTEGRATE TECHNOLOGY INTO THE CLASSROOM?

one

Technology can be used to enhance instruction and expand the limits of the existing curriculum. As an information tool, it can be used to obtain, organize, manipulate, and communicate knowledge and information. It can help to address the range of differing learning styles and the different modalities of individual learning strengths. By tapping into its power, students can expand their access to the world around them.[1]

What is the technology-integrated classroom? The technology-integrated classroom is a setting that uses tools such as computer-assisted learning, electronic access to information, multimedia applications, audiovisual aids, and distance learning to create a superior learning environment. It is information-rich, student-centered, and active. It is a classroom in which the variety of technology helps students acquire academic, social, and technological concepts and skills. The classroom is more than simply the use of computer hardware and software within a traditional setting. In the technology-integrated classroom, technologies are integrated with the best pedagogy in order to empower students and teachers to move toward a new vision of teaching and learning.

Why is technology in education important? What can we learn from research and past experience? What is the business community telling us about their employee requirements? What lies ahead? This first chapter will help you to develop a personal rationale for the integration of technology into the school curriculum. We believe that there are a number of important reasons for adopting the model of the technology-integrated classroom:

- Our students live in a world of technology.
- New technologies can enrich and expand learning, increase the productivity of teachers and students, and enhance their lives beyond the classroom.
- Research continually provides us with new information on how we learn and how technology can be of assistance in the teaching/learning process.
- There is an ever-widening diversity of student needs in every classroom and these students have different learning preferences.
- The workplace demands a new repertoire of skills and competencies.

Our Changing World

Technology continues to transform our world. As educators, one of our responsibilities is to prepare our children for a world that may be quite different than today's. In "Technological Trends," Willard Daggett, president of the International Center for Leadership in Education, encourages us to prepare "students to solve real-world unpredictable situations and problems."[2] He refers to the many future technologies that will be part of our students' lives so that we may see the importance of preparing them for their future.

- Internet 2: It was created in 1997. It consists of a high-speed, high-performance, high-bandwidth network called Abilene. Users can send all volumes of the Encyclopedia Britannica in less than one second.[3]
- Tele-immersion: It is like virtual reality. By entering a telecubicle, you can interact with anyone who also has access to a telecubicle. Kathy Foley in "Internet 2: The Sequel" writes of a business meeting between individuals in Paris and colleagues in Hong Kong. The business people in Hong Kong will see individuals from Paris in 3-D, walking around the office and touching things. They would shake hands and actually feel it.[4]
- Teleneurosurgery: Researchers are working on teleneurosurgery, which would allow a brain surgeon who could be in New York to operate on a patient who might be in Cairo.[5]
- Wireless access devices: These devices will allow Web services and information to become an integral part of our day-to-day lives.[6]

Today's students live in a technological environment. During the last few years we have seen the linking of computers through the Internet, and as a result there has been a significant role for the Internet in commerce, entertainment, and education. The World Wide Web gives students and teachers almost limitless access to knowledge and information produced by other teachers and students. Schools can link with businesses, community members, and government agencies. As a result of their Internet linkages, students can use the information gleaned to create reports, conduct research, analyze data, and present information to a broad audience. It is an important part of the student's experience.

> **"I**n a survey released in the spring of 1999, the [U.S.] Department of Education's National Center for Educational Statistics announced that 51% of the nation's 2.4 million public school classrooms had Internet connections as of last fall. In 1997, that figure was 27%, up from only 3% of classrooms in 1994."[7]

The power of technology is doubling every few years for the same cost, notes Christopher Dede, director of the Center for Interactive Education.[8] Our students may be taking their courses on-line and never set foot on campus until graduation. Not only are schools incorporating technology, but there are schools that exist only on-line. Established universities now offer courses on-line and these courses are being readily accepted in the workplace.[9]

> **"T**he student's toolbox of ten years ago, consisting as it did of pens, pencils, geometry sets and calculators, was easy to comprehend. The new tools, consisting of complex machines and vast computer programs, are far more complicated."[10]

Learning about the highly technological environment in which we live is critical to today's students. They will need to function comfortably in it and make intelligent decisions about the relationships among humans, technology, and the natural environment. In our society, important decision-making positions are held and will continue to be held by those who have developed the skills of obtaining, evaluating, and generating information. Parents and society expect educational institutions to prepare students for the world in which they will live. Although we cannot be certain about the exact nature of their adult world, we can predict that technology will continue to play a central role. Our students already live in a world of technology; our education system must now reflect their world and adequately prepare them for this reality.

> **"I**nformation technology is becoming essential to teachers' continued ability to do their jobs well, and to students' future success in a world where computer literacy is becoming as universal and essential as print literacy."[11]

Enriched Learning and Increased Productivity

"In the old order, the classroom depended heavily on textbooks, printed 'pre-digested' documents that are reviewed by adoption committees and then served as the main classroom tool for years until they are replaced. In the future, single mega-sources like textbooks will fade in influence as learners scan vast electronic resources to find the information they need."[12]

In previous years, the pen, pencil and textbook were the student's tools, and learning meant memorization demonstrated by performance on tests. Today, new technologies help teachers to respond to different learning styles of students and to develop new attitudes toward teaching and learning. Technology has the potential to help the teacher address other skills such as perseverance, collaboration, responsibility, confidence, and willingness to complete a task. We want our students to learn how to acquire information where and when they need it and to develop both their cognitive and communication skills. Information technologies can help students access information quickly, assist in the analysis and organization of data, and provide the ability to communicate with others. A learning environment enriched with information technology does more than provide the essential academic knowledge and skills.

Existing technologies can also play an important role in promoting authentic learning. Students' capacity to do research is greatly enhanced when they search beyond their classroom and local library. Teachers can expect that student research will be more current and more thorough. No longer is there an excuse for relying on out-dated material.[13]

Collaborative learning has also taken on a new perspective as students communicate with peers within their own communities and in other countries. In National Geographic's "Kids Network," students at different schools collect scientific data on problems such as acid rain.[14] Not only may there be communication between students, but telecommunications opens the door to "cross-age" communication between students and experts on a variety of subject matter.[15] Classroom work can be linked to current science events such as tracking the daily progress of a mountain climbing team. This type of activity brings authenticity to students' assignments by making connections between their work and the world outside the classroom. In a recent study conducted by The Center for Applied Special Technology, students attained higher scores in the areas of information management, communication, and presentation of ideas for experimental groups with on-line access than for control groups with no access to on-line learning resources.[16]

When computers were first introduced into the classroom, they were used primarily for drill and practice. Teachers frequently used access to computers as a reward or for enrichment. However, we know that students learn interactively, and educational technology integrated into the curriculum can enhance student learning.

The application of educational technologies now includes the use of complex multimedia products. Multimedia products on videodisc and CD-ROM bring images from the world into the classroom. Students can take a virtual tour of a national art gallery or visit a world-famous museum. Using multimedia reduces dependency on print resources. In addition, students' involvement with multimedia can result in their growth in a number of areas. In a study conducted at Jamul Primary School in California, where students were involved in a multimedia project, it was found that student motivation and self-esteem were high because of the small group interaction and the unlimited access to technology tools.[17] An increase in parents' participation and having an audience for student work were also important aspects in building motivation to communicate effectively.[18]

Initially, a technology-enriched learning environment was considered one in which technology was layered on top of an existing, traditional approach to learning. This approach to implementing technology led to little change in teaching and learning. We now know that to truly have a long-term effect, technology must be integrated into the teaching and learning experiences of the classroom.[19] In the technology-integrated classroom, technology is used to introduce, reinforce, supplement, and extend skills and to encourage students to produce and publish. The introduction of the technology-integrated classroom involves more than setting up the equipment. It often means that the teacher will need to adopt different strategies and assume a different role, moving from the teacher in control to the teacher as facilitator and coach.

It is generally agreed that technology can help create rich learning environments, for the motivational appeal of working with technology adds to both skill development and positive attitudes toward learning. Technology can increase the productivity of teachers and students through the effective use of word-processing and publishing tools, electronic and voice mail, authoring systems to create multimedia learning materials, and through access to information from the Internet and CD-ROM databases. Information and communication technology and the great variety of technology available today have the potential to change education as we know it.

> **"The** new technologies allow students to have more control over their own learning, to think analytically and critically and to work collaboratively."[20]

The Learner

We have a great diversity of students in our classrooms today, each with specific needs to be met. The individuality of students is reflected in their learning approaches. These learning approaches, or modalities, are the channels through which individuals receive and connect information to their existing knowledge base. Teaching to auditory, visual, and kinesthetic modality strengths can be an effective way to reach this diversity of students. Teachers can also plan the teaching of important skills and concepts considering Gardiner's intelligences.[21] The Florida Diagnostic and Learning Resources System/TECH and FDLRS/East linked specific software to Gardiner's Types of Intelligence, as summarized in the chart at the top of page 10.[22]

Generally, teachers need to select information and communication technologies that offer a variety of approaches through which students will have the chance to learn important educational skills and concepts while cultivating their multiple intelligences.

> **"When** educators allow students to interact with technologies in meaningful ways for significant periods of time, the growth that follows will encourage educators to try new things."[23]

Gardiner's Intelligence	Types of software
linguistic	word processors, crossword puzzle generators, word games programs, and prompted writing programs
logical-mathematical	database and spreadsheet programs, problem-solving and computer-programming software
spatial	paint-and-draw programs, hypermedia, and reading programs that use visual clues
musical	software that combines stories with songs, programs that use music as a reward, and music creation programs
bodily-kinesthetic	instructional games, software requiring alternative input devices, science and math programs with manipulatives and/or probes
interpersonal	group games, on-line tours, on-line communication, and programs that address social issues
intrapersonal	tutorial software, self-paced programs, and instructional games in which the computer is the opponent

The integration of technology into the daily learning experiences of the student leads to a student-centered approach in which students assume responsibility for their own learning. A number of studies have reported the many benefits to students who use technology. Reports from the Apple Classrooms of Tomorrow show that students who have regular access to technology
- explore and represent information dynamically and in many forms;
- become socially aware and more confident;
- communicate effectively about complex processes;
- become independent learners and self-starters;
- work well collaboratively;
- know their areas of expertise and share expertise spontaneously; and
- use technology routinely and appropriately.[24]

The benefits, however, do not end here. In a summary of the effects of computer-assisted instruction, Bialo and Sivin-Kach[25] reported that students felt computer-assisted instruction was valuable. They found that students felt more successful, were more motivated to learn, and had increased self-confidence and self-esteem.

"Modern technological tools allow educators to fulfill age-old dreams. We can individualize instruction. We can create simulations through which students discover important relationships**

and construct new knowledge. We can even put the reins into the hands of the students and watch as these tools take them to destinations they envision."[26]

The Workplace

"**T**o rekindle old debates about dropping the standards of the past misses the point. Educators debated the demise of writing when the fountain pen was replaced by the ball-point pen and the loss of mathematical skills when electronic calculators appeared. The world will not linger in the past in matters of employment skills. We must prepare our students to work in their future not our past."[27]

Preparing students for the workplace used to mean ensuring that there was a solid foundation in academic and social skills. Today, the workplace demands not only the basic skills of reading, writing, and computation but also basic technology literacy skills, the ability to work in a team, communication skills, and higher order thinking skills such as problem solving, and synthesis and analysis of information.

In studies conducted by the Canadian Corporate Council on Education, employers in both large and small businesses stated that they were looking for academic skills, personal management skills, and teamwork skills.[28] Similarly, in the U.S. Secretary's Commission on Achieving Necessary Skills (SCANS), a specific set of foundation skills and competencies was viewed as essential in the modern world. Competent individuals in the high-performance workplace were seen as needing
- basic skills — reading, writing, arithmetic, speaking, and listening;
- thinking skills — the ability to learn, to reason, to think creatively, to make decisions, and to solve problems; and
- personal qualities — individual responsibility, self-esteem and self-management, sociability, and integrity.

Effective individuals would productively use
- resources — they would know how to allocate time, money, materials, space, and staff;
- interpersonal skills — they would be able to work on teams, teach others, serve customers, lead, negotiate, and work well with people from culturally diverse backgrounds;
- information — they would understand social, organizational, and technological systems; they would be able to monitor and correct performance, and they would be able to design or improve systems;
- technology — they would select equipment and tools, apply technology to specific tasks, and use computers to process information.[29]

Both reports viewed the workplace as requiring multi-skilled workers and creative, collaborative team members who would be empowered to be decision-makers.

How can technology prepare students for the workplace? The Leader's Guide to Education Technology points to four possible ways.[30]

1. Technology helps students develop basic skills. "One way of looking at the new workplace is to understand that six out of every ten workers today can be considered, as the 1997 STAR Report notes, 'knowledge workers' — those whose primary job responsibilities are focused on creating, organizing, and communicating information." Workers need to be able to acquire information, evaluate, organize, maintain, interpret, and communicate information. As students engage in project-based, student-centered learning they apply these skills, work in groups, communicate ideas, defend their position, and convince and persuade others.
2. Technology use in schools simulates today's workplace. This can be accomplished by applying technology to authentic learning tasks.
3. Technology, by its very nature, is motivating. When technology is part of learning, students see the connection to the real world. "To be effective, technology cannot exist in a vacuum, but must become part of the whole educational environment."[31]
4. Technology is part of co-op placements, school-to-career programs, or internships that benefit both the student and the employer.

Why is business so interested in the nature of education? Profit and the nation's commercial advantage are strongly linked to how well the education system manages technology and innovation. The same technology that has produced such a change in the workplace has the potential to revolutionize education.

> "**B**usinesses are demanding from public schools what they call a 20th century technology-literate student." Terry Crane, the president of Josten Learning Corp.[32]

Past Experience

What have our past experiences and observations taught us? The success record of innovations in education is still not encouraging; in fact, the way most teachers teach has changed little since the days of the one-room schoolhouse. We tend to teach as we were taught or we adopt the teaching methodology of the teachers around us. Teachers still spend a significant part of each day lecturing, and the students are still viewed as one group rather than as individual learners requiring personalized programs. Emphasis is still on rote learning, following instructions, and performing routine tasks.

However, there is hope. Currently, student-centered and constructivist theories predominate in educational literature. There are many pockets of innovation and change, led by teachers who resist conformity to traditional practices and see the benefits of a constructivist environment that integrates technology. These teachers see their role as facilitating learning by helping students to access, interpret, organize, and transfer information in order to solve authentic problems. They require mentors, training, and support within their school environment in order to continue their work.

"**Y**ou're not going to get a technology-literate student if you don't have a technology-literate teacher." Terry Crane, president of Josten Learning Corp. and co-chair of the CEO Forum on Education and Technology[33]

Our understanding of technology has grown over the years. We now view it as a tool that not only has its own set of skills but also provides the means to develop and enhance subject-specific curriculum knowledge and skills. Our past experiences have taught us a number of things about the use of technology in the classroom. We know computers can improve education but not without planning on the part of the school system, and its principals and teachers.[34] On November 17, 1997, the *Wall Street Journal* outlined some specific lessons we had learned up to that time.

1. Computer labs are lousy locations for computers.
2. Struggling students often get more out of computers than average or above-average performers.
3. Most teachers still don't know how to use computers in class.
4. School systems must plan their computer use carefully.
5. Kids flourish when everyone has a computer but schools aren't spending enough to guarantee that.
6. Schools can't handle hand-me-downs.
7. Computers don't diminish traditional skills.
8. The Internet and e-mail excite kids by giving them an audience.
9. Kids love computers.[35]

Educators need to review the validity of the above statements in light of their educational experience and research.

"**T**he lab concept was to introduce kids to computers. We've come to understand that you don't want to introduce kids to computers. You want them to use computers." Linda Roberts, director of the U.S. Department of Education's Office of Educational Technology[36]

Future Trends

"**I** envision — as competitive necessity — the United States becoming one big school 'room.'" Stan Davis, one of America's most original management thinkers, says, "We should think about education as K–80, not K–12. School for life. Anywhere, Anyplace, Anytime, Any subject."[37]

Technology has the potential to change the face of education. Currently it is changing the role of the student and the teacher, the culture of education, and the relationship between business, education, and government. The future will include greater collaboration between business, government, and education. This is discussed in more detail in Chapter 2: Planning for Success.

The use of technology in the day-to-day life of the student will continue to grow. Students of the future will be learning in a technology-rich environment that is collaborative and knowledge building. We will see an increase in access and use of the Internet. The wide variety of technology tools currently available (see Chapter 2: Planning for Success and Chapter 3: Making It Work) will grow even richer, assisting students in becoming producers, developing products of real use to themselves and others.

In tomorrow's classroom, the ability to adapt to change, evaluate information and its source, solve problems, and apply new ideas will be skills that are cultivated daily. Students will be able to communicate with other students, their teachers, and experts in the community and follow current world events as they are happening. Teacher and student on-line mentoring will increase, for it is currently a promising technique for furthering educational change.[38] Students will be able to access applications from home, allowing them to create multimedia presentations demonstrating their learning and send them electronically to their teacher. Using multimedia technology, students will be able to present their work to the class. Although this is currently the norm in *some* classes, in the future it will be the norm in *all* classes. The teacher in the classroom of the future will be a facilitator, guide, co-learner, and explorer working with flexible groupings of students. A computer will be the teacher's daily tool. All teachers will be digitally literate, capable of evaluating the content of the Internet. Professional growth will be an on-going process with the sharing of teaching and learning strategies and curriculum packages just a mouse click away.

> **"The** beauty of new technology, within 10 years, is that we're going to have very broad bandwidths and thus much faster connections. A school's best teachers can become available to anybody on the Net. In Internet-based instruction you can attend class at 3 a.m. if you want to — whether it's a high school or a college class. You can communicate with class members and the teacher through e-mail, chat lines, and electronic forums. Video conferencing will enhance the 'live' aspects of virtual instruction."[39]

Communication with parents will be immediate and on-going using e-mail and Web conferencing. Community access to technology through the community centers and schools will bring technology to those who cannot afford it. No longer will the scheduling of parent-teacher conferences be a challenge. Technology will add interest, excitement, and authenticity to teacher presentations. Imagine a lesson on the functioning of the heart in which students view a cross-section of the heart showing the direction of blood flow and the operation of valves, followed by a discussion of transplant procedures with a heart surgeon or input from a fitness expert. With the incorporation of technology, teacher presentations become more motivating, interactive, and authentic.

As technology becomes an integral part of education, teacher training will become more and more a priority. The 1999 School Technology and Readiness Report (*Professional Development: A Link to Better Understanding*), a report released by U.S. business and education leaders, states that "hiring standards for teachers and administrators should include technology-integration proficiency by the fall of 2000 and that the standards should be mandatory by 2002."[40] You will read more about teacher training and competencies in Chapter 9: Technology Tools for Teachers.

"We knew that computers by themselves couldn't do anything without teachers." You have to have teachers, "who are trained to integrate technology into classroom instruction," says Tim Ireland, a Bell Atlantic representative.[41]

Research will continue to investigate how educational technology can increase teacher effectiveness and improve student performance. As a result of research and the requirements of the workplace, governments need to look at the future of education, an education that can extend from kindergarten up to and including retirement. The aim is to encourage technology-literate students and teachers and determine the steps required to attain this goal. As the challenge is embraced, it is important to remember that the keys to success in future schools include a technology-rich environment, a plan for the implementation of the technology, regular in-service of staff members, strong curriculum software and support from administration, the community, and government.[42]

President Bill Clinton and Vice-President Al Gore launched a technology literacy challenge that envisioned a 21st century where all students are technologically literate. Four goals defined the challenge:

- **All teachers in the country will have the training and support they need to help students learn using computers and the information superhighway (Internet).**
- **All teachers and students will have modern multimedia computers in their classrooms.**
- **Every classroom will be connected to the information super-highway.**
- **Effective software and on-line learning resources will be an integral part of every school curriculum.[43]**

Summing Up

With a sound theoretical and philosophical base established, you are ready to move on to the challenging and exciting task of creating a technology-rich school culture and classroom environment. The chapters ahead provide practical strategies and ideas that will help transform your vision into reality.

PLANNING FOR SUCCESS

two

"Nothing is more important in our society, by definition, than the education of our youth. Nothing in pursuit of educational excellence is more important than studying the models of things that work."[1]

B efore starting on any journey, you usually decide where you are going. In the journey to today's technology-integrated classroom, you need to do the same. What are your goals for the integration of information and communication technology (ICT) in your school or classroom? We suggest the following:

- To enable learners to use ICT to acquire the knowledge, skills, and attitudes they will need as functioning members of society
- To incorporate the appropriate use of ICT into all areas of the curriculum and at all levels
- To provide opportunities for learners to use ICT for a wide variety of purposes (e.g., accessing information, organizing data, exploring, creating, communicating, problem solving) that link directly to the curriculum
- To allow and encourage learners to use ICT seamlessly, independent of time and space, as an everyday part of the learning process
- To involve learners in using ICT on an equitable basis
- To help learners think critically about ICT in order to use it effectively, ethically, and appropriately
- To allow and encourage teachers to use ICT as an integral part of their instructional and professional duties

There are many models of information and communication technology integration that would complement these goals. They vary from a million-dollar facility to a classroom with one computer. You may be beginning with your own vision or working within the boundaries of an established plan. You may have only a limited effect on the vision toward which your school or school district aspires but you may have opportunities to influence decisions. It's better to help shape the future than to have it imposed on you. When you finish reading this chapter, you'll have an idea of the variety of potential ways to integrate information and communication technology.

The first step in implementing information and communication technology at the school level is to make your technology plan a part of the overall school plan. Schools that spend time doing technology planning reap the rewards. Whether this planning is done by the school as a team, a dedicated committee, or a single teacher with a personal vision, giving shape to the technology experiences can benefit learners, teachers, and community. Technology plans vary greatly in scope and complexity. In this chapter we provide you with some guidelines to assist you in the task of developing a new plan or reviewing an existing plan. The technology-integrated classroom is not a classroom for the future but a classroom for today. The comments from teachers and students that you will read throughout this book are testimony to the fact that it's a necessary and exciting change. Change is never easy, so in this chapter we look briefly at the change process. We also examine the range of digital and non-digital equipment available to enhance active learning.

You need not feel you are facing the challenge of technology alone. Partnerships with the business community can be of great assistance in achieving your goal of integrating information and communication technology into the daily life of students. We offer some practical considerations for establishing and maintaining such partnerships.

Examples of Technology Integration
The Technology-integrated School

Envision a school in which all ICT resources are networked and integrated to make information sources available to everyone who needs them. The communications network includes electronic mail, bulletin boards, electronic conferencing, and access to global telecommunications. Information is processed through the use of word-processing applications, databases, spreadsheets, multimedia presentation tools, and desktop and Internet publishing. Each student may be provided with a personal computer, or they are abundant enough that access is seldom, if ever, a problem. Teachers and students have curricula that fully integrate information and communication technology, multimedia products for teaching, and individualized learning and learning management systems that track and record student progress. In every unit you plan, you can include components in which students use ICT to access, organize, and communicate information. Any project described in this book is easy to manage—the possibilities are endless. Features of this high-tech model include

- computers in labs and classrooms,
- all computers with Internet connectivity,
- unlimited student and teacher access,

Figure 2-1

This "school of the future" is here today.

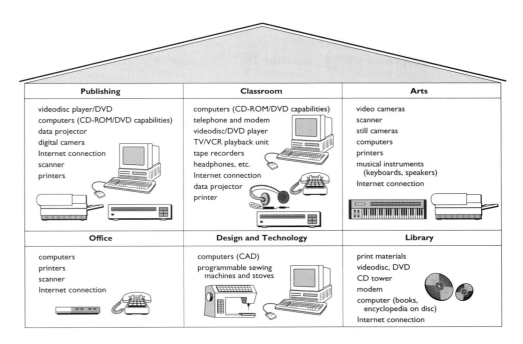

Publishing	Classroom	Arts
videodisc player/DVD computers (CD-ROM/DVD capabilities) data projector digital camera Internet connection scanner printers	computers (CD-ROM/DVD capabilities) telephone and modem videodisc/DVD player TV/VCR playback unit tape recorders headphones, etc. Internet connection data projector printer	video cameras scanner still cameras computers printers musical instruments (keyboards, speakers) Internet connection
Office	**Design and Technology**	**Library**

computers
printers
scanner
Internet connection
	computers (CAD)
	programmable sewing
	  machines and stoves
		print materials
		videodisc, DVD
		CD tower
		modem
		computer (books,
		  encyclopedia on disc)
		Internet connection

- multimedia room or workstations,
- equipment such as video cameras, digital cameras, scanners available,
- ongoing teacher training, and
- full-time technical support.

In fact, these schools do already exist today in many locations around the world. They are generally made possible through corporate partnerships, special grants from the business community, foresight by education officials in local districts, and the dedication of small groups of enlightened educators.

The Technology-integrated Classroom

The reality in many schools and school systems is that we are dealing with old buildings, limited funds for the purchase and maintenance of equipment, and a traditional curriculum. Despite these limitations, it is possible to establish very workable technology-integrated classrooms. The process begins with leaders who have vision and who consider the integration of ICT to be of the highest priority. It can be successful only through the efforts of committed, hard-working teachers who are willing and eager to change. You may find that, because technology allows you to optimize resources, you can redeploy funds to technology from other areas of the budget. By setting up some basic equipment and implementing curricula that assist in the integrated use of the equipment in daily activities, you can create a technology-integrated learning environment.

"We believe, however, that the eventual long-term success of computer education depends on widespread use of computers as teaching and learning tools in individual classrooms."[2]

We will explore this model in great depth, but to give you an idea of how much equipment you might require, we recommend the following:
- A minimum of three to five multimedia computers with Internet access
- A printer
- A digital camera
- A scanner
- A computer projection device
- A TV/VCR playback unit
- Two or three tape recorders
- A cordless telephone
- A CD and/or DVD burner
- A CD and/or DVD player
- Headphones

Put these items in your classroom, and things can change! Natural use of ICT as a tool can develop in this setting. You have the flexibility to organize a total learning environment that reflects the integration of the technology. The resources are available whenever students require them. You are not limited to specific subjects or time frames. In the chapters ahead, we will look at the many ways these tools can be integrated into the curriculum to improve and enhance student learning.

> **[The technology-integrated classroom] gives me the chance to see my kids as individuals and to work with them as individuals. I have 27 individuals and I can see 27 kids growing in leaps and bounds in every different direction because of the technology. It's not new to them, it's part of their education. It's part of their learning."**[3]

When each classroom has its own computers, a school computer lab takes on a new role. Rather than being a room where students go to "do" computers for a period of time, it is used for introducing new software, direct instruction, whole class activities, and allowing greater access to students as they explore and try out new software.

> **The Internet becomes a valuable tool when it is accessible to the greatest number of students. It is difficult to find a location (when you have only one shared phone line) to allow all students supervised access. The computer room is supervised only when there is a class in attendance; the library is run by volunteers on a part-time basis. Each classroom needs its own access."**[4]

The One-computer Classroom

We have seen teachers with access to only one computer discouraged by what they feel to be a situation with little potential. However, we have also seen what determination, creativity, and adaptability can accomplish. One computer can serve a lot of students if you keep it going at all times, and make sure that all students are scheduled equitably to use it. A little searching will probably turn up at least one piece of software that can be incorporated into each unit that you teach. You can use your computer as a teaching tool for large group instruction, as a workstation or learning center for an individual or small group, and as a personal secretary and record-keeper for you and your students. By pairing students at the computer and using cooperative learning groups, you can maximize usage. Hopefully, every student would get an opportunity to use the Internet in a classroom project at least once each term. You can round up simple technologies such as cameras and tape recorders. Remember that one of the greatest skills you can teach your students is fearless curiosity — the willingness to explore and learn about *any* technology. By working with the technology you have, you demonstrate that you are comfortable with technology, you view it as important, and you are ready and willing to move ahead when the opportunity arises. Many of the practical ideas we offer can be adapted for use in the one-computer classroom.

Five Categories of Classroom Computer Use

1. One computer and large groups
   - promote discussion
   - guide group explorations
   - demonstrate

2. One computer and small groups
   - introduce and practice skills in partners
   - undertake cooperative learning tasks

3. One computer as a lecture tool
   - implement Web-based lessons

4. One computer as a learning center
   - use for directed exploration
   - use for drill and practice
   - access information

5. One computer as your secretary
   - use for record-keeping
   - use for planning and assessment
   - create worksheets, letters[5]

Other Strategies

Because the integration of ICT can be such an expensive venture, we see schools experimenting with different adaptations to the technology-integrated classroom in their search for a cost-effective method. The variables of each situation are too numerous to mention, but you might consider the following options.

Shared Classrooms

One cost-effective idea is for two classes of students to share one set of equipment. Initially this seems like a good idea, given that there is a portion of the school day in which the equipment would be under-utilized (e.g., during physical education, vocal music, or drama classes). It facilitates maximum use of the technology, encourages teachers to plan and work as a team, and increases student interactions between classes. Schools that have tried this option, however, have experienced some disadvantages:

- The movement of students from room to room wastes valuable time and causes innumerable small problems with managing both students' and teachers' materials and possessions.
- Nobody takes ownership and responsibility for the care, storage, and maintenance of the equipment.
- Personality differences and different styles, standards, and expectations of the teachers involved can lead to an unpleasant working relationship.

Shared Computers

Some schools have purchased sets of laptop computers which they store on carts that can easily be moved from room to room. This is a good way to maximize use of the machines but requires teachers to plan and communicate well to ensure that the computers are available when required. In order to maintain the spontaneity of just-in-time learning (being able to quickly check a Web site, send an e-mail or look at a digital photo, for example) it's wise to keep at least one Internet connected computer in every classroom at all times.

" **C**lovis Unified School District in California combined Toshiba laptop computers and Microsoft Windows 95 and Office Professional software. To ensure that all students have access to laptops, the District bought 200 systems for in-class use and teachers coordinated classes to give all students maximum time with the computers. To increase computer exposure further, teachers within each school coordinated their teaching and pooled their PCs so students could share them. If students in seventh grade world history weren't using their computers for the first hour of a two-hour class, the machines were carried across the hall to the neighbouring science or language class, doubling the number of computers there. Careful coordination among four classes could quadruple the number of PCs in use when they were needed the most."[6]

School Technology Room

Another possibility is a special room within the school to which all classes have access on a rotational basis. This room can be equipped with the latest in digital equipment. You can imagine a 3-D scanner, electronic keyboards, digital still and video cameras with playback units, videodisc and DVD players, high-speed Internet access, desktop videoconferencing, multimedia software with assorted peripherals, and desktop publishing materials of all kinds! A site administrator or computer teacher can be assigned the responsibility of helping teachers and students, organizing the workspace, and caring for the equipment. At first thought this might appear very attractive, but it also has some serious drawbacks.

- ICT cannot be viewed as a tool to accomplish many specific tasks, because it is not available whenever the student needs it.

- The teacher cannot naturally integrate ICT into the daily experience of each student. It becomes a special event.
- The teacher doesn't have easy access to ICT for previewing resources or for personal use.
- Neither student nor teacher learns to take responsibility for the care and appropriate use of the equipment.
- Time-lines for the use of the room are artificial, arbitrary, and determined by administrative needs rather than student and teacher needs.

> **"W**hen computers are kept in special rooms, taught by special teachers for special students, the message is that computers are not for everyone. Who will shy away first? The kids who know who those special people are and that they themselves, aren't among them."[7]

However, any teacher would undoubtedly be happy to see the establishment of a school technology center *in addition to* technology-integrated classrooms, to be used for more specialized applications.

The High-tech Center

Some school systems extend the concept of the technology-integrated classroom to an even broader context by creating a high-tech center that serves several schools in a district. This allows for the purchase of the latest and greatest equipment and the specialists to operate it. Unfortunately, it magnifies all the disadvantages of the school technology center as well as adding transportation costs.

It has been our experience that none of these other alternatives serve students as well as when they have access to equipment in their own classroom, even to less sophisticated equipment.

School-based Technology Planning

In some cases, much of the technological equipment that has been purchased for schools remains dust covered from lack of use. Why has this occurred? One of the main reasons is lack of planning, before acquisition, for its maintenance and use. Pedagogically sound applications were not developed and teachers were not provided with opportunities to learn ICT skills. Without a plan it's easy to lose sight of your goals. A technology plan also addresses many issues besides the purchase and maintenance of equipment (e.g., procedures for evaluating software, equitable access, professional development of staff members, assessment procedures).

The number of choices available, especially in computer hardware, is enough to overwhelm even the most technology-literate person! The appeal of the latest "state-of-the-art" developments and "leading-edge" technologies can distract you from their actual use and cost effectiveness in educating students. Selection of hardware involves a variety of important factors.

- Goals for the use of hardware
- Inventory of current hardware
- Current and future hardware needs
- Compatibility with other equipment
- Supplier
- Price
- Uses by students and teachers
- Training required for students and teachers
- Amount of use
- Durability
- Ease of upgrading (if required)
- Ease and cost of repair
- Availability of parts
- Warranty
- Electrical requirements
- Safety
- Security
- Furniture required

Open a consultation process that will address all planning requirements. The purchasing officer of the school district brings a wealth of information about possible suppliers and costs. Most distributors are delighted to be invited to present their products. The latest tools, however, may not always be the best for your classroom or school so be sure that the salespeople are well briefed and have a clear understanding of your needs before they give proposals. A technical expert can provide maintenance and repair advice. You might find a person in the community, perhaps a parent, who is knowledgeable and prepared to act as a technical adviser. If your school district does not have a hardware technician, perhaps now is the time to plan for hiring someone.

> "**P**utting educational goals first also applies when selecting multimedia equipment vendors, notes Eliot Levinson, a senior consultant for Pelavin Associates, Inc., who helps school districts set up technology management organizations. Rather than letting vendors 'hustle schools...telling them that if they take [the vendor's] system, they can get anything out of it they want,' Levinson advises school leaders to ask the right questions and set up specifications for vendors to meet. 'For example,' says Levinson, 'lay out five problems that you would like solved, and give the list to the vendors. Let them demonstrate that they can help you solve your specific problems.'" [8]

A broad view of the potential management and use of the equipment by staff and students can be provided by the school principal. A superintendent or supervisory officer can articulate the vision and overall goals of the school system. The involvement of staff members representing various levels and curriculum areas is critical because they are in touch with the realities of using ICT in their unique teaching situations. These teachers can also provide a testing environment for trying out various products: field-testing potential purchases before investing can save time and money and avoid later frustration.

Input for the Decision-making Team

Trustees/Elected Officials	• What are the educational outcomes? • What is the associated cost?
Supervisory Officer	• What is the effect on teacher(s) and students at the system level and the classroom level? • What are the budgetary implications?
Purchasing Officer	• Who can supply the equipment? • Where can I get the best price? • What alternatives are available? • How reliable is the supplier? • Can the equipment be easily/cheaply upgraded? • Is it durable? • Is it compatible with existing equipment?
Technician	• How easy is it to repair? • Where can I get the parts? • What does the warranty cover?
Principal	• What will be purchased? • Where will I store it? • What about security? • What are the electrical requirements? • What about safety? • Who will pay for repairs? • Who will pay for replacements?
Teacher	• What training do I need? • How will students use it? • How will teachers use it? • Will the students find it easy to use? • How often will the students use it? • Where will I put it? • Will I need special furniture? • What training will the students need? • Is there a variety of ways in which the equipment can be used?

Figure 2-2

When the decision-making team consults with all individuals who will be affected by the purchases, they ensure that many different perspectives are considered.

The planning team should also include representatives from community stakeholders such as parents and business people, as this may be an appropriate opportunity to underline wider involvement in your school.

No matter what purchases you select, be prepared for something faster, easier to use, or with greater capabilities to soon emerge on the market. The goal of providing the latest and best hardware and software for students is constantly challenged by memory upgrades, special features, improvements in speed and portability, and greater compatibility with other technologies.

This should not concern you too much provided that your plan includes provision for upgrading, improvement, and replacement at regular intervals. Remind all involved that exposure to *any* hardware and software is still valuable, as it advances your intent of strengthening general technological competence. Assessment procedures must also be considered as part of the technology plan. Funding agencies, educational leaders, teachers, and parents want to know the outcomes of the investment that has been made. How well is it working? Is the technology doing what we hoped it would do? Keep the following in mind when planning this assessment:

- Clarify your assessment goals.
- Determine specific questions for which you want to find answers.
- Decide what type of data will help answer your questions, e.g., observations, surveys, interviews, test scores, evaluation of student work.
- Collect the data within your selected time frame.
- Analyze the information in a way that allows you to draw conclusions based on your goals.
- Share the results with all stakeholders.
- Use the information to improve what you are doing.[9]

Keep in mind that schools all over the world are going through a similar change process; there is lots of information available to assist you. You will find all sorts of reading and examples related to school-based technology planning by following the links we have provided at our Web site.

> **T**he School Technology and Readiness (StaR) Chart, developed by the CEO Forum, is a tool that can help all schools create and implement a plan for improving education with the help of ICT.
> You can get a copy from:
> **CEO Forum on Education and Technology**
> **1341 G Street, NW**
> **Washington, DC 20005**
> **http://www.ceoforum.org**

Change: Making the Journey

When you take the first steps in making ICT an integral part of the teaching/learning process, you begin a journey that will change you as a professional and will change your students' perspective and experience of school. Creating a technology-integrated classroom may require you to change your ideas about how teachers teach and how students learn. It's important to know that the transformation in your classroom will be ongoing and that every day might not be the success you hoped it would be.

Educational experts in implementation and the change process[10] state that

- change takes place over time,
- change is a process,
- change involves anxiety,
- technical assistance and psychological support are crucial,

Figure 2-3

Change brings with it a series of challenges. Your responses determine the effectiveness of the change.

- change involves learning new skills through practice,
- successful change involves pressure, and
- change implementers need to see why the new way works better.

We can try to turn back from change whenever the going gets tough or we can learn to embrace it by viewing challenges as opportunities. It is these very opportunities that for many teachers rekindle the excitement they felt at the beginning of their teaching career.

The nature of the change will determine to what extent the change is implemented. Some factors that may affect the integration of ICT into the classroom include

- the complexity of the change (e.g., How will the addition of technology to my classroom change my teaching role?),
- its explicitness (e.g., Are there specific measurable outcomes?),
- its practicability (e.g., Is there space for the equipment in my classroom?),
- its adaptability (e.g., Can it be useful to both teachers and students?), and
- its communicability (e.g., Will I be able to clearly explain to parents and administrators how technology is improving learning?).[11]

The innovation we describe in this book involves much more than just the addition of equipment to an existing classroom environment. It requires learning new technologies; restructuring the roles of teacher and student; developing strategies for cooperative and individualized learning, time-tabling, and organizational changes. Therefore, as an innovation, it is indeed complex and demands a significant amount of change.

After a decade of research on the instructional changes that occur during the process of integrating ICT into the learning environment, Apple Classrooms of Tomorrow (ACOT) identified the following five stages of professional growth:

1. Entry phase: educators struggle to learn the basics of using ICT.
2. Adoption phase: educators use ICT successfully on a basic level (e.g., integrate drill and practice software).
3. Adaptation: educators discover the potential of ICT for increased productivity (e.g., word processing, spreadsheets, Internet research).
4. Appropriation: educators have mastered ICT and use it effortlessly as a tool to accomplish a variety of instructional and management goals.
5. Invention: educators develop new learning environments that utilize ICT as a flexible tool to make learning more collaborative, interactive and customized.[12]

A project's outcome depends to a great extent on the characteristics of the project's setting — elements such as the school's climate, the leadership, staff relationships, and the physical environment. An orderly, secure, and supportive environment will make the introduction of a new way of teaching easier. If you are pursuing the integration of ICT as a personal initiative, you are responsible for convincing all the stakeholders of the validity of the change, obtaining funding, and pursuing the necessary expertise. Discuss with your principal exactly what you are planning to do and be ready to support your plans with research as well as practical classroom experience. The school principal is critical to the ongoing success of your innovation, and in the days ahead you may require monetary, philosophical, and/or pedagogical support. On the other hand, if your initiative is supported at the school and/or system level, you will find the change much easier, and support from both peers and experts will be available when you need it.

> **"As a veteran teacher of 20 years, I see educational changes every day. I realize that not all changes are good, but I know that change is a catalyst to improve. Technology is proving to be a great catalyst. Technology has opened the doors of communication for teachers. Teachers are sharing ideas, methods, lesson plans, tips, techniques, and bits of personal information. Communication among teachers has never existed like it exists today. Collaboration and communication is providing me with a portal into the minds of great teachers, and that gives me the opportunity to become a better teacher. Long gone are the days of locking up materials and hoping your cohort won't 'steal' your bulletin board idea. There are enough great ideas to go around. Who would have imagined it 10 years ago? I pass by classrooms today, and I don't hear teachers' lectures quite so often. I see portfolio evaluations of students on CD-ROMs. I hear sound clips of students' reports being played. I hear students discussing their group's PowerPoint presentations. I see students e-mailing their mentors or parents. I hear my 'you have mail' sound and I realize some concerned parent needs me to e-mail them their student's English grade. I see and appreciate progress. I see, am motivated, and have vision for education."[13]**

Part of this particular change involves improving teachers' technology skills. You may be wondering exactly what is expected of you in this regard. Many schools and school districts have developed frameworks of competencies in ICT that they expect their teachers to achieve. Find out if your school or district has specified expectations. Then find out what professional development plan has been put in place to help you achieve these goals. Much more about teacher competencies and training is coming up in Chapter 9: Technology Tools for Teachers.

What About Equipment?

Every technology-integrated classroom we visit seems to be equipped somewhat differently. Certainly, the success of your technology-integrated classroom rests much more on how you use the equipment than on what equipment you have, but some of the most difficult decisions *do* revolve around selecting, purchasing, and maintaining hardware. It is not our intent in this book to rate or promote various brands of hardware, but rather to provide you with general guidelines for selecting and maintaining hardware and specific considerations about certain types of equipment.

> **"What** we will be able to do with tomorrow's computer systems is a vast step forward from what we were able to do in the past. At the Institute for the Learning Sciences, we are now producing computer systems that interact with people in more engaging ways than before. Our systems allow children to try out things in simulated worlds of our own making, and sometimes of their own making; they allow children to fly their own ship to the moon, design their own animal, or direct their own newscast. This technology will allow us to support what is one of the most important parts of a good educational system: the cultivation of individual initiative in students."[14]

Computers and Computer Networks

In our experience, business partnerships, government grants, financial constraints, and personal preferences tend to be the factors governing the kind of computers used in schools. Once you have learned to use a computer, what you have learned is applicable to most other computers; the time invested in learning to use one type of computer is not lost when you switch to another machine. Before selecting a particular computer, however, speak to a number of suppliers and other educators. In addition to the general considerations previously listed, ask yourself the following questions:

- Is this computer reliable?
  Speak with others who use this brand.
- Will you need to move it regularly?
  Portable computers are constantly improving and becoming less expensive.
- Can features be added as required?
  In the future, you may wish to add more RAM, greater hard drive space, a faster modem, a CD burner, or a DVD drive, so plan ahead.

The choice of computer platform has little relevance to the successful integration of technology into the daily school life of students, provided that the computers can do what you want them to do. Therefore, when selecting which computers to buy, first consider the capabilities required. For example, a financially motivated decision to buy basic terminals for Internet use as opposed to fully equipped multimedia machines might be changed by consideration of the fact that there are still quite a few advantages to students' using CD-ROM disks rather than the Internet. They can be played on machines without Internet access, can be shared easily among teachers and classrooms, and offer much faster performance of video and graphics than the average school Internet connection. DVD versions, especially, have the potential for multimedia content that won't be available on the Internet for several years. So perhaps a better decision might be to use the school's existing older computers as Internet terminals and instead purchase new machines for multimedia applications.

What kind of applications will you most often use?

Kinds of Applications	Used For
databases	organizing information sorting information examining trends finding the highest, lowest, biggest, best...
desktop publishing	newspapers, newsletters worksheets, activity cards advertising, notices greeting cards, bulletin boards report covers, title pages
drill and practice	mathematics basic facts spelling and phonics keyboarding rote tasks
graphics utilities	illustrations, drawings, sketches, diagrams, maps visual communication graphic organizers drafting Web page design
multimedia	student and teacher presentations organizing resources research thinking skills communication skills Web page creation/enhancement
programming and control technologies	thinking skills problem solving programming languages robotics

Kinds of Applications	Used For
simulations	exploration, discovery
	topics difficult to explore otherwise in school
	imaginary topics
	identifying with the past, future
spreadsheets	calculating
	tracking costs or scores
	statistics
	lab results and calculations
	tables, graphs, charts
	student marks
word processing	writing, self-expression
	notices, letters, bulletins
	posters, banners
	tests, handouts
World Wide Web	communicating outside the classroom
	audio and video conferencing
	research
	distance education
	publishing student work

"**R**emember to keep the focus on how students can use the technology rather than on what the technology can do. The role of the technology is simply to enable human performance. It is more important to be able to say, 'My students are great because they have learned to send prepared datafiles via the system', than to say, 'The system is great because it lets my students send prepared datafiles.'" [15]

After deciding which classroom applications to use, you will have a basis on which to select computer hardware. We will look at these applications in greater detail in Chapter 3: Making It Work.

The next question that comes to mind after "What kind of computers?" is often "Where will we put the computers?" In our experience, secondary school teachers tend to be more comfortable with a lab setting, while elementary teachers prefer the computers in their classrooms. We believe this reflects a difference in school organization and teaching style. There are specific advantages and disadvantages to computers in labs and in classrooms, as described in Figure 2-4.

An important question when planning for computers in classrooms is "How many computers?" Teachers have invariably answered that they could never have too many computers, only too little physical space for them! Economics may limit many teachers' dreams of a computer for every student in every class for a while yet, but it is becoming a reality in more and more schools each year through the use of laptop and hand-held computers.

Figure 2-4

Give careful consideration to where to put computers. Naturally, computers in both labs and classrooms is the most ideal situation.

	1 to 5 Computers in a Classroom	15 Computers in a Lab
Number of students who can use computers at one time	2 to 10	15 to 30
Time at which computers can be used	All the time	Fixed amount of time per week
Using computers for whole group instruction	Difficult without projection device	Possible without projection device
Using computers for collaborative group work	Easy to organize	More difficult to organize
Using computers as an individual tool whenever required	Available any time; flexible	Available only at scheduled times; inflexible

Laptop Computers

When all students have their own computers, a computer lab is no longer required.

> **"T**here is ample research that shows that even if teachers have access to a computer lab, they don't use it," said Elliot Soloway, a University of Michigan professor. "Bringing a laptop to class eliminates that problem. If it is there, they will use it."[16]

Participation in laptop programs has recently come to be associated with improved student attendance and engagement with learning. Some of the advantages of laptops are the following:

- Students can share a laptop and take turns viewing, inputting, and analyzing data.
- Individuals or groups can transfer information using file sharing programs and/or wireless connectivity.
- Students at different locations can interact using e-mail or videoconferencing, using wireless connectivity or a modem.
- Students can check out laptops for use overnight or during vacations.
- Students have ready access to Internet resources from various locations
- Students are able to process and graph data immediately, check estimates, and make decisions about the next step of an activity in the field or laboratory.
- Students take responsibility for the computers and have more ownership in learning.
- Teachers can connect laptops to monitors or overhead projectors to review software, give multimedia presentations, teach from a Web site, and clarify assignments.
- Teachers can easily record and organize notes on individual student progress and use the computers in conjunction with digital cameras and/or voice-to-text applications to record events for later student assessment.
- Teachers are provided with a tool to facilitate changes in their methodology.

- Teachers have more flexibility for homework assignments knowing that all students have a computer and Internet access available.
- Laptops facilitate communication between students and teachers: using a laptop at home or in the field, students can submit assignments or questions via e-mail or wireless connectivity.[17]

Astudy conducted from 1996 through 2000 by Rockman Et Al, an independent research organization, found that students using laptops in Microsoft's Anytime Anywhere Learning program spent more time out of class on schoolwork, scored higher in reading and writing assessments, demonstrated improved research and analysis skills, were more confident in their computer skills, and engaged in more collaborative work than non-laptop using students.[18]

Laptops also proved to be a catalyst for teachers to use more constructivist teaching. Laptop teachers showed statistically significant change toward teaching practices that put students at the center of learning, use discussion rather than lecture, encourage student-led inquiry, and emphasize thinking skills. Laptop teachers had a greater sense of control over their classroom instruction and management of student learning and used computers far more often in a wider variety of learning activities than non-laptop peers.[19]

Expense often comes to mind when the idea of a laptop computer for every student is considered. How are schools managing the cost of laptop programs? We are seeing a variety of options including the following:

- Students and parents purchase laptops according to school specifications.
- Students and parents lease laptops from school district or an independent supplier.
- School and students and parents divide cost of either lease or purchase.
- School or district purchases laptops for students through re-allocation of funds.
- School or district applies for educational grants from the government or nonprofit foundations.
- School district creates an educational foundation.

You can find examples and tips for starting an educational foundation by following the links provided to two informative articles.

State-of-the-art laptops with lots of power and a variety of software applications may not be necessary in all situations. There are many options for less expensive portable technologies that will do some educational tasks very well. In Wyoming Elementary School in Millburn, New Jersey, students love to take their Alpha Smarts on class excursions. They use these portable word processors to take notes, transcribe interviews, and enter observations. When they return to school, they can upload their text to a desktop computer where they have access to software applications for producing stories, multimedia presentations, or newsletters. A Michigan school district in Flat Rock purchased a cart full of DreamWriters, keyboarding tools with an integrated LCD (Liquid Crystal Display) screen. In addition to helping all students with spelling, keyboarding, creative writing, and note taking, teachers find that the DreamWriters level the playing field for students with graphic problems. CalcuScribes are the tool of choice for Tully Elementary School in Kentucky.

They have small individual keyboards with screens. Students use them for text entry and editing and mathematical operations. Teachers have observed that the CalcuScribes have taken the labor out of writing assignments, especially for learning disabled and attention deficit disordered students. You can find out more about laptop programs at a variety of Web sites.[20]

Hand-held Computers

The "anytime, anywhere learning" theme also continues to be honed by hand-held devices of many kinds. The aim of the manufacturers of these devices is to compete with laptop programs for the most cost-effective and portable access to learning. Hand-held devices have come a long way since the first PalmPilots of 1996. For schools, the key advantage of these computers is that they are small, powerful, inexpensive, and easy to carry. The most common complaint at this time is that they cannot take the place of a laptop or desktop computer, but ongoing developments that expand the capabilities of hand-held computers promise to make them more viable very quickly. It is already possible to add peripherals such as digital cameras, scientific probes, and extra memory. Hand-held computers are used in schools for

- reading e-books;
- electronic calendars for teachers, students, and administrators;
- science experiments in the field, with the addition of scientific probes;
- managing information such as grades and seating plans;
- math calculations using specialized calculators downloaded from the Web;
- vocabulary work using dictionaries downloaded from the Web;
- recording, storing, and playing MP3 music files;
- taking snapshots for Web pages by attaching a digital camera;
- sending and receiving e-mail; and
- learning tasks with "pocket" versions of Microsoft Word, Excel, and PowerPoint.[21]

For a look at some of the models available, check out the manufacturers' Web sites.

> **C**onsolidated High School District 230, in a suburb of Chicago, has put nearly 3,000 palmtop computers into the hands of their students in one of the largest educational initiatives of this type. This program offers students the option of purchasing a Palm IIIxe model or renting one if they wish to take it home; otherwise students have access only during the school day. The Palms have become an integral part of the school district's program. Students use them for activities such as note-taking, outdoor science experiments and data gathering, and analyzing personal fitness and nutrition data.[22]

Many schools have chosen to network their computer labs and technology-integrated classrooms to a central file server. A group of computers that are physically wired together is called a local area network (LAN), although wireless LANs are now also available. They can be in the same room or building, or on the same campus. LANs do not require modems for computers to communicate with one another; instead, they use appropriate LAN interface cards. One computer, called the server, manages the network. The advantages of a network are the following:

- There are financial savings due to shared drives and printers.
- Only one copy of each program is required with a site license.
- Students can choose software from a menu without the teacher having to find individual disks.
- Students do not require a floppy disk to save work.
- Students can share data over the network.
- Students have the ability to communicate with one another over the network.
- Teachers can control individual screens and demonstrate on-screen.
- Students require less training than if they had to manage a computer desktop and handle individual disks.
- One person within a school is usually responsible for maintaining the hardware and updating and supporting software.

There are also some disadvantages:
- One problem can bring down the whole system.
- More training is required for the system manager.
- The computers are generally slower, especially during start-up periods when many users are logging on simultaneously.
- Internet connections can be slow, depending on bandwidth.
- There is less individual teacher control and technical management is more difficult.
- File management is different from what teachers are used to on their home computers.
- Access to software is limited to those programs loaded on the central file server unless each workstation also has its own drive(s).

Wireless Technologies

Wireless networks may operate on microwaves, cellular systems, radio frequencies, or infrared light. Cell phones and hand-held devices are the popular gateways to the wireless world, but schools have been exploring the possibilities of wireless networking for some time now. Wireless networks circumvent the need to retrofit older buildings and can be set up on a needs basis in a variety of different settings. The ability to bring resources to students rather than students to resources provides true flexibility for active learning. Project-based learning is enhanced by the ability of students to communicate and access information anytime, anywhere. Wireless networks do not necessarily replace the school network; they enhance it and make it more flexible. A simple explanation is that computers are fitted with adapter cards, allowing them to interact with data made available through a network access point. A typical access point supports 15 to 20 users who can then move about without losing connectivity. Mobile Wireless Labs generally include a set of notebook computers, a mobile cart, and a wireless access point. Several leading technology companies have developed solutions to help schools go wireless and the costs of this technology is declining. For a look at some of these offerings, try the Web links provided.[23]

Texas Instruments' TI-Navigator system combines their TI-83 graphing calculator with local wireless networking. Students plug their calculators into hubs on their desks, which are wirelessly linked to the teacher's computer. The teacher can download curriculum material, send questions to groups, and monitor student progress.

Internet Connectivity

Although most schools are now connected to the Internet, many connections are less than ideal. Speed is usually the issue; it seems that a school's Internet connection can never be fast enough! Students tend to find unproductive ways to occupy their time when faced with long waits for sites to load. Those who have quick Internet connectivity at home are impatient when working through the school's local area network, which is inevitably slower. Many teachers long for the capability for 30 students to access the same Web site simultaneously, but this is rarely the case. Consider these strategies if you have a limited or slow connection:

- Divide the class into teams and have each visit a different topic-related Web site.
- Use an Internet-related activity as a learning center through which individuals, pairs, or groups rotate.
- Schedule students to take turns throughout the day when Internet access is required.

Some schools have several phone lines, each with a modem-equipped computer, located around the school. Although students may have to leave the classroom, they can still have easy Internet access provided that the number of terminals is adequate for the student and teacher population of the school. Other schools have several modem-equipped computers but are limited to only one phone line. Many schools have high-speed data lines, but often they do not have enough bandwidth to handle the school's volume of on-line traffic. In our experience, most Internet terminals are located in the school library/resource center and the computer lab. This configuration allows each class structured Internet use for an hour or so per week but makes it difficult to integrate activities into the curriculum in a seamless, natural way. This model also works best with older students, with whom teacher supervision is not an issue. You'll need to plan for individuals or pairs of students to move freely to wherever the terminals are located at the times that they need them. The cooperation and teamwork of all staff members help to make this work. A schedule might be needed, especially in larger schools, so that all classes get a fair share of time. You'll also have to arrange for someone to be available to assist these students as they work, especially at first. Often, the librarian or computer teacher can be available. Parent volunteers and student experts are also invaluable. With younger students, the most useful location for an Internet terminal is in the classroom.

For more advice, go to a set of Web pages prepared by Wayne Fischer, Internet program specialist with the U.S. Department of Education. You'll find documents that focus on issues for schools regarding wiring a building and connecting directly to the Internet. The pages are designed for educators and administrators who have little or no technical background. They provide enough details to make them "wise shoppers" as they work with equipment vendors and installation contractors.

Security of School Networks

Now that most school districts have LANs (local area networks) connecting computers within buildings and WANs (wide area networks) connecting networks among buildings, security of data is an important consideration. A popular solution is to establish an Intranet. We do not wish to get into the technical details here, but basically an Intranet is a scaled-down version of the external Internet that uses Internet Protocol and common Web browsers, but restricts information to those who are allowed access. Most Intranets contain confidential information such as student names, grades, and personal records and possibly internal e-mail. A firewall, which is a set of programs that filters network information and requests, is used to secure the Intranet from the broader Internet. This means that when teachers wish to access student grades from home, for example, they require a password to gain access. Currently, most school districts put school data and applications together on their in-school network or Intranet. These days, however, increasing complexity is constantly adding to the cost of building and maintaining such a system, causing some schools to seek outside solutions for their data management. Figure 2-5 shows a brief comparison of these two choices. A third option, of course, is some combination of the two.[24]

	Pros	**Cons**
In-school LAN or Intranet	Customized to meet specific needs Local control of data	Hard to get ICT technicians Teachers end up doing tech-work Possible platform incompatibilities Expensive hardware and software upgrades
Outside Application Service Provider	Easy to install, maintain, and upgrade Lowers cost of IT specialists Experts handle data Easy access for all	Dependency on outside source Internet companies come and go Confidential information stored off-site May not meet individual school needs as closely On-line applications may not be as powerful as locally hosted versions

Figure 2-5

The costs and benefits of choosing an outside service provider to handle school applications and/or data must be carefully considered.

One example of the outside **ASP** model is **PowerSchool Student Information System**, a Web-based application that allows users access to important data while minimizing support and training costs (http://www.apple.com/education/powerschool/). Instead of incurring an upfront charge for software, hardware, and installation, schools pay a subscription fee for each student per year. **PowerSchool** features include student demographics, a master schedule builder, attendance records, automated reports and form letters, and student/parent access.

Printers

A fast reliable printer in the lab is a necessity. Access to both a black and white and a color printer is ideal. Printers also belong in classrooms along with computers. Teachers and students are far too busy to waste time going down the corridor to pick up their documents. Some schools provide black and white printers in each computer-equipped classroom and keep a color printer in a more central location to be shared by all.

Scanners

A scanner is used to transform a printed image to digital form for storage, manipulation, and presentation on a computer. Now that scanners are relatively inexpensive, they are an easy accessory to be added to the lab or classroom computer station. They are extremely simple to learn to use — just follow the steps that are provided or ask a colleague to show you. A scanner is useful for

- capturing student work to be added to an electronic portfolio;
- copying documents (with appropriate attention to copyright);
- obtaining images from books and magazines for student projects (with appropriate attention to copyright);
- using images to embellish class presentations and resource material; and
- scanning photographs for printing, e-mailing to others, adding to print or electronic presentations, and all the other uses listed below for digital cameras.

Scanning tips
1. Images take up a lot of disk space. A couple of photos can fill a diskette, and collections of photos taken by various classes can take up huge amounts of space on the school file server.
2. Keep your file size small; it will be faster to save, copy, and paste the item. You can usually adjust the size once the image is in your application.
3. Use a high-quality image as your original and your copy will be almost as good.
4. The basic quality setting, 640 × 480 pixels, is adequate for posting on the Web.
5. If you intend to print your scanned image, scan it at a slightly lower resolution than your printer is capable of producing. This allows you to create scans that match the capabilities of your printer.
6. Place a dark sheet of paper under the picture being scanned to avoid traces of what might be on the other side.

Cameras

Both still and video cameras are recognized as extremely useful educational tools in any classroom. Teachers and students have been using still and video photography for years, but the digitization of these technologies creates many more possibilities for creative uses in combination with the power of computers.

Digital cameras allow you to capture and view photos on your computer. The photos are transferred from the camera to the computer by a cable, by a Flash Path memory chip, or on diskette, depending on the type of camera. Once you have the photos stored in the computer, you can make all kinds of photo image and editing adjustments and then import the photos into other applications such as word-processing, presentation, or Internet publishing software. As the prices of digital cameras decrease, they are becoming one of the most popular school purchases. Ideally, each teacher or classroom should be provided with one. Many digital cameras take not only still pictures, but short movie clips also. Digital cameras such as the QuickTake, Sanyo, ZapShot, QuickCam, FlexCam, Polaroid Digital Camera, Intel's Create and Share Camera, and Sony's Mavica floppy disk camera make great additions to the classroom.

When shopping for a digital camera, look for one that has an interface compatible with your current computer equipment. There is wide variance in the types, features, and prices of digital cameras, so consider the age of the intended users and what will be the primary purposes.

The least expensive cameras, as you might expect, tend to have fewer features: small storage capacity, a lens that cannot be manually adjusted, and low image resolution. These will suit your needs if you want a simple, point-and-shoot camera for snapshots and Web pages. Cameras that save images directly to a floppy disc are popular with teachers because files are readily transferable to computers for viewing and editing, ensuring that students spend more time on the subject than on technological housekeeping. The creation of a library of images stored on CDs could be an ongoing project for a class or school.

Students and teachers use digital cameras for

- preparing individual student profile pages;
- creating a classroom seating plan, especially useful for supply teachers;
- adding to author descriptions for student-published books;
- gathering first-hand data of all sorts;
- enhancing pieces of creative writing by adding images to word-processed documents;
- collecting images for projects and Web pages;
- sharing images with others via slide shows or e-mail;
- recording products such as art works and student-built structures and mechanisms;
- capturing special events;
- self-evaluating performances; and
- making the yearbook.

You can find more ideas for using cameras by visiting the publisher's Web site.

Pros of a Digital Camera
- **faster than a regular camera**
- **cheaper to process images**
- **more environmentally friendly**
- **easy to transfer pictures from one person to another**

Cons of a Digital Camera
- **initial purchase is expensive**
- **images require a lot of storage space**
- **images not usually the quality of traditional cameras**
- **batteries may need frequent charging and replacing**

Students and teachers can find many uses for a video camera. As you explore the possibilities, you may discover that some students are already quite comfortable with the operation of a video camera. A video camera may not be required on a daily basis, but it's great to have access to one when students need it to enhance multimedia presentations, collect visual data, practice public speaking, or prepare news broadcasts and drama. Keep durability and portability in mind when purchasing a video camera for classroom use. Select special features according to your anticipated uses of the camera. A tripod is a good investment that may add years to the life of your video camera!

Digital video is initially more expensive than analog, but it is more flexible for a variety of educational uses. Students can document school events, post video clips of school activities to the school Web site, or record classroom activities. Digital video also has some other advantages over analog:

- It's more easily edited.
- It can be compressed for easier storage.
- It can be edited and shaped in ways analog video cannot.
- It lends itself readily to the Internet, CD-ROM, and DVD.

Video is said to be "captured" when it is transferred to your computer. A regular video camera records in analog format, whereas computers use digital formats. A video capture card changes your video from analog to digital format. Many capture cards are available; basic ones are only a modest investment.[25] At the publisher's Web site you will find a few links to the manufacturers of video capture cards.

As part of a statewide initiative to rewire schools, **Farmington High School** in Farmington, Minnesota, has constructed a state-of-the-art video and video-editing facility with the help of **Alpha Video**, a consulting company that specializes in helping schools incorporate video into their classrooms.

"It is truly amazing how cool this stuff is to work with," says **Matt Ruby**, the school's television instructor. "But even more amazing is how quickly the students learned to use it in daily curriculum projects."

Students at Farmington record and professionally edit school plays, sporting events, and assemblies using Panasonic **DVC PRO** Digital camcorders, **JVC** Professional edit stations, and Alpha Video's **Edgecast** character generator. Sophisticated post-production effects are added using Panasonic digital video mixers.[26]

CD and DVD Burners

Many computers come with built-in CD burners, or you can attach an external CD burner. This greatly enhances file storage capacity and increases the flexibility for creating large items such as multimedia projects and student portfolios. Some computers now include the hardware and software for creating DVD discs. Teachers can film videos of classroom projects and burn them onto DVD for storage and viewing.

Projectors

The addition of an LCD (liquid crystal display) panel or a data projector to a classroom opens up new doors for teaching and learning. This equipment allows projection of your computer screen for whole-class viewing. An LCD panel is a projection panel that, when placed on top of a high-intensity over-head projector, allows you to show the computer image on a wall screen in a darkened room. It attaches to the computer with a cable, in place of (or in addition to) the monitor. LCD panels are now being replaced by data projectors made by companies such as InFocus or Lightware. An overhead projector is not required for a data projector; you attach the computer directly to the projector with a cable. Most data projectors can do both front and rear projection. With a good one, there is no need to worry about putting your students in the dark. Alternatively, you can attach your computer to a large-screen TV (at least 32 inches/80 cm) for whole-class viewing.

A scan converter is one tool that allows the user to connect the computer to a TV or multiple TVs. The room does not have to be darkened and the set-up time is shorter. You can also use the scan converter to make videotapes of whatever is on the screen, videotape student computer projects for parents to view at home, and keep video records of student computer work.

Groups of teachers can create whole-group lessons using presentation tools such as PowerPoint or Corel Presentations and share them among colleagues. In Chapter 9: Technology Tools for Teachers, we elaborate on this topic and provide a sample.

TV/VCR

A combination TV/VCR can be used for whole-class, small-group, and individual viewing. There are a number of advantages to selecting a combination unit. One of these is its portability, an important consideration when teachers share equipment. Also, combination TV/VCRs have fewer wires, thus there are fewer connections to be concerned about, and they take up very little space in the typically crowded classroom.

TV/VCR units can be purchased with either vertical or horizontal loading. With younger students in mind, horizontal loading is the logical choice because it is the type with which children are most familiar. Most units wisely have the fine-tuning controls out of sight, but find out where they are located in case students decide to experiment! A TV/VCR can be adapted for headphones by the simple addition of a jack and switch. The jack is required for the attachment of headphones while the switch is used to switch the audio back and forth from the headphones to the speakers. Add a U-bolt so that the equipment can be secured to a table or wall. Always check with the manufacturer before opening the casing, otherwise the warranty might be invalidated.

Videodisc and DVD Players

Videodisc and DVD players can be an exciting part of the interactive instructional system. They can be used to enhance large group presentations or as a research tool for small groups or individual students. Their most attractive features include the excellent quality of the image and the flexible use of content that is possible. The interactive capabilities of videodisc and DVD players make them far superior to VCRs, although they may cost up to twice as much. Many new computers now include built-in DVD players. Unlike videotape, no tedious rewinding is necessary with videodisc or DVD. The teacher or student can move immediately to a particular image or video clip in order to demonstrate a concept or stimulate discussion. Many videodisc packages come with what are called "bar coded lesson guides." When purchasing a videodisc or DVD player, explore its capabilities to make sure that it will suit your needs.

Audio and Videoconferencing

The potential of telecommunications for education is obvious in the burgeoning field of distance learning. Though you may not yet be involved or contemplating involvement in this specialized field, it's exciting to think of the possibilities ahead, such as audio conferencing, audiographic conferencing, and videoconferencing. Audio conferencing allows a group of learners to interact using telephone handsets or speaker phones. Audiographics allows for transmission of graphics at the same time as voice messages using a standard telephone line. Computers with special software packages and modems are required, and an electronic tablet and pen can be used to write or draw on-line. With the appropriate software, you can add computer-generated text and graphics, video clips, photos, and scanned images. Videoconferencing involves the transmission of full images and sound. In other words, a group of learners in one site can see and speak with learners in another using cameras and TV or computer screens.

If you are eager for a school or classroom videoconferencing experience, first define how you want to use the technology: to provide access to remote experts, collaborate with students in a distant location, and/or provide on-line training. The most common means of getting access involves transporting students to a community facility or local business that houses the equipment and has fast, broadband access. As well as all the large organizations that own their own videoconference systems there are thousands of public videoconference bureaus located in 72 countries. Commercial options are also available, such as EyeNetwork (http://www.eyenetwork.co.uk/), an international booking service with over 1500 affiliate public bureaus around the world. All you need to do is to tell them where you want to conference with and they book your nearest location. It is now possible to videoconference to almost anywhere in the world.

Headphones

Headphones are essential when using any kind of audio equipment in the busy classroom environment! Good-quality headphones will help you maintain a quieter work environment. The "Walkman" type of headphones may survive for a year or so, but they cannot stand long-term constant use.

When headphones are used for a variety of equipment, teachers and students quickly discover that some pieces of equipment require a large plug while others require a small one. Adapters sound like the answer but they are small and quickly lost. A better solution is to provide headphones with a variety of plug sizes. Many companies will customize the headphones to suit your needs.

Microphones

Microphones provide students with the option of recording their own speech as well as environmental sounds. These audio clips can easily be incorporated into multimedia presentations. Many computers have built-in microphones that will suffice, but the quality varies.

Tape Recorders

Studies have shown that students spend nearly 50% of their classroom time listening, yet most schools offer no formal classes in listening.[27] Audio equipment is used to address the needs of those students who learn best by listening, to remedy weak listening skills, to support written text, and to enhance student presentations.

Although almost all computers now integrate audio input and/or output, students in a technology-integrated classroom also find it useful to have access to a large tape recorder as well as the smaller, hand-held variety. Larger tape recorders are suitable for groups as they listen to stories, newspaper articles, poems, or musical selections. The smaller hand-held variety is ideal for speaking activities as well as individual assignments such as review of multiplication tables.

Battery-operated hand-held tape recorders give students the flexibility to move to where they can quietly do a speaking activity or an interview. The most obvious disadvantage of this type of equipment is its relatively short life span. If it's damaged or dropped, it may not be financially worthwhile to repair. With adequate care, however, these small tape recorders can give students two or three years (and sometimes longer) of trouble-free use.

Audiocassette tapes have been used in many classrooms for a number of years. You can record cassettes yourself or buy commercial productions. Be aware of copyright laws when making your own tapes for classroom use. To prevent the accidental erasing of these selections, simply break the plastic clips at the top of the cassettes. Tape over the holes once again if you want to erase work. Even very young children can use this technology easily.

CD Players

A portable CD player has many uses. Teachers require one for music and physical education activities. Some teachers like to play calming music to ease the transition between active outdoor activities and quiet indoor listening time. Students enjoy listening to their favorite music or story during lunch breaks.

Calculators

It is a given these days that students at all levels will use calculators to extend their understanding of mathematical concepts, perform complex operations, solve problems, and predict or check calculations. Sophisticated graphing calculators such as those made by Texas Instruments, Casio, and Hewlett Packard are required learning materials for many senior mathematics and science courses. The range and capabilities of these calculators is so diverse that they could be the focus of an entire book, thus we have chosen not to delve into this topic in detail here.

You can find support, teaching strategies, lesson plans, and product information for graphing calculators by going to Web sites prepared by the following companies and groups:
- **Texas Instruments**
- **Hewlett Packard**
- **The High School Student's Guide to Programming the TI-86 Graphics Calculator**
- **The Calculator Program Distribution Site**

Power Bars and Extension Cords

These small items are often overlooked in budgeting for technology-integrated classrooms, but they are, in fact, usually essential because most classrooms are notoriously short of power outlets. Teachers should not be expected to purchase such items themselves; every school needs a good supply.

Furniture

Classroom furniture has improved in recent years, becoming more functional, durable, ergonomic, and stylish. Desks and tables are designed to hide cords, balance laptop computers, incorporate keyboard trays and monitor pedestals, and create pods for collaborative learning. Specially designed computer carts, shelving, printer stands, and whiteboards are readily available from educational supply companies. In most schools, however, traditional desks and chairs are still the norm and space is at a premium.

Regular classroom tables are often used to accommodate computers and printers. With the simple modification of large holes drilled through the tables, the multitude of power cords and connecting cables can be bundled on the lower shelf out of sight. School custodians will appreciate the fact that cords are kept off the floor, allowing their brooms to pass under the furniture unobstructed. Another alternative is to have built-in shelving or counters specifically for equipment.

Business-Education Partnerships

As you embark on your journey, explore the possibilities of establishing a partnership. When a business and a school make a commitment to a mutually beneficial venture, a partnership is established. Technology often serves as the meeting ground for business-education partnerships because both rely on ICT to accomplish their goals and because technology-based projects can be specific and achievable. You'll find that many of the grants and award programs available today require evidence of one or more business partnerships.

> **"P**ick up almost any issue of the many K–12 technology publications or even K–12 publications that are not focused strictly on technology, and you will very likely read about teachers who have not only designed and facilitated a compelling technology-based classroom project, but who also located the funds to acquire the tools their students needed. Those of us who have gone 'digging for dollars' to fund digital tools can't begin to estimate the number of digital cameras or scanners that have been acquired through 'mini-grants' from local businesses or Parent-Teacher Organizations."[28]

Establishing a business partnership is different from asking a business for a grant or donation. True business-education partnerships are collaborative relationships in which partners share values; human, material, or financial resources; and roles and responsibilities, in order to achieve desired learning outcomes. For example, a local Internet service provider might give your school reduced access charges if teachers enroll in their training courses.

The Conference Board of Canada states that "employers and educators support business-education partnerships that

- enhance the quality and relevance of education for learners;
- mutually benefit both partners;
- treat fairly and equitably all those served by the partnership;
- provide opportunities for all partners to meet their shared responsibilities toward education;
- acknowledge and celebrate each partner's contribution through appropriate forms of recognition;
- are consistent with the ethics and core values of all partners;
- are based on the clearly defined expectations of all partners;
- are based on shared or aligned objectives that support the goals of the partner organizations;
- allocate resources to complement and not replace public funding for education;
- measure and evaluate partnership performance to make informed decisions that ensure continuous improvement;
- are developed and structured in consultation with all partners;
- recognize and respect each partner's expertise;
- identify clearly defined roles and responsibilities of all partners; and
- involve individual participants on a voluntary basis."[29]

Partnerships can be formed with individual companies, colleges, and universities, or with groups of individuals representing several related businesses. For a school, the benefits of forming a business partnership might include leadership from experts in a particular technology, gifts or loans of equipment, development of curriculum materials, opportunities for student internships, and/or the provision of support services. From the perspective of a business corporation, for what reasons would a company enter into a partnership with an educational institution? The reasons might include

- public relations and media exposure;
- immediate or long-term financial gains;
- brand-name recognition at an early age;
- testing ground for new products;
- opportunity to learn from educator expertise;
- need for graduates trained in high-technology areas; and
- altruism.

The shareholders of a company are generally more interested in increasing the value of the company's stock than they are in public relations. If their product can be showcased in the school or if its use in the school leads to an increase in sales, the company would obviously be more interested in getting involved in a joint venture.

When considering a business partnership, keep in mind the importance of dialogue — a better understanding from both sides. For example, how many people in business realize that a professional teacher does not usually even have a phone? On the other hand, a partnership with business will underline for teachers how important their work is in preparing students for the workforce. Tolbert[30] suggests the following guidelines to establishing a good relationship between business and education:

- understand the unique roles, needs, and expectations of each party;
- understand the responsibilities of each partner;
- provide an agreement between institutions, not individuals; and
- use peer review and/or endorsement by outside experts.

Finding a corporate partner with whom to join forces may not be easy. As educators, most of us possess neither the skills nor the strategies we need to approach the wider community for support. We may feel naive and in danger of being victimized by business marketing skills. How do you go about it? There is no guaranteed recipe for success, but here are some hints that we have found to be helpful.

- Identify companies in your local area and companies whose products you are already using.
- Explore personal contacts, such as parents within your school.
- Find out as much as possible about potential partners and their needs.
- Establish credibility by showing people from the business community some of the great things that are already happening in your school through the use of technology. Proposals in which the school raises a

portion of the money and the business matches the amount raised are often successful.

- Generate as much publicity as you can for your venture. Try to establish your school as an innovative leader. Everyone likes a winner.
- Provide a detailed plan of your project and its benefits to all parties.[31]

Keep in mind that the most beneficial partnership for both parties is accomplished through long-term planning and cooperation rather than an isolated donation or a special project. By keeping the communication lines open, setting clearly defined and measurable goals, ensuring accountability of both partners and problem solving together, you can enhance the success of your partnership.

As an alternative to approaching businesses, consider this innovative solution to technology funding. "Technology-based student businesses have sprouted as authentic responses to problem-based learning scenarios. At Palos East Elementary School in Palos Heights, Illinois, for example, fifth graders were inspired by a real school problem, a lack of printers to accompany classroom computers. Mrs. Deb Balayti's students decided to form a classroom business to earn money to acquire the needed equipment. The project was a huge success and the student business an instant 'local legend.' Each year since 1996–97, Mrs. Balayti's students have formed a technology-based school business, producing and selling products to the many visitors to Palos East during American Education Week. Thanks to scheduled 'Mom's Day,' 'Dad's Day,' and 'Grandparent's Day' each year, hundreds of adults become customers and clients for the fifth grade entrepreneurs. Products have varied; students have taken digital pictures of grandparents and their grandchildren (set in front of a colorful student-designed backdrop) and designed and filled orders for customized gift labels and stationery.... Although the financial gain is impressive, Mrs. Balayti reports that the student learning that occurs as students brainstorm, strategize, plan, organize and implement their business is even more exciting. Math skills, writing skills and interpersonal skills are all strengthened. Multiple intelligences are needed and showcased. Students analyze building needs and wants, research products, interview vendors, and conduct rigorous 'cost-benefit' analyses in making their purchasing decisions. The criteria they establish to guide their purchasing decisions and the exhaustive questions they pose to vendors provide clear evidence of strategic higher order thinking."[32]

Summing Up

Sound planning is essential to the success of your ICT initiatives, whether they be at the district, school, or classroom level. It's easy to be captivated by the bells and whistles of new technologies, and it seems to be human nature to wish for the latest and greatest hardware. We are bombarded daily by media reports of what's new in technology, but sometimes it's not clear exactly how this technology will make our students better learners or more productive workers. Because technology changes so very quickly, you will find that you are continuously revising and updating your plans; the five-year plan is a dinosaur of the past. In this chapter, we have provided some guidelines and food for thought, not only for beginning the technological journey but also for along the way. With a plan in place, you are ready to move on to careful consideration of the classroom issues: the software and curricula that will make ICT an integral part of your teaching and your students' learning.

MAKING
IT WORK

"Barring some major social or technological cataclysm (a plague of millennium bugs, perhaps), computers, faxes, modems, home pages, CD-ROMs, the Internet, e-mail, virtual products, conference calls, ... search engines, data bases and other elements of communication and information technology will continue to be an important and growing part of our lives, our work, and our education systems. If these technologies are not available in public education, young people will not be adequately prepared for their future lives and careers, and formal schooling will become increasingly irrelevant and discredited as a serious learning institution."[1]

Facing new equipment at the beginning of a new school year can be a more overwhelming experience than facing a roomful of eager students! Questions come to mind such as "What will I actually do with all this? What software should I be using? How will this improve my students' learning? How will I choose the best and most appropriate technological learning materials for my students?" One teacher described her initial experiences this way:

At first, I used any learning materials and computer software that I could get my hands on. Our school was supplied with a variety of useful programs and I was eager to try them all. As the year went on, I became more selective. I learned what software was best for certain tasks from talking with other teachers and reading articles in educational magazines. I listened to my students as they expressed their likes and frustrations about using specific pieces of hardware and software. I also found that sometimes a print resource worked better in meeting my curriculum goals than an electronic resource or vice-versa.

Computers can play such a variety of roles in schools today that attempts to classify software and hardware into categories are problematic. For example, does one label Web authoring software as a communication device, a productivity tool, or a creative publishing program? Thus, for the sake of simplicity, we have chosen to group hardware and software according to their role as tutor, tool, or tutee.[2] It's an old model, but it still provides a framework for looking at the variety of hardware and software available today. As tutors, computers and video can deliver complete courses, lessons, short tutorials, simulations, or drill and practice exercises. As tools, various technologies can help students and teachers perform all sorts of tasks more productively. Programming and control activities put computers into the role of tutee — that is, they "learn" to perform the programmed tasks — as the computer responds to the commands of the user. Increasingly, there is overlap between these categories, but they may be viewed as a continuum toward a more constructivist paradigm.

In this chapter, we examine these roles in more detail by describing different applications, suggesting appropriate uses for students, and featuring key pieces of software as examples. In Chapter 9: Technology Tools for Teachers, we discuss how teachers can use these applications for their own tasks.

The value of each piece of hardware discussed in Chapter 2 depends on the pedagogy and content of the materials you use with it; this includes videotapes, CD-ROM, cameras, etc. Teachers cannot be expected to be aware of the complete line of educational materials that are flooding the market on a weekly basis. You can, however, stay informed about the new materials specific to your needs by attending workshops, consulting resource people in your school or district, reading journals, joining an on-line forum or listserve, and talking with your peers.

> **"R**egardless of which tools, and how plentiful the tools, educators are being offered staggering amounts of technology activities to 'weave' into the existing curriculum. These are multiplying daily — truckloads of software which provide the learner with interactive experiences on everything from algebra to zoology. Add to that the Internet with its hundreds of thousands of homepages. Teachers are now preparing for new broadband technology which will dish up software, the web, old and new television — as well as a new breed of interactive programming at 50–100 times the current speed. It's coming at us fast and furiously."[3]

Evaluating Computer Software

The quality of early educational software was poor. In 1983, the Educational Products Information Exchange, a non-profit organization that provides consumer information about education materials, reviewed and rated available educational software and identified only 5% of programs as highly recommended.[4] Software was authored either by educators who were new to programming or by programming experts who lacked knowledge about the curriculum and how children learn. Despite the fact that developers have since learned more about education and educators about development, it's still not a good practice to order software sight unseen. Try to get a demo disk or, better yet, the complete program.

Evaluation of software is becoming an important factor in the professional development of teachers. Before investing a lot of time developing your own evaluation criteria, find out if your school or school system has already adopted an evaluation procedure. Consult experts and curriculum specialists if they are available. In many cases software is recommended by a review committee and purchased centrally by school systems. If you prefer to do your own evaluation, simply decide what criteria you wish to use and find or develop a good evaluation form. You know your students and objectives and outcomes best. Educational journals and magazines are also good sources of software evaluation criteria. Common criteria include the following:

1. Instructional quality
   - What mode of instruction is used?
   - Does it reflect good pedagogy?
   - Are goals and objectives and outcomes clearly stated?
   - Are thinking skills part of the objectives and outcomes?
   - Is the content appropriate?
   - Is there a variety of problem-solving situations?
2. Production quality
   - Is the quality of the graphics and sound acceptable or better?
   - Does it have prompt and appropriate feedback?
   - Is material presented in a clear and logical sequence?
3. Flexibility
   - Is it easy to use?
   - Are there levels of difficulty or can the program be modified to address student needs?
   - Is it suitable for a cooperative learning environment?
   - Is it accompanied by useful documentation?
4. Cost
   - How many students will benefit?
   - Does it utilize available computer capabilities?
   - Will additional peripherals be needed?

One way to learn about new software is by scanning reviews in educational magazines, journals, and books. Some reviewers have a vested interest in promoting specific software, so take into account the reviewer's qualifications, educational and/or technical expertise, and whether he/she has actually tried the software with students. A more time-efficient way to learn about new software might be to access a special interest group on an educational network on the Internet. This allows you to communicate directly with other teachers who have used a piece of software and can share their experiences. Alternatively, you can access on-line resources for software evaluation using the links provided at the publisher's Web site.

How you plan to use the software to support your curriculum is the final determining factor. Let's take a look at some common software applications and how and why they might be useful to students.

Figure 3-1
You may find that a checklist is the easiest format to use when evaluating software.

Software Evaluation Checklist

Program Title _____

Package Title _____

Cost _____ Copyright Date _____

Publisher _____

Address _____

Required Hardware _____

Prerequisite Skills _____

....

Rate the software using the following key: Y: Yes N: No N/A: Not Applicable

Documentation

	Y	N	N/A
Hardware requirements are clearly stated.	Y ___	N ___	N/A ___
Program installation is easy to follow.	Y ___	N ___	N/A ___
Goals/objectives are clearly defined.	Y ___	N ___	N/A ___
Teaching ideas/suggestions and/or additional activities are provided.	Y ___	N ___	N/A ___
Prerequisite skills have been stated.	Y ___	N ___	N/A ___

Operating of Software

	Y	N	N/A
Instructions are clear.	Y ___	N ___	N/A ___
Help screens are provided throughout the program.	Y ___	N ___	N/A ___
Screen display is well designed.	Y ___	N ___	N/A ___
Software is reliable and free of bugs.	Y ___	N ___	N/A ___
Student controls the pace.	Y ___	N ___	N/A ___
Student can exit the software at any time.	Y ___	N ___	N/A ___
Students can re-enter the program where they stopped.	Y ___	N ___	N/A ___
Student can access previous screens.	Y ___	N ___	N/A ___

continued...

Figure 3-1
continued

Presentation

Reading level is appropriate for the intended
   audience.   Y ___   N ___   N/A ___

Sound enhances the program.   Y ___   N ___   N/A ___

Graphics are appropriate.   Y ___   N ___   N/A ___

Feedback is immediate and motivating.   Y ___   N ___   N/A ___

Feedback after an incorrect response is
   immediate and helpful.   Y ___   N ___   N/A ___

Content

Content is accurate.   Y ___   N ___   N/A ___

Content is free of biases/stereotypes.   Y ___   N ___   N/A ___

Content reflects the objectives.   Y ___   N ___   N/A ___

Content is suitable for the intended audience.   Y ___   N ___   N/A ___

Content is presented in blocks.   Y ___   N ___   N/A ___

Content is presented in a variety of ways.   Y ___   N ___   N/A ___

Management

Student records are saved.   Y ___   N ___   N/A ___

Clear reports are provided on student
   achievement.   Y ___   N ___   N/A ___

Student records are private.   Y ___   N ___   N/A ___

Teachers can access records easily.   Y ___   N ___   N/A ___

Recommendation

Excellent ___ Good ___ Fair ____ Poor ____

Computer as Tutor

Computer Assisted Instruction

Computer assisted instruction (CAI) facilitates the learning of specific skills
and/or knowledge through a lesson or series of lessons. Practice sessions
and quizzes or tests often follow these lessons. Interactivity, engaging visuals,
carefully structured learning experiences, immediate feedback, and the use

of sound learning principles are important elements of good CAI software. Often called courseware, CAI has a variety of potential applications: whole-group instruction, small-group teaching, review, remediation, enrichment, and individualization of student programs. Research and reports from students about the effectiveness of learning course content from the computer are varied. Much depends on the quality of the software and the learning style of the user.

You need frequent, regular access to a computer lab if you want to use CAI as a main component of your unit or course of study, but two or three computers are adequate for review, remediation, or enrichment purposes. To take advantage of on-screen lessons for whole-group teaching, a data projector or LCD tablet is required.

Figure 3-2

Why not involve students in the selection process? This software evaluation guide is simple enough that it can also be used with students with a little explanation of terms such as program type and graphics.

What Do You Think?

Check Yes ____ or No ____

1. Did you understand the directions?   Yes ____ No ____

2. Can you use this program easily?   Yes ____ No ____

3. Was the text easy to read?   Yes ____ No ____

4. Do you like the graphics (pictures)?   Yes ____ No ____

5. Are there sound effects?   Yes ____ No ____

6. Did you like the sounds?   Yes ____ No ____

7. Did the program tell you immediately if your
   answer was right or wrong?   Yes ____ No ____

   - or -

   Did it give you the information you wanted?   Yes ____ No ____

8. Was the program too easy?   Yes ____ No ____

9. Was it too difficult?   Yes ____ No ____

10. Would you like to use this program again?   Yes ____ No ____

Comments: _____

_____

_____

_____

Featured CAI Software: Science Trek 4,5,6

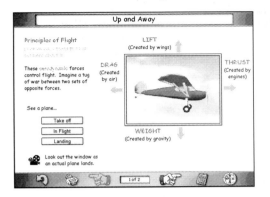
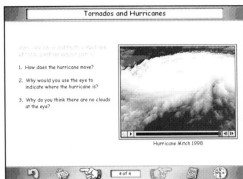

Figure 3-3
These Science Trek lessons use animation to demonstrate the principles of flight and a video clip to demonstrate the power of a hurricane.

Some of the newest courseware offerings, designed for particular subjects and grade ranges, are more like productivity tools than the traditional rote learning software of the past. This trend reflects a more constructivist view of learning and may well lead to both a decrease in textbook use in favor of computers and some measurable improvement in test scores attributable to computer use. Do not be surprised if the curriculum of your school district mandates the use of this type of courseware. These applications are generally well supported by Web sites, discussion groups, and a plethora of ready-to-use classroom activities both in books and on-line. Examples of this type of courseware are ArcView and Arc Explorer, and The Geometer's Sketchpad.

Featured CAI Software: ArcView and Arc Explorer

ArcView and Arc Explorer are geographic data analysis tools developed by Environmental Systems Research Institute, Inc. (ESRI). With more than 500,000 users worldwide, ArcView may be the world's most popular desktop mapping and GIS software. It puts hundreds of mapping and spatial analysis capabilities at your fingertips. ArcView makes it easy to create maps and add your own data to them. Using the software's powerful visualization tools, you can access records from existing databases and display them on maps. You can make great-looking publication-quality maps and create interactive displays by linking charts, tables, drawings, photographs, and other files. Arc Explorer is designed to change the way geographic data can be viewed and shared. You can use Arc Explorer to view and query geographic data stored on your computer or on the Web. With tools such as query, address match, measure, and map creation, you can

- locate street addresses or intersections on a map,
- measure distances on your map,
- find features,
- identify and query geographic and attribute data,
- create maps using classifications, symbols, and labeling,
- pan and zoom through multiple map layers, and
- view and download data published on Web sites that use ESRI's Internet Map Server (IMS) technology.

Featured CAI Software: The Geometer's Sketchpad

The Geometer's Sketchpad was developed by Dr. E. Klotz (Swarthmore College) and Dr. D. Schattschneider (Moravian College, Pennsylvania) as part of the Visual Geometry Project, funded by the National Science Foundation. It is now widely used for 2-D Euclidean geometry in classrooms in many countries. The approach is research-based, encouraging students to engage in a process of discovery in which they analyze a problem and make conjectures before attempting a proof. Using The Geometer's Sketchpad, students can explore relationships dynamically, seeing the change in geometric figures as they manipulate them.[5] Students can import diagrams into their word-processing documents, where they explain their calculations and thinking. The Geometer's Sketchpad, an example of constructivist courseware, is supported by a host of on-line activities, lessons, and tutorials:

* The Geometer's Sketchpad materials, including lesson plans, scope and sequence, and teacher inservice
* The Geometer's Sketchpad Tutorial
* examples of what The Geometer's Sketchpad program is capable of doing
* lesson plans for The Geometer's Sketchpad

Figure 3-4

The Swarthmore site is a great place to look for resources to support your use of The Geometer's Sketchpad in the classroom.

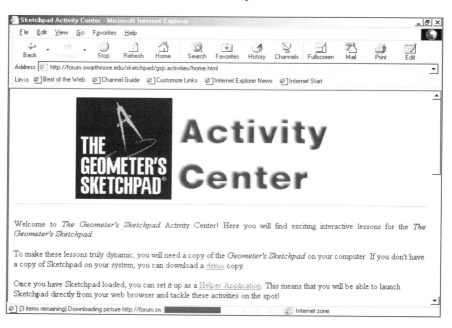

Drill and Practice Software

Because drill and practice software is specific for subject, age level, and skill, we can consider it only in general terms. Its purpose is to improve student performance in a specific task or skill. It is most often used for rote learning tasks such as keyboarding, math drills, phonics, and memorizing of subject-related facts. From a teacher's point of view, it is often difficult to assess the actual learning that takes place unless you work directly with the student, assign a follow-up activity, or use software designed to keep track of student progress. In addition to the great variety of drill and practice software available for purchase, you can find drill and practice exercises at Web sites. Look for these characteristics in drill and practice software:

* different skill levels

- modifiable for students with special needs
- teacher-controlled input and options
- ability for students to create their own tasks and tasks for others
- relevant and immediate feedback
- built-in motivation
- self-directed and self-paced setup
- on-line help
- attractive graphics
- randomly generated questions
- access to students' work by teachers
- helpful support materials

Ted S. Hasselbring, the co-director of the Learning Technology Center at Vanderbilt University's Peabody College in Nashville, Tennessee, identifies three broad steps that are necessary to mastering basic skills — developing the skill initially, becoming fluent at it, and being able to apply it across different activities and content areas. Drill-and-practice, he says, addresses only the second step — fluency. Educators, unfortunately, have not always understood that, he says. "People have assumed that drill-and-practice will teach kids skills, but drill-and-practice was designed to develop fluency. That's the only reason why you use a drill-and-practice program."[6]

Featured Drill and Practice Software: Reader Rabbit

Reader Rabbit has long been popular with teachers and parents alike. The software's engaging graphics, sound, and interactivity make it appealing to young learners. You need to spend some time playing the games yourself in order to determine exactly what skill students will be practicing. A parent volunteer or older student should sit with the young child; otherwise, the predominant strategy may be simply guessing the correct answer with very little learning.

Featured Drill and Practice Software: Math Baseball

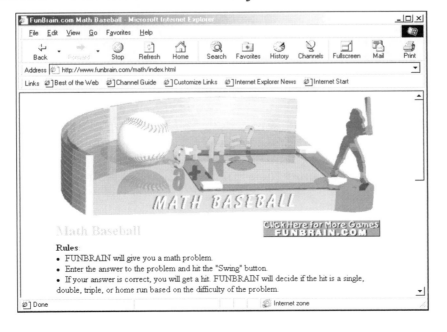

Figure 3-5

In the math baseball game (http://www.funbrain.com/math/index.html), the computer gives you a math problem and if your answer is correct, you get a hit. The computer decides if the hit is a single, double, triple, or home run based on the difficulty of the problem. If your answer is wrong, you get an out. The game is over after three outs. You can choose from the four basic operations and the difficulty level can be set from Easy to Superbrain, making the game usable at many levels.

Simulations

Computer simulations are useful for exploring concepts that may be too dangerous, complex, expensive, time-consuming, or otherwise impossible within the confines of the classroom. They can allow for manipulation of variables in an efficient manner so students can construct and test hypotheses, make inferences, and draw conclusions. Students might use a simulation to

- develop and sustain an ecosystem (e.g., Digital Field Trip to the Wetlands);
- design and build a robot to cross a specific terrain (e.g., Robot R & D);
- design a building (e.g., KidCad);
- dissect a frog (e.g., Digital Frog);
- establish and maintain the economy of a town (e.g., SimCity);
- experience life in a different time or culture (e.g., Underground Railway at http://www.nationalgeographic.com/features/99/railroad); and
- plan a trip (e.g., CrossCountry Canada).

Many such simulations are available on both CD-ROM and the Web. It is a matter of selecting good ones that fit your curriculum. Students are highly motivated by the game-like nature of most simulations and will happily return to them regularly. Sometimes an on-line simulation can provide just the right activity without substantial preparation by the teacher. For example, directing students who are struggling with a concept such as the physics of flight to a simulation of the airflow over a wing in which they can manipulate certain variables can visually and interactively demonstrate and clarify the concept in ways that are not possible using the chalkboard. Although software can also be used, a Web page may be more convenient if you have easy access. Keep in mind that these simulations are often Java applets (small programs) that must be downloaded before they run, a process that can take a minute or two. Others are Shockwave programs, so you need the plug-in to run them. Some of the developers may allow you to download the files and place them on your school Intranet or server, which will speed up student access. Thousands of simulations, particularly on Science topics, are now readily available. Find and bookmark the best of these by referring to the jars.com directory of Java-based science resources at: http://www.jars.com/jars_categories_java_science.html.[7] You will find a few others to get you started at the publisher's Web site.

Teachers want students to develop important skills such as critical thinking, decision-making, and problem solving while enjoying the activity. A common difficulty, however, is that students learn to manipulate the simulation through trial and error until they get the desired result without really determining the rules and principles that produced it. By asking students to explain their results or apply their learning to a new situation, you can focus student use of the simulation.

Electronic Books and Stories

Reading stories to children has long been considered an important contribution to their success as proficient readers. Electronic books on CD-ROM, with their engaging components of animation, voice, and interactivity, are now familiar to many young children and their parents and teachers. In particular the Living Books series (Broderbund, Random House) and the Discis Books (Knowledge Research) can be found in most schools. The stories selected for this medium are usually written by well-known children's authors, beautifully illustrated, and read in pleasant voices. Sometimes you can choose between male and female voices, child and adult voices, or different languages. Highlighted words can be pronounced and defined with a click of the mouse. These "talking books," as they are often called, are especially beneficial to beginning readers, reluctant readers, and students learning English as a second language. The computer never gets tired of reading the same story repeatedly. Price determines the number of special features, but the cost of these products has rapidly declined over the past few years, making them affordable for schools and individual teachers.

One recent case study comparing electronic to paper books demonstrated that the electronic storybook can yield similar, if not in some cases the same, outcomes as those generated by a human-read story. The electronic books held students' attention, and students retained more information from the electronic versions of the stories. The author suggests that time spent with electronic stories can indeed give children some building blocks to aid their acquisition of literacy.[8]

Electronic books and stories are also available on the Web. The Internet Public Library (http://www.ipl.org) is a good place to begin looking for on-line stories to accompany your learning units. Check the teen and youth sections. The Children's Literature Web Guide (http://www.acs.ucalgary.ca/~dkbrown/stories.html) maintains an excellent list that will provide another starting point in your search for different types of online stories.

WHAT CAN STUDENTS DO WITH ELECTRONIC BOOKS AND STORIES?
- read and share
- read with a peer tutor or parent volunteer
- use as a model for producing their own electronic stories
- make vocabulary lists and dictionaries
- learn English as a second language

For other **WWW** sources of electronic books and stories, go to the publisher's Web site.

FEATURED ELECTRONIC BOOK: DO SPIDERS LIVE ON THE
WORLD WIDE WEB?
(http://www.ipl.org/youth/StoryHour/spiders/mousepg.html)

Figure 3-6

This beautifully illustrated book from the Internet Public Library can be used to help young children learn the vocabulary of computers. It introduces terminology such as mouse, Net, Web, laptop, and window by contrasting them with their non-technological synonyms.

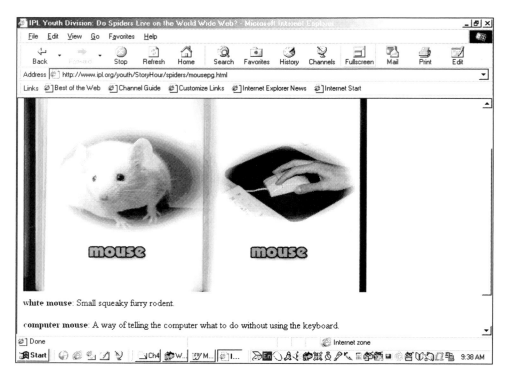

E-books are digitized versions of books that can be downloaded from a Web site and read on a desktop or laptop computer, a hand-held device, or a dedicated e-book reader. Dedicated e-book readers are inexpensive, ergonomically designed for reading, very portable and offer good screen resolution. You can find out more about them at the manufacturers' Web sites.

The obvious advantages of e-books are their capacity for easy updating, savings in the traditional costs of printing, shipping and storage, and relief from the 20-pound backpack. In a teaching and learning context, the potential of e-books is exciting. Imagine integrated reference and testing tools, opportunities for teachers to add and customize content, embedded hyperlinks to Web sites, and information search capabilities. To try out some of the free e-book readers and titles available on the Web, you can download Microsoft Reader (http://www.microsoft.com) or Adobe Acrobat eBook Reader (http://www.adobe.com) along with copyright-free books. Until publishing companies receive enough demand from schools, lack of content in e-book formats may continue to be problematic, but this exciting technology holds a great deal of promise for the near future. From the publisher's Web site you can link to some on-line spots where you can presently find e-book titles for downloading.[9]

Computer as Tool (Productivity)

Word Processing

Speed, power, and ease of revision make writing on the computer more productive than using pencil and paper. Word processing is the most widely used computer application in both work and home settings. Students adapt easily to composing on screen once they get used to it and often resist returning to "old-fashioned" writing tools. Manual skills continue to be necessary, however, and should not be ignored. When using word processing, the focus can be on the writing process — prewriting, composing, revising, and editing, not just on the content. Students can plan their stories and reports using the outlining tool available in many word-processing applications. Many students experience increased self-esteem due to the professional appearance of their completed work, especially those with poor manual skills. Students also enjoy having their collected works readily accessible in their electronic portfolios.

There are many types of word-processing software and each is unique, hence we treat this type of software generically here rather than highlighting one program in particular. When selecting which word-processing software to use in your classroom, consider ease of use for the particular age range of students and invest some time in teaching students how to effectively use the features available. Special features are more important for older students, but all students benefit from features such as

- spell check
- grammar check
- glossary
- thesaurus
- on-line help

What Can Students Do With Word-Processing Software?

- create alphabet books
- keep a journal
- document science experiments
- prepare factual reports
- write collaborative stories
- compose content-area class books
- use outline features to plan stories and reports
- create surveys and questionnaires
- make charts and tables

Learning Tips and Tricks for Word Processing:

- demonstrate features within the context of a learning activity
- tackle only the special features that you need for a particular task — you can learn others as you need them
- post "how-to" cards or signs at the computer
- create exercises or task cards to provide students with practice in such skills as text editing, using the spell checker and thesaurus, adding charts and graphs, and moving and resizing clip art

Figure 3-7

Students create a simple chart using WordPerfect in which they can organize their research about life in medieval times.[10]

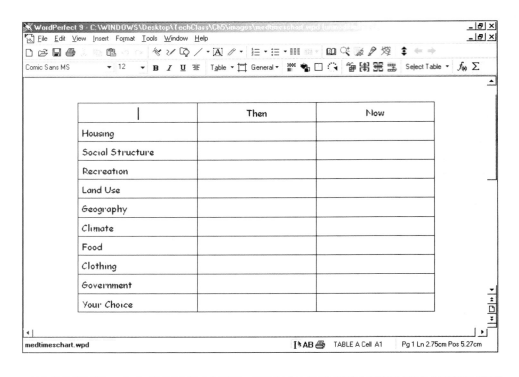

Figure 3-8

Most word processors can produce so much more than text these days. Here students use the chart function of Microsoft Word to create a radar web comparing two characters from the novel they are studying.[11]

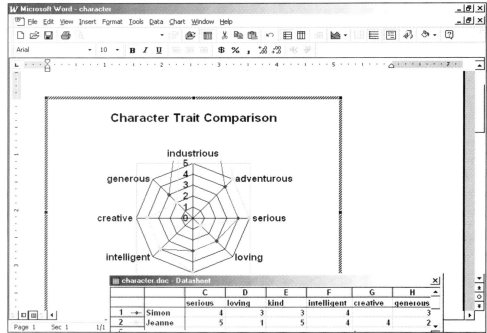

Collaborative Internet Applications

Collaborative Internet tools are changing and growing rapidly, allowing greater possibilities for communication than ever before possible. The potential of these technologies in learning is just beginning to be explored by creative educators worldwide. The following is merely a sampling of the most accessible of these applications. For those interested in distance education, where these tools are used extensively, we suggest you consult other resources specifically on that topic.

E-mail

Virtually everyone is now so familiar with e-mail that sending an e-mail is comparable to making a phone call. In fact, e-mail is the "hook" that gets a lot of people started using computers, even those who have been resisting. E-mail has now become the primary way that most of us keep up to date with both work and social commitments. Most school districts maintain an internal e-mail system that also connects to the world via the Internet and provide a free account for all employees. Teachers are expected to access current information, download forms for both personal (e.g., health insurance) and professional (e.g., student Individual Educational Plan templates) use, find out about professional growth and career opportunities, and correspond with their colleagues. Some school districts provide e-mail accounts for students; others rely on students having their own personal accounts either from home or through one of the free Web services such as HotMail (http://www.hotmail.com).

WHAT CAN STUDENTS DO WITH E-MAIL?
- correspond with a keypal
- ask a question of an expert
- collaborate with peers on a common project

Listserves

Listserves are simply topic-related mailing lists that send messages to all subscribers. Once you have joined the list, messages appear automatically in your e-mail inbox. Teachers often find listserves to be a time-effective way to stay current in teaching issues or subject content areas.

WHAT CAN STUDENTS DO WITH LISTSERVES?
- probably nothing at school, but may subscribe at home to a listserve of personal interest

Newsgroups

Your Web browser has a feature that allows you to access newsgroups, which are on-line discussion groups. You can participate in the discussion or search through the archives of all messages. Most public newsgroups contain little of educational value, but a teacher can set up a private newsgroup, accessible only by students, for a special purpose or project.

WHAT CAN STUDENTS DO WITH NEWSGROUPS?
- pose a question to teacher or peers
- collaborate with peers on a common project

Web Conferencing

Web conferencing is a generic term for personal interaction in a Web-based environment. Interaction is asynchronous, that is, the people interacting may not be on-line at the same time. All comments are listed and archived, allowing you to read through the dialogue and respond at your convenience. Many different free and commercial programs are available for Web conferencing, each with a variety of features. Teachers can create their own private Web conferences — go to the publisher's Web site for a link that will take you to a Web page that will show how.

WHAT CAN STUDENTS DO WITH WEB CONFERENCING?
- collaborate with peers on a common project
- chat with teacher or peers
- share files such as text, images, and music

Internet Relay Chat

Internet Relay Chat (IRC) allows for "real-time" (synchronous) interaction, which is motivating and fun but can become hectic. An experienced moderator is most helpful in directing and ordering incoming questions and comments. A chat client software program is required for IRC.

WHAT CAN STUDENTS DO WITH IRC?
- collaborate with peers on a common project
- chat with teacher or peers
- access information and opinions from outside the classroom
- interview an expert

Desktop Videoconferencing

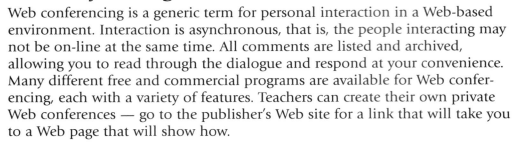

As described in Chapter 2: Planning for Success, videoconferencing involves the transmission of full images and sound. Desktop videoconferencing will bring this possibility out of the studio and into your classroom. You need a color video camera, a microphone, videoconferencing software (free or purchased), and an Internet connection. The quality of the video and audio, however, will depend on the speed of your Internet access. Despite the fact that most of the examples we have seen to date feature miniature, distorted images with halting, jerky audio, this technology may well be ready for the classroom much sooner than you expect. CU-SeeMe is a popular videoconferencing software application. You can find out more about it or download a free copy at the company's Web site.

Databases

Any information that is stored in an organized fashion is considered a database. Some databases that you use regularly include telephone directories, address books, dictionaries, and recipe files. A database serves to organize information so that it can be easily read, analyzed, and accessed. When the information is entered into a computer, it becomes an electronic database. An electronic database allows you to locate information quickly, update and add information easily, alphabetize and sort information, rank information in order of importance, and merge with a word processor to put information onto envelope labels, parent letters, and certificates. A database is often included as one component of an integrated software package or suite. Both Microsoft Works and Apple Works include a simple database appropriate for elementary students. FileMaker Pro is another powerful database commonly used for educational applications. In Chapter 9 you will find out how a database can be a teacher tool. Databases are useful to students within any discipline, as they are simply tools for gathering, organizing, and analyzing information. Follow these steps in introducing the use of databases to your students using any appropriate content from your curriculum. Students will describe a database and name its parts using the phone book as an analogy, use a simple teacher-created electronic database to find information, add information to a teacher-created template in which the fields are already set up for them, design a curriculum-related database template on paper, collect data to be entered in each field of a database, and create a simple electronic database.

Parts of a database
- **A file is a subset or part of the whole database; for example, if all the people in the phone book are a database, all those who have a 613 area code constitute a file.**
- **A record is all the information about each element of the database; for example, in the phone book, the record about one person might include that person's last name, first name, address, and phone number.**
- **A field (or category) is the single item of information from any record in the database; for example, in the phone book, "last name" is a field, "phone number" is another field.**
- **An entry is the data that is put into a field; for example, in Mary Smith's last name field, the entry is "Smith."**

WHAT CAN STUDENTS DO WITH AN ELECTRONIC DATABASE?
- collect information about all the leaders of your country to create a class database with fields such as name, date of birth, term of office, political party, major accomplishments
- create a database of plants, animals, or insects with fields such as habitat, food, size, adaptations, use to humans
- collect data from science experiments and organize it into a database
- keep a record of books read using fields such as title, author, type of book, length, date read, evaluation

Featured Database Software: AppleWorks Database

Formerly known as ClarisWorks, AppleWorks is perhaps the most commonly used software in the educational market. Whether you use the Macintosh or IBM platform, you are sure to come in contact with this user-friendly word-processing, database, and spreadsheet suite. The database in AppleWorks is an easy-to-use basic database. Students can enter and view their data as either a running list of records or a summary chart. Records can be sorted alphabetically, numerically, or by category. The extensive Help menu will address most of your questions as you explore this software.

Figure 3-9

A database is an excellent tool for a science unit on the topic of classification of animals because it allows students to sort by various criteria and draw conclusions based on the reorganized data. This animal database is shown as it appears in List layout (left) and in Browse layout (right).

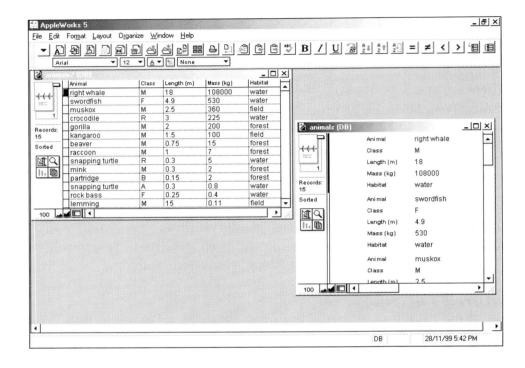

Figure 3-10

A Reading Log is one of the most popular uses of a database at all levels. Students can customize their Reading Logs by adding check boxes and drop-down choice menus. Electronic Reading Logs can follow students through many grades and provide an important component of cumulative portfolios.

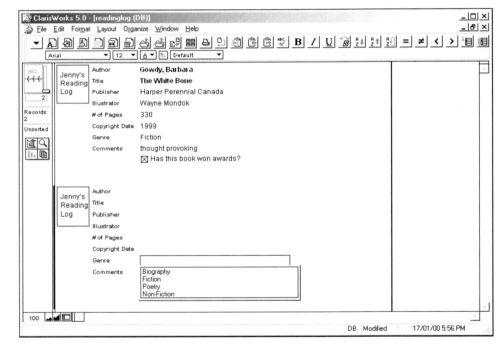

LEARNING TIPS AND TRICKS FOR APPLEWORKS DATABASE:

- Begin by browsing through the introductory tutorial included within the software. Follow this with a trial-and-error practice session.
- For other tutorials and ideas, go to the publisher's Web site.
- Decide which fields you need before you begin to create your database.
- With younger students, create the fields and have them simply enter the data they have collected to create a class database.

Making It Work **67**

- "Layout" controls the way information will appear on the screen or on paper when printed. A file can have many layouts, each serving a different purpose and having a different appearance while not changing the content of the data.
- There are lots of books available for ideas, including
  - Caughlin, Janet. *Claris Workshop for Students K-6.* [United States]: Visions Technology in Education, 1995.
  - Kitto, Rick, and Rob Scott. *Works Across the Curriculum.* Toronto: Addison-Wesley Publishers, 1994.
  - Smith, Irene, Sharon Yoder, and Rick Thomas. *Classroom Activities with AppleWorks 5.0, Revised Edition.* Eugene, Oregon: ISTE, 1999.
- You do not need to enter your records in any particular order — the "sort" function allows you to do that later.
- The "match" function helps you to find records that fit more complex criteria — for example, all the birthdays in January.

Featured Database Software: Filemaker Pro

FileMaker Pro is a much more powerful and sophisticated database than those included in either Microsoft Works or AppleWorks, hence there is more to learn. Filemaker Pro is often used for creating electronic portfolios because it allows storage of graphics, sound files, and QuickTime movies. You can find out more about this in Chapter 8: Assessment and Evaluation. FileMaker Pro offers prepared templates, which, if appropriate, can save a lot of time. You might begin with a template and then customize it as you go along.

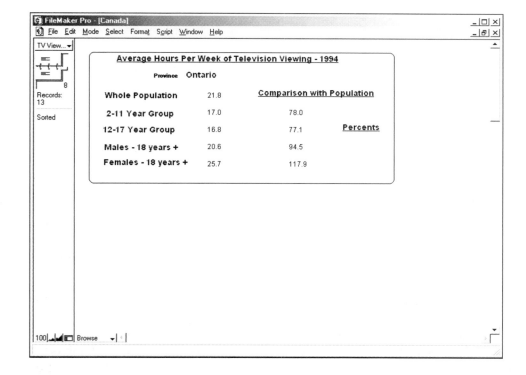

Figure 3-11

Students use a FileMaker Pro database to organize data from which they can make inferences and draw conclusions about the TV watching habits of various groups.

LEARNING TIPS AND TRICKS FOR FILEMAKER PRO:
- Give yourself lots of time to learn this software.
- Take a one-day workshop.
- Read some resources before starting to free explore.
- Specify the field type from eight options, including text, number, date, time, and container (for graphic, sound, or movie).
- Scriptmaker is used to execute a series of commands.

Desktop Publishing

WHAT CAN STUDENTS DO WITH DESKTOP PUBLISHING SOFTWARE?
- make a travel brochure or a newspaper
- make business cards
- make flyers for classroom and school events
- create book covers or CD covers
- make greeting cards and thank-you notes
- make posters for school rules, safety, or environmental awareness
- print banners for sporting events, fund-raisers, dances

Featured Desktop Publishing Software: Microsoft Publisher

Microsoft Publisher is one of the easiest and most useful applications for teachers and students to learn. If you are a beginner looking for a good starting point, we suggest Microsoft Publisher. It may be comforting to know that if you are familiar with Microsoft Office, you are well on your way to learning Microsoft Publisher, as it uses the same menu bars, rulers, and short-cuts where appropriate. Your students may already be familiar with it, as it has been around for a while. The newer the version, the more intuitive and versatile the software. The CD contains a useful clip art gallery; you can also import your own images. Students are invariably pleased with the professional appearance of the publications they create using MS Publisher.

LEARNING TIPS AND TRICKS FOR MICROSOFT PUBLISHER:
- Take the tutorial.
- Use the helpful wizards and cue cards.
- Think about the intended audience and the layout of your publication before beginning.
- Play with Word Art.
- To get a quick idea of what the chunk of text or graphics that you are working on will look like, use the F9 key to enlarge to 100% and reduce back to 33%.
- Older versions of MS Publisher may not accept your imported graphic unless it is in bitmap (.bmp) format.
- Once you have created a format you like, simply copy and paste it onto a new page and change the text to suit.

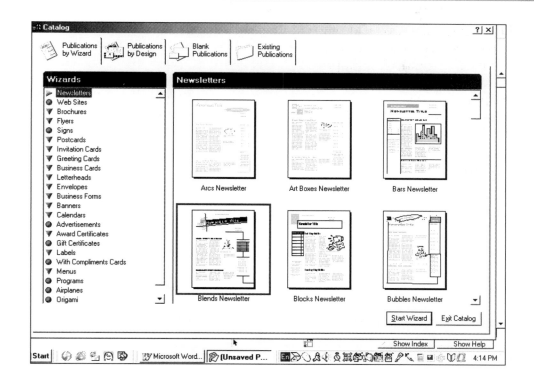

Figure 3-12

You can select the type of product you wish to create from an extensive list of options. A variety of templates are provided for each, or you can choose to create your own from scratch.

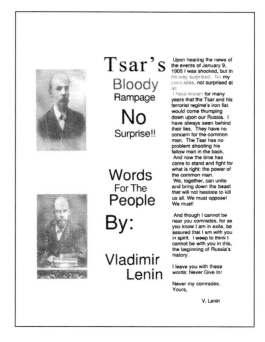

Figure 3-13

After discussing the causes of the Russian revolution, students use Microsoft Publisher to create a propaganda flyer illustrating a particular point of view.[12]

Graphics Software

Sophisticated graphics software is the tool of choice for more and more professional artists and designers these days. Many Web site builders use powerful graphics programs such as Adobe Photoshop and Adobe Illustrator, Macromedia Flash, and CorelDRAW to create images for their pages. Good graphics software is also invaluable for educators. Graphics software is not difficult to learn, and once you have experience with one graphics program, you will find it easy to learn another. The painting and drawing tools tend to be similar, though they vary in their complexity. Most computers come with a basic graphics package already installed, such as Windows Paint or MacDraw. Some graphics programs have been developed for personal and professional use; others are specifically for young children.

WHAT CAN STUDENTS DO WITH GRAPHICS SOFTWARE?
- match pictures to letters
- make patterns and graphs with the stamp pad
- explore symmetry with the kaleidoscope feature
- create notebook covers, project covers, and title pages
- write and illustrate a children's story or book
- design a simple or complex machine
- draw a plan for something they are to design and later build
- design a logo for a product
- make a slide show to describe or announce an event
- create posters for clubs and events
- produce bulletins and notices
- illustrate stories
- create graphic organizers such as Venn diagrams and flow charts
- learn and demonstrate art concepts such as perspective, 3-D modeling and shading
- design projects involving drawings; for example, a bridge structure made out of sticks, a complex food web, or a model of the atom

Featured Graphics Software: Kid Pix

Kid Pix is a multimedia graphics program that was designed by a father for his three-year-old son. It was specifically designed for children who cannot yet read, but it has a much wider application. It allows young students to create graphics and multimedia slide shows, encouraging their creativity by giving them hundreds of tools, choices, and options. The program is easy to learn and use, yet has enormous potential for classroom applications. All you need do is show students some of the basics and then let them discover the rest through free exploration. Kid Pix is full of sounds: tools make sounds while you work with them, sounds can be selected from a bank to add to projects, and you can record sounds. Fortunately, teachers can turn this sound off if headphones are not available! Digital video clips can be pasted into Kid Pix pictures, viewed in the Wacky TV feature or used as slides for a slide show. The Teacher's Guide provides a multitude of lesson plans for using Kid Pix at all grade levels.

LEARNING TIPS AND TRICKS FOR KID PIX:
- Play, play, and play.
- Look in the various Teacher's Guides for integration ideas and lesson plans.

- Go to the publisher's Web site for a link that will take you to the tutorial.
- Books about Kid Pix:
  Ballweg, Judy K. *Kid Pix ABC — Art, Books and Computers*. Eugene, Oregon: ISTE, 2000.

Ballweg, Judy K. *Kid Pix Digital Gallery — Cameras, Scanners and Computers.* Eugene, Oregon: ISTE, 2000.

Kampman, Marybeth. *Fat Crayon Multimedia Using Kid Pix.* Eugene, Oregon: ISTE, 1998.

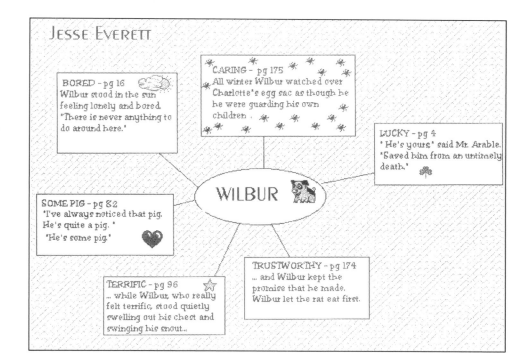

Figure 3-14

Grade 3 students use Kid Pix to arrange critical information from the book Charlotte's Web *by making a graphic organizer.*[13]

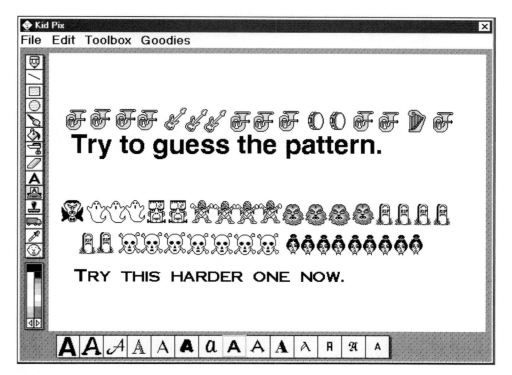

Figure 3-15

The Kid Pix tool bar is simple enough for very young students. Here a young student uses Kid Pix to demonstrate patterning and a pictograph.

Figure 3-15
continued

Featured Graphics Software: CorelDRAW

CorelDRAW, one of the most popular pieces of software in the world, is an intricate graphics program offering numerous features for older students. You can prepare, modify, import, and export graphic images. Options such as word art and the volume of available clip art and photo CDs make it flexible for a wide variety of cross-curricular projects. Students can design pictures with CorelDRAW for use in your school or class Web site. (Notice that your CorelDRAW files save with the extension ".cmx." This is one of the formats acceptable for use on the Web.) There are many versions of CorelDRAW. The more recent versions (e.g., CorelDRAW 8 and 9) require a moderately powerful system for optimal performance. Be careful to save your pictures in the correct format if you plan on taking them to another computer or network. The only limit on what CorelDRAW can do for you is your imagination, as you create anything from a simple poster to elaborate engineering designs.

 See the Corel Features in Action Web Page at the company's Web site.

Learning Tips and Tricks for CorelDRAW:
- Give yourself lots of time to learn this software.
- Work with a peer or student expert who can get you started.
- Take a one-day workshop.
- Check out the tutorial, Corel TUTOR, before starting to explore.
- Tutorials can be found at the company's Web site.
- A good way to begin is to see what everything on the toolbar does. Right click on each icon to get the options of "What's This?" and "Properties."
- Text can be curved by going to the "Effects" menu and selecting the "Envelope" feature.

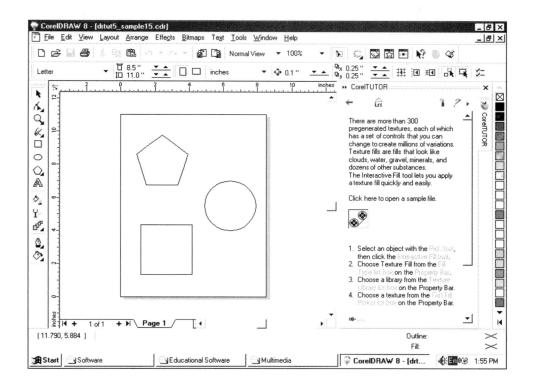

Figure 3-16
Corel TUTOR, which you can access at start-up or from the help menu, will take you step by step through the many and varied features of this powerful graphics program. You can use the sample files to teach yourself — so can your students.

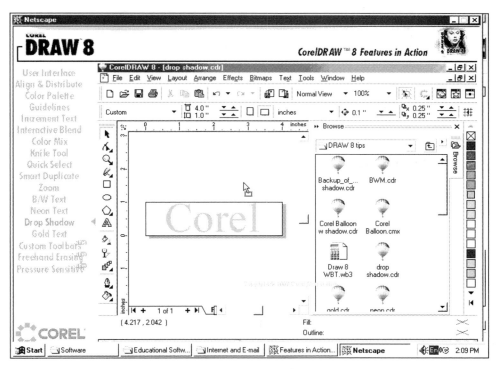

Figure 3-17
Corel Learning has begun to develop visually enhanced Web-based tools that provide interactive training and information on how to use their products. To run the modules, you need a screen resolution of 800 by 600 (the recommended minimum), a sound card and speakers, Netscape Communicator 3.0 (or higher) or Internet Explorer 3.0 (or higher), and QuickTime movie player 3.0 (link provided for download).

- The "Transformation" menu includes graphics manipulations such as mirror images, rotations, and skewing.
- Shift-F4 re-centers the drawing page and Ctrl-z undoes your last action.
- Your on-screen images will appear at the maximum resolution of the output device, such as printer or monitor, so to get a high-quality image you'll need a good printer.

- CorelDRAW is a large and powerful program, but don't let its initial appearance of complexity put you off — explore, use the available help, and remember to save your pictures regularly.

Multimedia Software

Multimedia refers to software that incorporates several media — text, graphic objects, clip art, audio, and video. "Multimedia is...woven combinations of text, graphic art, sound, animation, and video elements. When you allow an end user — the viewer of a multimedia project to control what and when the elements are delivered, it is called interactive multimedia. When you provide a structure of linked elements through which the user can navigate, interactive multimedia becomes hypermedia."[14] The use of multimedia tools for student projects supports a student-centered constructivist view of learning.

Figure 3-18

Hyperlinking allows presentations to be webbed (as opposed to linear), which is much more in keeping with the way the brain works.

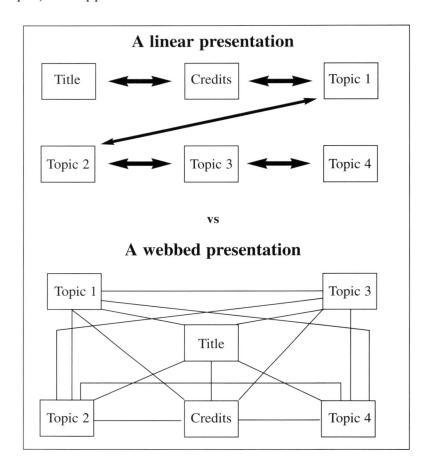

WHAT CAN STUDENTS DO WITH MULTIMEDIA SOFTWARE?
- prepare personal portfolios
- present projects in any subject area
- create a learning game
- build an electronic library of stories
- create "choose your own adventure" stories

- create a visual tour of the school or community
- make interactive book reports or poems
- compare art styles, music, architecture, or different cultures

Featured Multimedia Software: HyperStudio

HyperStudio is used not only by schools in grades K–12, but in college courses as well. You don't have to be a programmer — the program does all the programming for you. In HyperStudio, you create a "stack" with a set of cards. A stack is formed from cards in the same way that a book is formed from pages. Each card can contain text, graphics, audio, and/or animations. Cards are linked to one another by "buttons," allowing them to be inter-linked and multiply linked in an endless variety of ways. Buttons are simply objects on the screen that make things happen when you click on them, so they can also be used to play sounds, animate objects, or show video clips. Invisible buttons can be used to run the stack as an automatic slide show. HyperStudio buttons can direct Netscape or Internet Explorer to open to a specific URL location. This can be used to integrate particular Web pages right into a project. The HyperStudio CD-ROM contains some video clips, sounds, graphics, and animations from which you can choose if you do not have time or need to create your own.

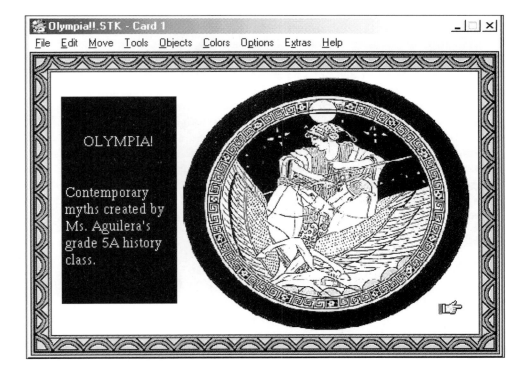

Figure 3-19

In this activity, each student creates a myth and the myths are compiled into a class HyperStudio presentation.[15]

Figure 3-20

Students create a storyboard or planning guide to their HyperStudio project. They show it to the teacher for feedback before beginning to create screens.

My Project Planning Sheet

Title Card
Links to: _____
Notes: (sound, animation) _____
_____
_____

Contents Card
Links to: _____
Notes: (sound, animation) _____
_____
_____

Card 1
Links to: _____
Notes: (sound, animation) _____
_____
_____

Card 2
Links to: _____
Notes: (sound, animation) _____
_____
_____

Broward County Digital Storytelling Project
"Broward County students are spreading stories all around, and they're using HyperStudio to do it! More than 50 schools in the Fort Lauderdale, Florida district are creating digital stories that are started in one classroom and grow in length as they are passed among other classes. Each school will choose three 'masterpieces' to send to district-level competition, where judges will select the winning entries. Those chosen will be displayed at the Broward County Public Library's Children's Literature Conference, Children's Reading Festival, and at other local, state, and national conferences. Students will be using their reading skills while learning the writing process, and then publishing their stories using HyperStudio. What a wonderful way to integrate technology into the curriculum!"[16]

LEARNING TIPS AND TRICKS FOR HYPERSTUDIO:
- There are a lot of features so allow a minimum of one or two hours for training in the classroom.
- Projects can be big — too big to fit on a diskette, so save to the computer's hard drive, use a Zip diskette, or learn how to compress files.
- Take 15 to 20 minutes to walk through the built-in tutorial.
- Before you begin your project, have a storyboard of what you are going to do. Plan ahead so that you know what your next step will be.
- Check out the different sample projects on the HyperStudio CD for curriculum integration and design ideas.
- When scanning images to go into your HyperStudio project, scan them at a good size. HyperStudio reduces pictures well but enlarging produces a grainy effect.

- Provide students with a clear assessment guide or rubric to keep them focused.
- Teach students that the esthetics and multimedia extras such as available music clips, animations, and video clips can distract from the actual content.
- The main HyperStudio site features sample projects, resources, tips, and user forums.
- There are a multitude of books available for teachers about using HyperStudio in the classroom, such as the following:

  Cochran, David W., and Robert A. Straats Jr. *HyperStudio Express*. Florence, Kentucky: Thomson Learning, 1997.

  Kitto, R., and Rob Scott. *Student Projects with HyperStudio*. London, Ontario: KS Publications, 1998.

  Ivers, Karen S., and Ann E. Barron. *Multimedia Projects in Education — Designing, Producing and Assessing*. Englewood, Colorado: Libraries Unlimited Inc., 1998.

  McBride, Karen Hein, and Elizabeth DeBoer Luntz. *Help! I Have HyperStudio...Now What Do I Do?* [United States]: McB Media, 1996.

  Muir, Michael. *But How Do I Use HyperStudio with Kids? Designing and Doing Curriculum-based Projects*. Eugene, Oregon: ISTE, 1997.

  Sharp, Vicki F. *HyperStudio in One Hour*. Eugene, Oregon: ISTE, 1999.
- For tutorials go to the publisher's Web site.

> **"I**t is best to follow the 'K-I-S-S' rule of multimedia, especially when you are just getting started:
>   **Keep It Simple to Get Started!**
>   **Keep It Short and Sweet!**
>   **Keep It Simple to Survive!"**
>   **(D'Ignazio[17])**

Photo Editing and Working With Photos

Photos greatly enhance communication and students enjoy using them to add a personal flavor to their work. One of the important considerations when saving images to insert into documents is the file format in which you choose to save them. Digital images can be saved in a variety of graphic formats. You can tell the format of a file by its file extension, which is the part of the file name that comes after the dot; for example, mydog.gif is a gif (Graphics Interchange Format). Some of the most common types are

- bmp (Windows Bitmap) These tend to be very large files.
- gif (Graphics Interchange Format) This is a compressed graphic often used on the Web (so you can take big graphics and make them much smaller memory-wise).
- jpeg/jpg (Joint Photographic Experts Group) This is another compressed Web-type of graphic, but it's more often used for graphics such as photos.
- TIFF/tif (Tagged Image File Format) These also tend to be very big files.
- pct (Macintosh PICT) These are the Mac version of the bitmap (the default graphic format used). They also tend to result in large files.
- pcd (Kodak Photo CD)
- pcx (PC Paintbrush)

The end use of the image will determine the software into which you plan to insert it and, hence, the format in which you choose to save it. You can insert many popular file formats into your documents either directly or with the use of graphics filters built into the software. Get to know what types of image files are supported by the software you most frequently use in order to avoid wasting time experimenting.

FEATURED PHOTO EDITING SOFTWARE: MGI PHOTOSUITE SE

MGI PhotoSuite SE is quite typical of the majority of beginner software in this field. The photo editing options include applying special effects; changing brightness, colors, and image size; cloning parts of a photo to another part; adding text or drawing onto your image; resizing; and cutting/pasting selected areas (see Fig. 3-21 and Fig. 3-22).

Figure 3-21

Like most photography software, PhotoSuite provides a number of creative ways to use your digital images. You can group photos to make albums, create slide shows of your photos, make cards and calendars, or add text.

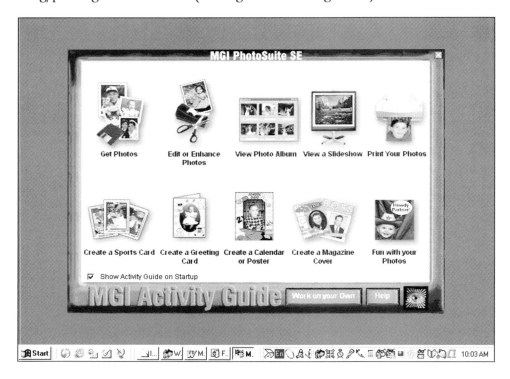

LEARNING TIPS AND TRICKS FOR MGI PHOTOSUITE SE:

- Explore.
- Make all the changes you want to an image, and when you get in trouble just choose not to save your changes.
- Use the HELP menus.

Presentation Software

Why use chalk and blackboard or a dull series of black and white overhead transparencies when you can share dazzling lessons and student projects from your computer? All you need is the ability to project the computer screen using an LCD panel, data projector, or large-screen TV. Although presentation software was designed with the boardroom rather than the classroom in mind, it can be used to organize and present any information in a variety of formats.

Figure 3-22

In this example, a student adds a word balloon to a photo that will then be incorporated into a poster for a fund-raising drive to help homeless animals.

Information can be shown on colorful slides with interesting backgrounds and a variety of transitions from screen to screen. Presentations can be enhanced with the addition of charts, graphs, pictures, and video clips. Once a presentation has been prepared, it is easy to store and modify for use in a different setting or during the next school year. Students will be proud of the professional-quality presentations they can make to the class.

WHAT CAN STUDENTS DO WITH PRESENTATION SOFTWARE?
- report on a field trip
- share curriculum projects with the class
- teach a topic to their peers
- work at their own pace to review a lesson or presentation
- create electronic books or book reports

Featured Presentation Software: PowerPoint

Using PowerPoint, you can produce on-screen presentations, overhead transparencies, or 35 mm slides. You can choose to print an outline, speaker's notes, and/or handouts to accompany your presentation. The software contains many different templates from which to select one that suits your taste and topic. The addition of pictures, clip art, video clips, charts, or audio clips can make the presentation dynamic and visually appealing. You can import these from a variety of sources. PowerPoint allows you to quickly and easily rearrange and modify any piece of information. Because PowerPoint was designed for the boardroom, not the classroom, its presentation options include company meeting, marketing plan, and financial overview. However, many teachers and students have adapted and adopted it as their presentation tool. This software is far easier than it looks, and a presentation can be simple and effective or as complex as your imagination, time, and ability allow.

Figure 3-23

In this activity, a group of students has created a brief presentation based on a mathematical problem. The presentation includes a title page slide, a slide containing the history of the problem, a slide containing a description of how they solved the problem, including equations and diagrams, and a bibliography. The slides will then be presented to the class, with each of the groups presenting their own problem.[18]

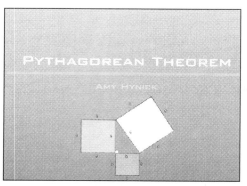

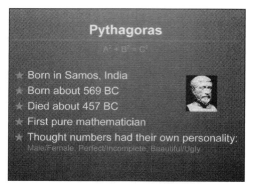

Pythagoras

$A^2 + B^2 = C^2$

★ Born in Samos, India
★ Born about 569 BC
★ Died about 457 BC
★ First pure mathematician
★ Thought numbers had their own personality:
Male/Female, Perfect/Incomplete, Beautiful/Ugly

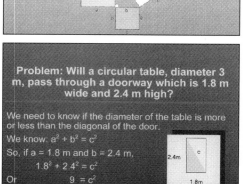

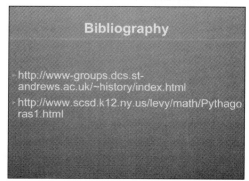

Problem: Will a circular table, diameter 3 m, pass through a doorway which is 1.8 m wide and 2.4 m high?

We need to know if the diameter of the table is more or less than the diagonal of the door.
We know: $a^2 + b^2 = c^2$
So, if a = 1.8 m and b = 2.4 m,
$1.8^2 + 2.4^2 = c^2$
Or $9 = c^2$
$c = 3$
Therefore, the table will fit through the door.

Bibliography

• http://www-groups.dcs.st-andrews.ac.uk/~history/index.html
• http://www.scsd.k12.ny.us/levy/math/Pythagoras1.html

Figure 3-24

A student presents a book report as a multimedia presentation.[19]

A Door in the Wall
by Marguerite de Angeli

Awarded the Newberry Award and
the Lewis Carrol Shelf Award
Publisher: Scholastic

About the Author

✓ Marguerite de Angeli is the author of 23 children's books. Her first 3 books were based on the activities of her own children. She was born in Michigan on March 14, 1979.

Characters - #1 Robin

✓ Robin is a 10 year-old boy of nobility who lives in London in the Middle Ages.
✓ Robin is supposed to become a knight but he is stricken with an illness and cannot walk.
✓ Robin learns to read, write, swim and walk on crutches with the help of Brother Luke.
✓ Robin devises a plan to escape through the door in the wall to save Lyndsay Castle.

Central ideas and Themes

✓ survival
✓ war and peace
✓ growing up
✓ finding your own identity
✓ courage

LEARNING TIPS AND TRICKS FOR POWERPOINT:

• To find out how to get a step-by-step tutorial go to the publisher's Web site.

- Use the AutoContent Wizard, Pick-a-Look Wizard, and Cue Cards to guide you along the first few times.
- Provide students with a storyboard template (such as the one shown in Figure 3-20) so that they can organize their thoughts prior to creating screens.
- You must use the PowerPoint software to create your presentation, but you can show it from any computer that has just the free PowerPoint Viewer installed.
- Transition is an option for choosing how the elements of your slides will be presented. They can zoom, chug, or flash onto your screen. Text can zig-zag, zip, or scramble into place. Play with this option to individualize your presentation, but be careful not to overdo the variety of transitions in any one presentation.
- Animating parts of a screen to appear just when you want them is creative and focuses your audience's attention, but keep in mind that too much action can distract from the content.
- Find out the lighting conditions in the room in which you are going to present. If you cannot make it fairly dark, use a lighter background on your slides.
- Use a large enough font to be readable from a distance.
- Present no more than three or four points per slide.

Spreadsheets

A spreadsheet is a calculating tool often used for financial planning, budgeting, and record keeping. The real power of a spreadsheet is that you can enter formulas that automatically recalculate when you make changes to the data, and you can present and analyze your data in the form of many different types of charts and graphs. These charts and graphs can be easily exported into a word-processed document or an electronic presentation. A spreadsheet is generally included as one component of an integrated software package or suite. Both Microsoft Works and AppleWorks include a simple spreadsheet appropriate for early and middle years students. Corel Suite includes the more sophisticated spreadsheet, Quatro Pro, and Microsoft Office includes Excel. Marks management is greatly facilitated by using a spreadsheet; commercially available grade management programs are based on spreadsheets. You can find out more about a spreadsheet as a teacher tool in Chapter 9. Although math teachers naturally make the most use of spreadsheets in their content area, they are also useful to science and social studies teachers and students for gathering, organizing, and analyzing numerical data. Follow these steps in introducing the use of spreadsheets to your students, using any appropriate content from your curriculum. Students will

1. use an existing spreadsheet to produce a simple graph,
2. use existing data to create a spreadsheet and a graph,
3. conduct a survey, collect data, and create a spreadsheet and a graph.

Parts of a spreadsheet:
- **A spreadsheet is a grid of rows and columns; rows are horizontal and columns are vertical.**
- **The boxes where rows and columns intersect are called cells. Your data, formulas, or the results of calculations are stored in the cells.**
- **Each cell has a unique address that is based on its location — for example, cell A5 is at the intersection of column A and row 5.**

WHAT CAN STUDENTS DO WITH SPREADSHEETS?
- record and graph the nutritional value or content of various foods
- record and graph data collected from weather observations
- record and graph flight distances of paper airplanes
- experiment with a variety of displays of the same data and select the type of graph that best represents the data
- produce and analyze a quotation to complete a job in the home
- conduct a school energy or recycling audit
- create and maintain a budget for a school club, ski trip, or special event

"The real power of spreadsheets lies in the way students can ask 'what if' questions. By simply changing an entry in the spreadsheet, it is possible to see the effect of that change on the system as a whole. This 'what if' question serves two purposes — it lets students explore the system represented by the spreadsheet, and it also lets them make and test their own hypotheses."[20]

Featured Spreadsheet Software: AppleWorks spreadsheet

The spreadsheet in the AppleWorks suite is an easy-to-use basic spreadsheet. For beginners with spreadsheets, this is a great starter program.

The software provides a variety of graphical formats for displaying data. Only simple formulas, such as those for the basic operations, are available.

LEARNING TIPS AND TRICKS FOR APPLEWORKS SPREADSHEET:
- Begin by browsing through the introductory tutorial included within the software.
- You might wish to print out the help file for ongoing reference.
- For other ideas and tutorials go to the publisher's Web site.
- For printing, you can remove the column and row headings and/or grid lines.
- Use the CD-ROM The Cruncher (MECC) to help younger students learn how to use a spreadsheet.

Featured Spreadsheet Software: Quatro Pro

Quatro Pro is a sophisticated spreadsheet that can be used by both teachers and secondary school students. It is extremely useful because of the large number of calculations it can perform as well as its extensive graphing abilities. Math, geography, business, and science are typical classes where a software program such as this may be helpful.

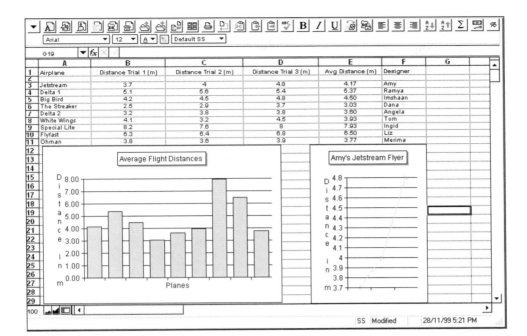

Figure 3-25

One of the most popular activities in a unit on flight is to conduct paper airplane trials. When students enter their data they can quickly and easily generate graphs and charts, as seen in this AppleWorks spreadsheet.

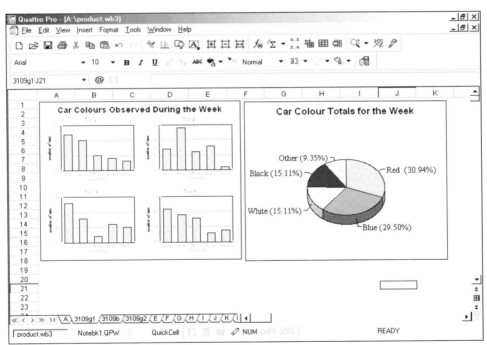

Figure 3-26

In this data management activity, students observe car colors at regular intervals and graph their data.[21]

LEARNING TIPS AND TRICKS FOR QUATRO PRO:

- Give yourself lots of time to learn this software if you want to use its powerful features.
- Sit down with a peer or student expert who can get you started.
- Take a one-day workshop.
- Read the available Help before starting to explore.

Figure 3-27

After recording their running or walking times over a course for a given number of trials, students demonstrate their progress using graphs generated in a spreadsheet.[22]

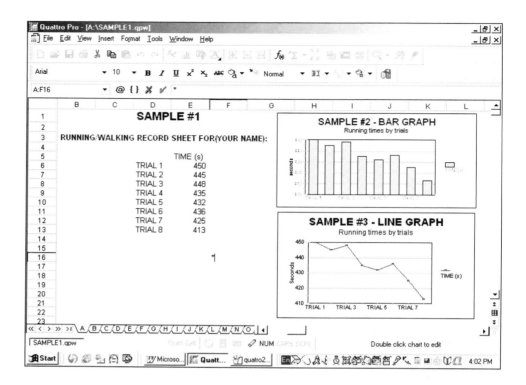

Video Technology

The use of video technology as a teaching tool is well established; TVs and VCRs are commonplace at most schools. The big difference between VCR video and computer video is interactivity — instead of sitting and viewing in linear fashion a presentation created by someone else, computer video allows students to "do": to exert control over the creation and/or viewing. A videodisc or DVD can be a visual database; you can easily sift through the visual materials in any order and at any speed you want. Think of the videodisc and DVD not as merely the modern replacement for the videotape, but rather as a tool that allows greater quality, flexibility, motivation, interactivity, individualization, and student control. Students and teachers who *use* video instead of just *showing* it, greatly increase its value as an educational tool.

> **D**on't forget about TV in the midst of all this — it can educate as well as entertain! Look for TV programs that address appropriate content and skills, fit your available time frame, are flexible, and are of good quality. Many networks offer curriculum guides jampacked with ideas. Consider ways of *using* newscasts, documentaries, dramas, sports events, weather reports, bulletin boards, and commercials as well as instructional programming.

Be sure to preview videos and videodiscs before selecting them for classroom use, with these questions in mind:
- How well does the content fit the curriculum you are teaching?
- What can students *do* with the content presented?
- Is the vocabulary age appropriate for students?

- Is the program true to life in its portrayal of characters?
- Is the narrative powerful and meaningful?
- Is there variety in presentation of content?
- Is it free of bias and are minorities represented?
- Is the quality of audio and video excellent? (The resolution of a videodisc or DVD should be better than that of a video.)
- Does it have a teacher guidebook? (A guidebook can help you locate information quickly and may also contain suggestions for meaningful learning experiences.)

Many teachers have a camcorder readily available to them. The camcorder is now moving from the role of recording and documenting special events to that of a teaching, learning, and assessment tool. You will have noticed by now that there are many software applications, such as HyperStudio and PowerPoint, into which video clips can be inserted. Students can use a camcorder to obtain primary-source video data for their projects. Alternatively, they can capture a short video clip from TV, videotape, videodisc, or DVD with proper consideration given to copyright. Some schools now have video-capture hardware and software, usually found as part of a multimedia workstation or room. Video capture is generally not a difficult process and might be best handled by a team of student experts.

> **"E**ver since January, when Columbia Basin installed video equipment with a $14,000 federal Carl D. Perkins grant for vocational and applied technology programs, many of the students involved in video communications have undergone a transformation of sorts, school officials say. They come to class regularly and act out less. They work as a team on projects. Some even take time out on weekends to film community events, or 'remotes', such as ... an elementary school play. 'Some of these kids weren't doing anything before, now I can't get them out of my classroom,' [Bob] Schroeder [a teacher of video communications at Columbia Basin Alternative High School in Moses Lake, Washington] says. 'The discipline problems have been going away. They're excited about class.' "[23]

WHAT CAN STUDENTS DO WITH VIDEO TECHNOLOGY?

- produce a weather broadcast
- film their science and technology inventions at work
- tape their own TV commercials
- keep visual records of products for their electronic portfolios
- perform a play and share it with other classes
- produce a weekly news show
- interview a doctor, architect, senior citizen, etc.
- present research findings through drama, music, or dance
- create travel videos for tourists
- add exciting, meaningful video clips to their multimedia projects
- explain a math concept

> **D**eborah Trimble asked her eighth-grade students at St. Charles
> School in San Carlos, California, to design a video to explain
> Newton's laws of motion. "The resulting film, 'Did Newton Get it
> Right?' uses images such as NASA rocket launches and skating
> basketball players to illustrate fundamental laws of physics. The
> students also used HyperStudio to create an interactive test so the
> fifth-graders who watched the video could demonstrate how much
> they had learned."[24]

Web Browsers and Plug-ins

A Web browser is the software that allows you to view Web sites. Netscape
Navigator and Internet Explorer are the Web browsers that most people use.
Some people have a preference for one over the other, but for most of us,
either will do the job. Virtually all new computers come equipped with a
Web browser. The features of Web browsers are constantly improving, so
having the latest version is always nice, but not essential. A plug-in is a piece
of software that enhances the capabilities of your Web browser. At most sites
where a plug-in is required, you will find a hyperlink that takes you to the
site of the product manufacturer, from which you can download the required
plug-in. The good news is that plug-ins are free. The bad news is that some
time may be required to download the plug-in. Since this process is generally
an unwanted interruption to your task, it's a good idea to set aside some time
in which to update the plug-ins that reside on your computer. For a step-by-
step guide of how to download a plug-in, see the Web link on the publisher's
Web site.

Featured Plug-in: Adobe Acrobat Reader

When you browse the Web in search of lesson plans for your classroom, you
may find that some are posted as Adobe Acrobat (.pdf) files. In order to view
these files, you will need to download the Acrobat Reader plug-in. Because
.pdf files are a convenient means of publishing, you will find that Adobe
Acrobat is used often for posting materials on the Web.

Featured Plug-in: Shockwave

Shockwave is a plug-in that lets you experience interactive Web content like
games, business presentations, entertainment, and advertisements from your
Web browser. You've probably seen Shockwave used on business and entertainment sites such as Disney.com, Intel.com, SharperImage.com, Palm
Computing, and others. Many interactive Web sites for students, such as
the exciting on-line exhibits at the Learning Studio of the San Francisco
Exploratorium (http://www.exploratorium.edu/learning_studio/index.html),
require Shockwave for viewing. On-line games, product demonstrations, and
e-merchandising are other common applications of this technology. To get
Shockwave on your computer, you simply download the free player from
http://www.macromedia.com/shockwave/download/. The download takes
about 10 minutes. Shockwave 7 provides convenient automatic updating of
the player.

Web Publishing

Web publishing is highly motivating to most students; it allows them to showcase their work to a world audience! Working through an activity that involves organizing a set of links or interrelated pieces of information is directly related to developing analytical skills. Designing your Web page or site begins with planning the purpose, deciding what the content will be, and laying out how you want to structure it. A well-designed Web site can make it easy for your audience to navigate and get the information you want them to receive. It can also make it easier for you to manage and update later on.

"Take a rather routine assignment, such as writing a news article based on the latest results of the Olympics. When the possibility of Web publishing was added to this simple task, the results were dramatic indications of the power of the Web to transform education. Students finished articles within deadlines with real enthusiasm and genuine pride when they knew that their articles were to be posted daily at the PBS Olympic Cyberschool site. In fact, because I had announced the project to the entire upper-school student body, many worked late at night and e-mailed articles round the clock, while others were ready to fill in as needed on short notice by means of e-mail. At the close of the Olympics, the project was extended, and students were eager to continue writing articles for two more weeks. By this time, submissions from around the globe complemented those of the students at our school."[25]

It's increasingly simple to publish on the Web these days without learning the programming language of Web publishing (hypertext markup language or HTML). Most Web editors let you place text and graphics using WYSIWYG (what-you-see-is-what-you-get) editing, while allowing for more advanced users to toggle to the actual HTML code. Web authoring software is abundant and easy to use. You may have heard of some of these Web editors:
- Claris HomePage (Apple)
- Dreamweaver (Macromedia)
- FrontPage 2000 (Microsoft)
- GoLive 5 (Adobe Systems)
- Web Workshop (Sunburst Technology)

Web publishing tools are included in many software packages or suites such as Microsoft Office. Most new versions of word processors and desktop publishing packages allow you the option of saving your text document as an HTML document.

WHAT CAN STUDENTS DO WITH WEB PUBLISHING SOFTWARE?
- create Web-based lessons for other students
- create and maintain a school or classroom Web site
- point to excellent topic-related information at other Web sites
- publish exemplary work
- share data with others through a cultural exchange

Featured Web Publishing Software: Claris HomePage

Claris HomePage allows you to build Web pages and entire Web sites without spending precious hours learning HTML. Your creations can range from simple to sophisticated. Claris Homepage works very much in the same way as a word processor.

Figure 3-28

You will recognize icons in the Claris HomePage toolbar such as the bold, italic, and justification symbols and find familiar options in the drop-down menus. Text formatting is somewhat different, however, as you choose from various heading sizes, lists, and normal text.

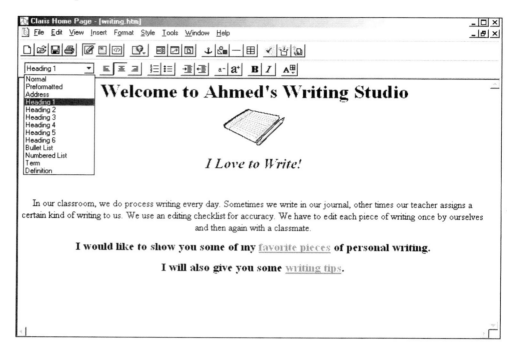

Figure 3-29

The School Site Assistant in Claris HomePage will walk you step-by-step through setting up your first school or classroom Web site. It's a great way to begin and enormous fun to learn!

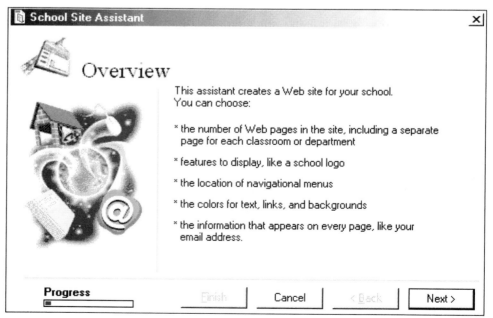

You can insert .gif and .jpeg images from the Homepage library, your scanner, the Web, or your own collection (respecting copyright). Backgrounds and colors are easy to change. It is simple to create links to parts of your page, other pages, or other Web sites using the link editor.

LEARNING TIPS AND TRICKS FOR CLARIS HOME PAGE:
- Read the manual and use the HELP file.
- Use assistants and/or a template for your first attempt.
- Spend some time planning your page or site so that the organization and visual presentation communicate your intent effectively.
- For the latest information, visit the company's Web site.

Computer as Tutee
Creating Books and Stories

For many years, teachers have known the value of having students publish their writing for others to read. School libraries are enhanced by the addition of student-created books, and parents are often enlisted to manage the school publishing center. Now young students can easily create their own stories and books using software such as Storybook Weaver and EasyBook Deluxe. This type of software allows them to input their own text and add graphics either of their own design or from a selection of clip art. Even very young students can program the computer to show their ideas and creativity to others.

Featured Authoring Software: Storybook Weaver

Storybook Weaver is user-friendly and appropriate for students in the early grades. Students write their own story and create pictures using the large assortment of clip art and borders provided. It is self-contained, thus does not accept imported images and sounds. One good way to share or to peer edit is to have students move from computer to computer reading one another's stories.

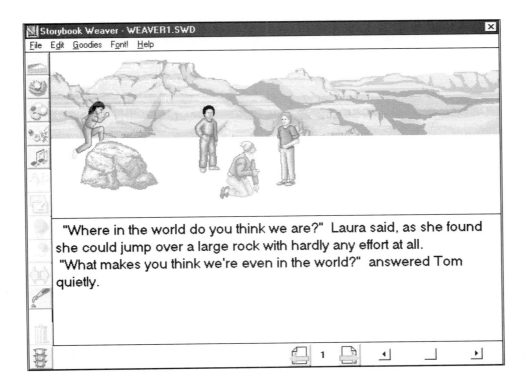

Figure 3-30

Stories came alive with the addition of clip art to create backgrounds and objects as colorful illustrations. They can be viewed on-screen or printed.

Programming Using Logo

Logo is a computer language, developed by Dr. Seymour Papert and his colleagues at MIT during the late 1960s. It is intended to make the computer "an object to think with."

It is designed to be easy enough for young children, yet also support complex explorations and sophisticated projects by experienced users. Logo programming environments are designed to support constructive learning, and activities can be used in mathematics, language, music, and science. Logo can also be used to develop simulations and create multimedia presentations.

Papert and his colleagues originally programmed a turtle-style robot that drew patterns on a sheet of paper laid out on the floor. Soon the turtle migrated to the computer graphics screen where it is now used to draw shapes, designs, and pictures. It moves around according to the programmer's instructions, leaving a line that traces its movement in response to simple commands. You combine commands to form more complicated procedures. Find out more about Logo at the company's Web site.

www

Lego Logo was an innovation of the mid-eighties developed by Mitchel Resnick and Steve Ocko at the MIT Media Lab. It is a system that interfaces Logo with motors, lights, and sensors that are incorporated into machines built out of Lego bricks and other elements. Lego Logo was a commercial success and is still used by thousands of teachers and their students.

"The fifth grade at The Blake School studies gears in the classroom using the Lego Dacta Pulley Set #9614. Throughout this unit, students keep journals where they address several questions: 'What did we do today?' 'What problems did we encounter?' 'How did we solve these problems?' 'What will we do in the next LEGO session?' Teams describe what their project will do in English before writing programming code. Projects must use a pulley system and incorporate lights, sound, and a sensor. At the end of the unit, teams present their project to parents, friends, classmates, and teachers."[26]

By the early 1990s some educators in the United States began to see Logo as old and out of date, and it did not attract much interest among many new computer-using educators in the United States and Canada; however, this was not the case in other parts of the world where Logo continued to be an essential element of the curriculum. The introduction of MicroWorlds Project Builder in 1993 revived interest in Logo, as it included major changes in the Logo environment and language. Control Lab and Control System are new Lego Logo products whose software is built on the same core as MicroWorlds. Another recent Lego Logo innovation is the Programmable Brick. In earlier Lego Logo products, the computer received instructions through wires connected to a computer. The Programmable Brick has a computer inside it, allowing for wireless robotics. Robolab and Mindstorms are commercially available robotics kits that use this programmable brick.

Featured Logo Software: MicroWorlds

MicroWorlds is a true programming environment and as such is limited only by the student's imagination. MicroWorlds includes many new features, such as drawing tools, a shape editor, a melody maker, and the ability to import graphics and sounds that work along with Logo to support the creation of multimedia projects, games, and simulations. With a good implementation of Logo, children in grades 3 to 8 can enjoy programming. At the easiest level, the program can be simply an excellent drawing program or scene creator. It has a complete set of drawing tools and 140 colors and includes a point-and-click shape center with dozens of beautiful multicolored shapes. Students can draw scenes, using the shapes as stamps, or dress a programmable turtle with a shape. At a more advanced level, they can add movement to the scene. Each turtle (dressed as trees, cars, people, etc.) can be programmed to move, or to move and change shapes (for animation). A turtle can be programmed using a simple program dialogue box. Very little programming is needed to create lots of action. As students' skills improve even more, they can develop complete working models. The samples included with the software are a great way to learn how to program and a good source of ideas for your own projects. For example, one of the complete programs included in the package models a fish ecosystem. The user adjusts the speed at which the fish reproduce and eat trying to reach a delicate balance.[27]

Figure 3-31

In this project, the start button begins an animated race between the horse and dog, with the crowd jumping and waving as they cheer the contestants. This was created and programmed by 11-year-old Nicole Sleeth. You can see more of her work on the Web. One small piece of the programming code for this sequence looks like this:
      to ColourRedHit
      DoJump 100 95
      End[28]

Learning Tips and Tricks for MicroWorlds:
- You can get Logo lessons at http://members.aol.com/mckoss/logo.htm
- The "Kids Can Program" site has Logo lessons and sample projects. You can print them out simply by e-mailing the author, Don Sleeth, for permission.

- Books about MicroWorlds Logo
  The following three titles are included with your software purchase:
  MicroWorlds Project Builder Projects Book
  MicroWorlds Reference
  MicroWorlds Project Builder Teacher's Resource
  Moursand, D., and Sharon Yoder. *Introduction to MicroWorlds 2.0 —
  A Logo-Based Hypermedia Environment*. Eugene, Oregon: ISTE, 1996.
  Yoder, Sharon. *MicroWorlds 2.0 — Hypermedia Project Development and Logo
  Scripting*. Eugene, Oregon: ISTE, 1997.

Robotics

Programming today does not have to involve a textual language. It can be part of the user's application environment, using pictures, sound, and animation. Robotics kits such as Robolab and Mindstorms (available from Spectrum) provide all the components necessary for students to design and build working robotic models.

Basic programming allows students to use computers to control machines they build. Commercial construction sets are most often used for these types of activities. A simple easy-to-use interface provides the communication link between the computer and the student-constructed models. Construction sets combined with control technologies provide students with a hands-on problem-solving environment in which they come to understand the role of computers in today's technology.

The problem solving that takes place using robotics can be open-ended exploration, guided investigation of concepts and skills, simulation of real-life examples, or invention. Using control technologies, students can tackle activities like these:

- Design and build a safe, reliable merry-go-round for the fair. It must carry four passengers. Each ride must take a specific length of time and then the merry-go-round must stop to let people off. Music would make the ride more enjoyable!
- You work in a rest home, in which the elderly people sometimes leave the bath water running. Design and build a system to warn that a tap has been left running. Remember that elderly people may be short-sighted or hard of hearing.
- Design and build a machine to move pallets in a warehouse. It must be able to pick up a pallet of ten bricks, move it a distance of 1 foot (30 cm) up a ramp, and place it on the ground next to another.

Students come to these kinds of activities with a background of problem solving in a technological environment. In a well-designed sequential design and technology program, computer control is but one aspect in a hierarchy of skills that include

- building with soft materials (water, sand, Plasticene),
- building with hard materials (cardboard, plastic, wood, junk, construction kits),
- desire for movement (wheels, pivots, hinges, pulleys),
- motorizing (elastics, balloons, wind, water, electric motors),
- action (lights, bells, pumps),
- control (manual, electric, computer).

Summing Up

The list of software in this chapter is not exhaustive by any means; it is a sampling of the variety of good educational software and hardware that is available. Look for these products in your school, ask your peers and students about them, and try them out yourself. Determine which best fit your curriculum goals.

It is curriculum that determines what and, to some degree, how we teach. A random-sample survey of more than 700 educators helped Socratic Technologies, a research firm specializing in new technologies, to identify the most important factors affecting educational software purchases. These factors included

- depth and breadth of curriculum content,
- usefulness in extending core curriculum,
- likelihood of improving students' scores on standardized tests, and
- usability in individualized instruction.[29]

Curriculum is the driving force behind technology use in schools. In the next chapter, we'll look at curriculum issues in detail.

> **"C**onsider this quote: 'The age of illustration is upon us and illustrate we must if we hope to gain the attention of young and old.' When was it written? Go ahead, take a guess…. Of course, [this] 19th century quote refers to the magic lantern. For those of you who don't still have the magic lanterns in your school, the device resembled an early slide projector, except the slides were big and made of glass and the light source came from flame. The magic lantern could display a big picture on a blank wall, so you can see why this equipment was highly touted. In the mid to late 1800s, some educational reformers complained that there was just too much teacher talk in the classroom. That's just not how kids, or adults for that matter, learned."[30]

WHAT ABOUT CURRICULUM?

"Blue Sky High School (a fictitious name) had fallen into the trap of confusing software programs with purpose. The high school operated on the premise that teachers would integrate technologies into the classroom if they had just enough time to learn basic software programs....In making this assumption, the school effectively placed the cart before the horse and ignored the most important learning issue of all, which is how to use these technologies to enhance student thinking and performance.... We need to untie the cart and place it where it belongs...behind the four horses of curriculum, learning, teaching and exploration."[1]

Let's assume that you have decided to plan a unit in which information and communication technology is an integral component. You want to use this technology to enhance your child-centered classroom, to assist in teaching and learning, to motivate and excite students. Whichever subject(s) you choose, you will find that the steps to successful planning of a technology-integrated unit are similar to planning any unit of study — straightforward and logical. We recommend an eight-step process. In each step, consider the possible advantages that various technologies have to offer.

Step 1: *Establish Learning Outcomes*

What do you want the students to know and be able to do? Become familiar with the knowledge, skills, and attitudes that your students are expected to develop. Whether you select these learning outcomes or they are designated by the central core curriculum of the school, school district, or province or state, keep them foremost in your mind as you proceed through the planning process. They are your guide for students' process and products and the focus

95

Figure 4-1

These curriculum planning steps can be used to create a successful technology-integrated unit. The dotted lines indicate that some steps are particularly inter-related and interdependent.

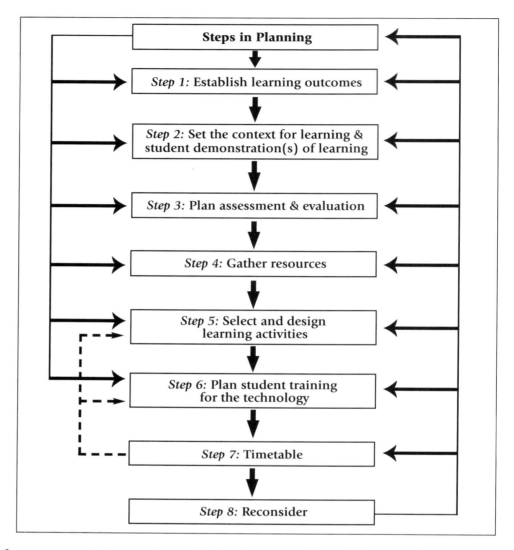

Steps in Planning

Step 1: Establish learning outcomes

Step 2: Set the context for learning & student demonstration(s) of learning

Step 3: Plan assessment & evaluation

Step 4: Gather resources

Step 5: Select and design learning activities

Step 6: Plan student training for the technology

Step 7: Timetable

Step 8: Reconsider

for assessment. Some school districts have established frameworks and standards specifically for technology-related outcomes. These generally begin with broad outcomes such as "Students will use technology to locate, evaluate, and collect information from a variety of sources"[2] and are then broken down into grade-specific skills such as "Use keyboards and other common input and output devices (including adaptive devices when necessary) efficiently and effectively."[3] Go to the publisher's Web site to find links to on-line examples of school districts' scope and sequence of ICT skills.

www

You can obtain a copy of the National Educational Technology Standards for Students developed by the International Society for Technology in Education by contacting ISTE Customer Service at 1-800-336-5191 or visiting their Web site at http://www.ISTE.org.

Step 2: *Set the Context for Learning and Decide on How Students Will Demonstrate Their Learning*

How will you know when students have achieved the specified outcomes? If you have free choice of the context into which to place student learning, consider that curriculum contexts may stem from a wide variety of places and experiences. Some possible sources are

- an experience or problem appropriate to the age level,
- a design or building project,
- the need for a service in the local community,
- an incident from the news or some everyday or local event that has had an impact on the students or sparked a particular interest,
- a presentation or competition such as a dramatic, musical, or sporting event, and
- a play, book, or story.

Brainstorming the topic with colleagues and students results in the consideration of related ideas and concepts. It gives you an idea of the prior knowledge that students bring to the topic. Motivation and interest are also enhanced when students are involved in planning. Ideas can be grouped on a flowchart or list. Your goal of enhanced inclusion of technology will be already apparent in this first step of planning.

There is an enormous variety of products that students can use to demonstrate their learning. You might choose to focus on one culminating demonstration or collect a portfolio of smaller demonstrations throughout the unit. Students are often motivated by using technology to create an exciting product such as

- a HyperStudio presentation,
- a Web page,
- a slide show with PowerPoint, Corel Presentations, or Kid Pix,
- a computer-produced story or book, or
- a flyer, brochure, or newspaper prepared with a publishing application.

Step 3: *Plan Assessment and Evaluation*

Diagnostic, formative, and summative evaluation are components of all units. Teacher, peer, and self-assessment are common strategies. One of the many purposes of assessment is to improve student learning. By carefully planning assessment prior to the task, teachers are able to provide students with clear guidelines and criteria for success. Rubrics, checklists, and rating scales are examples of tools for assessing both subject-related and technology-related concepts and skills. Computer technology can be of great assistance in the evaluation process. This issue is considered in greater detail in Chapter 7: Assessing Student Progress.

Figure 4-2

In their development of a technology-integrated activity, these teacher candidates have clearly identified the ways in which they plan to have students demonstrate their learning.

Grade 1 Language Arts
Students will produce a simple typed sentence about themselves and their special friend and illustrate their sentence using Kid Pix.
(Melissa Fryer, Student, Faculty of Education, University of Ottawa, 1999)

Grade 4 Social Studies
Students will
* produce a medieval legend using a word-processor,
* plan a medieval village using Sim City,
* visit a minimum of three different medieval Web sites for research,
* contribute to a class database of famous castles of the world, and
* print and assemble a paper castle from Elmer's Cut and Build Castle and House CD-ROM.
(Katherine Azar, Student, Faculty of Education, University of Ottawa, 1999)

Grade 6 Science
Each student will use the Internet and the CD-ROM, Experiencing the Solar System, to research a specific planet, recording their results on a worksheet provided. Students will then use the information gathered to produce a spreadsheet and graph that calculate and display their weight on each of the planets. They will also create a poem about a planet, word-process it, and print it for inclusion in a class book.
(Lissa Jianopoulos, Student, Faculty of Education, University of Ottawa, 1999)

Grade 8 Math
Students will design a questionnaire using ClarisWorks word-processing software. They will compile and analyze the data collected by constructing ClarisWorks spreadsheets and generating graphs from them. Students will prepare a word-processed report of their findings, importing their graphs to support their analysis.
(Janice King, Student, Faculty of Education, University of Ottawa, 1999)

Grade 8 Physical Education
Each pair of students will be assigned a physical activity/ or sport skill to teach to the class. After researching the specific activity/ or skill using the Internet, they will break the skill down into teachable steps and record these steps using either a digital or conventional camera. Students will then create activity cards to be posted in the gym to enhance their presentation.
(Erin Rakus, Student, Faculty of Education, University of Ottawa, 1999)

Grade 9 Science
Students will use the Starry Night software to select a constellation that will be visible in the early evening at the particular time of year. They will then use the Internet to search for information and pictures about it. On a class field trip, students will photograph the selected constellation. The picture will be scanned and used in a class presentation, along with the Internet-researched material. The presentation will take the form of a multimedia report (Corel Presentations), pamphlet (MSPublisher), or Web page (Claris Home Page).
(Peter Cudmore, Student, Faculty of Education, University of Ottawa, 1999)

Grade 10 Social Sciences
In this problem-based activity, students will pretend to be hopeful immigrants planning to come to Canada. They will search the Internet to find out how this process works and what they must do to immigrate successfully. They will word-process a report of their findings.
(Mike Hengeveld, Student, Faculty of Education, University of Ottawa, 1999)

Grade 11 History
Students will take an interactive journey on the Underground Railway at the National Geographic Web site (http://www.nationalgeographic.com/features/99/railroad). They will keep a multimedia diary of their travels and stops, collecting images and sounds in addition to a written record of what they see, whom they meet, and how they feel. Each student will present her/his diary to the class using Corel Presentations.
(Katherine Caldwell, Student, Faculty of Education, University of Ottawa, 1999)

Step 4: *Gather Resources*

In the development of a technology-integrated unit, teachers usually find that gathering learning resources challenges them to expand their horizons. In the past, when we thought of resources, we tended to think of various print resources and videos, but thanks to the advancements of technology, there is now a much greater variety of learning resources from which to choose.

Print Resources

Regardless of the non-print resources you select, a classroom library of books related to the topic or concept is still essential. Encourage students to use these print resources. Plan on searching through the available readers and anthologies in the school to find stories that relate to the topic. Use newspaper and magazine articles for variety and to provide more current information for your students.

> **T**his advice comes from two very computer-savvy grade 4 students. "Tip from Laura and Ashley to other kids: Don't even bother going on the Internet when you start a project. If you're smart, you'll begin by going to the library."[4]

Videos

Videos can usually be borrowed through a central media outlet. Educational TV channels provide some excellent programming. Check your local program guide to see if any shows or series currently being aired relate to the topic you have chosen. The time that a particular program is aired on TV may make it difficult or impossible to integrate into your timetable; however, some television broadcasts may be taped for classroom showing at a time more appropriate. You might consider asking a parent volunteer to be responsible for taping specific broadcasts for you. These videos can then be added to the collection in your school resource or media center. Again, be aware of copyright laws.

> **C**able in the Classroom is a service that offers teachers the opportunity to tape off-air, at no charge, specially selected television programs and use them in the classroom for the specified period of copyright clearance. Viewing guides and lesson plans are often available. Participating cable companies provide a cable hook-up and free monthly service to thousands of schools. For more information visit their Web site by following the link provided at the publisher's Web site.

When selecting videos to accompany a unit, think about the different ways they can be used. It is not necessary to show the whole video to the whole class every time. Sometimes showing a short clip as part of a lesson is the most effective way to illustrate a concept or provide a real-life view of a situation or setting. Viewing a video or video segment can be a learning experience for a small group or an individual student. Students can also capture a video clip and use it in a multimedia project or presentation.

Videodisc, DVD, and CD-ROM

If a videodisc, DVD, and/or a CD-ROM is available on the topic, preview it carefully in order to determine its best use. These resources have a great deal of potential for student motivation and learning. You may wish to use the same item several times over in different ways. The following questions can be used as a previewing guide.

1. Is it appropriate for the targeted age group?
2. Does it include specific content or skills that I wish students to master in this unit?
3. What part or parts do I wish the students to view?
4. Is it best used as a student resource or research tool or would it be best included as part of a lesson?
5. Are there specific points at which to stop for discussion?
6. Does it lend itself better to whole group discussion? small group discussion? or individual reflection?
7. Should a follow-up activity be based on this viewing? If so, whole group? small group? or individual?
8. Are there helpful suggestions in the teacher's guide?

An encyclopedia on CD-ROM may be available in a technology-integrated classroom, computer lab, or school resource center. It is difficult to imagine a unit in which this resource would *not* be useful. The challenge is to design student activities that incorporate the use of this resource to achieve specific learning outcomes for your students.

Computer Software

> **"J**ust as teachers plan subject areas, so should some time be devoted to planning for classroom computing....Using the computer in a haphazard manner or on the spur of the moment often results in many classroom disruptions and few educational benefits."[5]

In compiling resources for a unit, explore the applications of classroom computers. Here, you are limited only by your imagination and the available hardware and software! Consider the following issues when deciding on how to use computers in the study of a specific topic.

1. How can students best use a word processor in this unit?
   - writing notes
   - creative writing
   - research reports
   - letter-writing
   - drafting
   - formatting and editing
   - other
2. Is student use of a database appropriate in this unit to search, sort, and analyze data? If so, is there a ready-made database available that relates to

this topic? Would student creation of a database assist in the development of the selected knowledge, skills, or attitudes of this unit?

3. Would a spreadsheet be useful for any activity that students might pursue, either individually or as a group?

4. Would the use of a graphics program provide another way to learn skills, reinforce knowledge, and/or present findings using multiple intelligences?

5. Is there any other software available that relates to this topic?
   - simulation
   - problem-solving
   - drill and practice
   - electronic stories or books
   - other

6. How can students enhance their presentation of products by using desktop publishing or multimedia tools?

7. How might the knowledge available on the World Wide Web or the communication allowed through the Internet contribute to student learning?

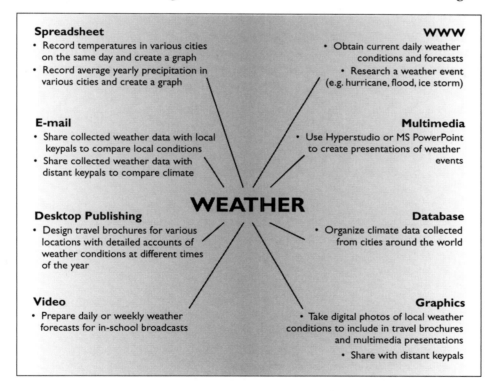

Spreadsheet
- Record temperatures in various cities on the same day and create a graph
- Record average yearly precipitation in various cities and create a graph

WWW
- Obtain current daily weather conditions and forecasts
- Research a weather event (e.g. hurricane, flood, ice storm)

E-mail
- Share collected weather data with local keypals to compare local conditions
- Share collected weather data with distant keypals to compare climate

Multimedia
- Use Hyperstudio or MS PowerPoint to create presentations of weather events

WEATHER

Desktop Publishing
- Design travel brochures for various locations with detailed accounts of weather conditions at different times of the year

Database
- Organize climate data collected from cities around the world

Video
- Prepare daily or weekly weather forecasts for in-school broadcasts

Graphics
- Take digital photos of local weather conditions to include in travel brochures and multimedia presentations
- Share with distant keypals

Figure 4-3

Laying out your unit from a technology point of view is one way to ensure that a variety of technologies are integrated. This example illustrates teacher planning for a unit about weather.

Telecommunications

The World Wide Web provides access to a vast array of information. Not only are there substantial text-based resources on topics ranging from planets to politics, but a wide range of resources is available for electronic field trips involving pictures, text, sound, and sometimes interactivity. Today's "push technologies" can put you on the receiving end of a customized project rather than having to sort through the massive amounts of material on the Web. Push technology automatically delivers news and other specified information from the Internet to users' desktops. Electric libraries are on-line research

services that can be accessed through both school and home computers. They offer students access to extensive databases of sources such as newspapers, magazines, maps, images, and TV and radio transcripts. Students search the database with a simple question or a series of related keywords. This fast, friendly, and easy-to-use format saves the time and frustration associated with searching the Web.

You will find that some Web sites are most useful for background information, some as sources of lesson plans and ideas, and others for student on-line activities. Develop your own collection of favorite Web sites to complement your curriculum or rely on some of the excellent collections you can access by visiting the publisher's Web site.

> *The Teacher's Complete and Easy Guide to the Internet*, by **Ann Heide** and **Linda Stilborne**, was awarded the best Education Title in the **Small Press Book Awards** 1997. The book and accompanying **CD-ROM** offer a wealth of great educational sites.

Possibly the most powerful feature of the Internet is its potential as a communication tool. Students delight in being able to connect with people around the world. They can contact an expert, collaborate with peers studying the same topic, or publish their work for a global audience.

Figure 4-4

There are many ways the Internet can be used in the classroom.

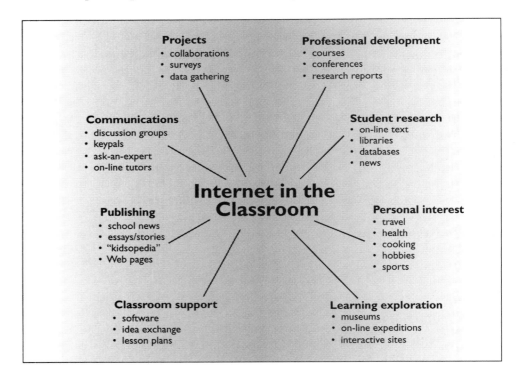

Concrete Materials

Do not overlook the simple but valuable hands-on materials such as hammers, pulleys, tangrams, and the many other manipulatives so useful in an active learning environment. The term *active learning* reflects a particular belief in the way that children learn — by actively investigating the world that surrounds them, by interacting with people, and by manipulating concrete materials. An active learning program provides the child with opportunities to explore materials, ideas, and relationships. Although technology is engaging for children, it should enhance, rather than take the place of, the real experience. Watching a video of life in the forest may give the student a feeling for it, but it isn't equivalent to being there. For the young student, moving numbers around on a computer screen to make a 3+5=8 number sentence may be useful, but it doesn't replace the concrete experience of counting out blocks.

> **"We learn...**
>   **10% of what we read**
>   **20% of what we hear**
>   **30% of what we see**
>   **50% of what we both see and hear**
>   **70% of what is discussed with others**
>   **80% of what we experience personally**
>   **90% of what we teach to someone else."[6]**

New technologies can guide and complement hands-on explorations. Software such as Tom Snyder Productions' Science Court Series combine multimedia with manipulatives to create powerful learning situations. For example, in Science Court: Pendulums, students watch an animated video on the computer about a ski race that is timed with a homemade pendulum. The loser of the race challenges the results and takes the timekeeper to Science Court. Students are prompted to conduct their own pendulum experiments to generate data for judging the case. The CD-ROM leads students sequentially through the case, keeping them on task and motivated. It also provides a built-in timer that students can use to ensure accuracy in their experiments. A wide variety of topics such as fossils, gravity, flight, heat, soil, seasons, and inertia are available in the Science Court Series, which is designed for students in grades 2 to 6.

Human Resources

Your community can provide wonderful resources such as places to visit (e.g., museums, businesses, and manufacturing industries) and people who will come into your classroom to share specialized knowledge and interests. We have often been surprised to see what community resources show up when a "parent letter" is sent home announcing the beginning of a new and exciting unit of study! With telecommunications, virtual visits make it easier to connect with the many resources in your local community and around the world. A good place for your students to look for an expert to consult is at Pitsco's Ask an Expert site at http://www.askanexpert.com. Visit the publisher's Web site for more links to experts.

Step 5: *Select and Design Learning Experiences*

With student learning objectives and outcomes, the flow chart of the topic, and the list of learning resources you have collected and researched, you are well prepared to begin the challenging task of creating learning experiences for students. In designing these learning experiences, try to maximize the use of all the equipment and ICT available. The organization of these learning experiences will reflect your desire to balance whole group involvement, small group activities, and individual pursuits, and also to include both teacher-directed and student-centered activities.

Resource books, teachers' manuals, the guides that accompany audiovisual materials, workshop handouts, education courses, etc., can all trigger the creation of exciting and educationally sound learning experiences. Opportunities for the students themselves to make choices and pursue investigations of sub-topics and issues in which they are interested will enhance motivation and learning.

> **"S**trategic teaching requires thoughtful choices. An effective teacher has a toolkit of strategies that can dramatically modify student performance when the choice of tool fits the situation and the individual student."[7]

It is sometimes difficult to decide among a wide variety of possible learning experiences. Try asking these questions when selecting and designing learning experiences.

- Does this learning experience focus on specific knowledge, skills, or attitudes that I wish students to develop, master, or review in this unit?
- Do I have, or can I easily get, the materials required for students to complete this learning experience?
- Do I have the space to store these materials and for students to work with them?
- How long will it take students to complete this learning experience?
- Do I have enough time to include this learning experience?
- Are most or all of the students in my class capable of successfully completing this learning experience?
- Can the students read the directions?
- Can the students follow the directions?
- Do the students have the prerequisite skills?
- For those students who are not capable, can the learning experiences be easily modified?
- Can exceptional students work with a partner or have the support of a group?
- Is this learning experience too easy or basic for the more advanced students in my class?
- Is it open-ended or can it be modified to suit more advanced students' needs for enrichment?
- Will students have access to the resources and/or technology required at the time they need it to complete this learning experience?

- How will I evaluate the outcome of this learning experience?
- Is it more appropriate to evaluate process, product, or both?
- How well will this learning experience meet the perceived needs and interests of the students as they were expressed at the time when we explored the topic together?

Activity Title:
Grade:
Subject:
Expectations:
These will come directly from the appropriate school or district guidelines.
The activity may span several subjects.
IT component:
What kind of application(s) will students use? e.g., graphics, word processing, database, spreadsheet, digital camera, Web authoring.
Software/hardware required:
IT expectations:
These will come directly from the appropriate school or district guidelines.
Prerequisite IT skills:
With what IT skills would the students have to be familiar before tackling this activity?
Description/demonstration of learning:
Approximate time required:
Student grouping:
Will students be working as a whole group, small group, pairs, or individually?
Activity Plan:
Step-by-step, clear instructions to guide the activity from start to finish: prior to the task, during the task, and at the end of the task. You may or may not require a student recording sheet/activity card.
Assessment:
How will this activity be assessed and who will assess it (teacher, peers, self)?
Extensions/differentiation:
What follow-up activities might be appropriate? How could this plan be modified for exceptional students?
Resources:
Are there any other books, videos, Web sites, etc. that could be used in conjunction with this activity?

Figure 4-5

A sample planning template for a technology-integrated learning experience.

In Appendix 1 you will find examples of detailed technology-integrated lesson plans at four different levels using the template provided in Figure 4-5. These plans were prepared by teacher candidates at a university. Various educational institutions and organizations maintain databases of technology-integrated lesson plans. You may find inspiration, ideas, or exactly the lesson you want provided by one of the following institutions or organizations:

- North Carolina Public Schools, Computer Skills Lesson Plans
- Bellingham Schools Lesson Plans
- Florida Center for Instructional Technology (Teaching N' Technology)
- Forefront Curriculum
- South Central Regional Technology in Education Consortium

Filamentality is a fill-in-the-blank interactive Web site that guides you through picking a topic, searching the Web, gathering good Internet sites, and turning Web resources into activities appropriate for learners. You can create a Hotlist, Scrapbook, Treasure Hunt, Sampler, or WebQuest. These online activities include everything the learner will need on one Web page.

Task Cards

A task card format is often appropriate for individual assignments and sometimes also for cooperative learning tasks. In order to successfully work from a task card, students need to read; follow directions; organize appropriate materials, resources, and work areas; and make some decisions on their own. If your students are used to a more teacher-directed approach, spend some extra time practicing these skills before requiring independent work from task cards. The following sample task cards, written at various levels of difficulty, illustrate how student use of technology can be integrated with concept and skill development on a task card.

Figure 4-6

In this simple activity integrating science and visual arts, young students use Kid Pix to demonstrate their understanding of both plants and colors.[8]

Title Page for
"Plants in Our Environment"

1. Type the title in a **cool** color.
2. Be ready to tell your teacher why you picked this color.
3. Use the stamp to put **coniferous** trees and **deciduous** trees on your title page.

4. Use the stamp to include at least one **flower.**

5. Put **animals** and **people** on your page because they depend on plants from our environment.

6. Type your name in the top right hand corner using a **warm** color.
7. Be ready to tell your teacher why you picked this color.

The Different Layers of Soil

1. Choose MSPaint from the Program Menu
2. Click on the pencil and then click on the line width tool. Select a wide line.
3. Draw the shape of the large jar that you used in your experiment.
4. Select a narrower line width.
5. Draw several straight lines across the jar until you have the number of layers you see in the settled soil.
6. Fill each layer with a different color or texture pattern. You might wish to use the airbrush tool, the fill tool and/or the paintbrush tool to make it look like the real thing.
7. Label each layer in the proper order and with its correct name.
8. Raise your hand to have your work checked before you print it.

Figure 4-7

After completing an experiment in which soil has been mixed with water and settled out into layers, students use a graphics program to illustrate their observations.

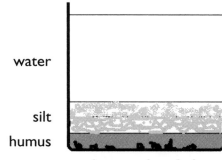

water

silt

humus

rocks, gravel, and clay

Who is responsible for this Web site?

Under what category does the Web site fall?
____ Activity-based
____ Writing
____ Photographic

When was this site last updated? _____

For whom is this site intended? _____

Describe the site.

How does this Web site relate to what you have learned about labor history?

What was the most useful part?

Figure 4-8

After students have used various Web sites to research labor history, they are required to evaluate one of the sites they have used.

Figure 4-9

In this task, senior students create an electronic interactive travel brochure and a Web page.[9]

 Interactive Travel Brochure

You are making an electronic interactive travel brochure for the fictitious company, Astronomical Tours, using Hyperstudio and a web page.

The web page will be your destination title page (e.g. Beyond the rings on the lovely moon of Rhea!) and be the launch site for your stack. Your web page will link back to the class main page for Astronomical Tours.

Your Hyperstudio presentation will be a stack of cards — no more than 4 cards please — plus one bibliography card.

Cite your sources, (books, software and Internet sources), for information, graphics, sounds, video clips and animations on the bibliography card.

Make your writing style persuasive — you are trying to attract clients to your destination.

You must include the following information in your stack:
- how far is it (in kilometers and in astronomical units)?
- how long will it take to get there?
- how will people get there (be creative e.g. for very long trips, induced hibernation may be required).
- what do people need to pack in their suitcase (type of clothing, food, oxygen, protective gear, equipment).
- biogeophysical information such as type of atmosphere, gravitational force, planet density, planet day length, year length, direction of rotation (from which direction does the sun rise?), number of moons and any special characteristics.
- why would people want to go there—for minerals, sunshine, atmosphere, view of the galaxy)?

Incorporate the data required into the sales pitch, for example, instead of saying Jupiter has 13 moons, say something like "Experience the marvel of a steady progression of 13 moons across the night sky!"

Include a home button or icon in your stack to return browsers to the main page.

Possible destinations:

Sun	Saturn	Uranus	Mercury	Jupiter
Neptune	Venus	Mars	Pluto	Earth
Moon	Comets e.g. Hale-Bopp			

Asteroid belt and the largest asteroids are Ceres, Pallas, Vesta, and Hygeia
Jupiter's largest moons Io, Europa, Ganymede and Callisto
Saturn's largest moons Titan, Rhea, Dione and Tethys

Figure 4-10

When you are developing task cards that direct students to use Internet sites, consider using an electronic worksheet instead of paper. Most new software allows you to embed a hyperlink into the text. By clicking on this link, students go directly to the site from which they will gather their information.[10]

CONGRATULATIONS!
You have won a school lottery and you get to pick
an adventure to anywhere you would like to go!
Take your family, take your friends, take your pets; it's up to you!

Imagine that you get this news in the mail when you get home from school today. Find a trip that you and your partner would like to take. Discover as much as you can about your trip. Be sure to include all the information someone would need. Keep in mind the 5 W's and "How" questions.

Here is a list of adventure Internet sites to get you started:
http://www.adventurepages.com/
http://www3.sympatico.ca/bushman
http://blueloon.baynet.net
http://www.telusplanet.net/public/catchem/index1.htm

POSSIBLE QUESTIONS TO ANSWER
Where are you going?
How long is the trip?
What will you do and see?
Who are you taking with you?
How much will it cost?
When will you go?
Why did you choose this trip?
What kind of clothes should you bring?
Do you need any special equipment?

How High will the Ping-Pong Ball Bounce?

The only variable you can change is the height of the ball drop.
Begin with a drop from 20 cm, then 40 cm, 60 cm, 80 cm, etc.
Measure and record the height of the first bounce on each drop.

But first, predict...

We think

Drop (cm)	Bounce (cm)
20	16
40	36
60	42
80	54
100	62
120	64
180	65
220	77
300	78

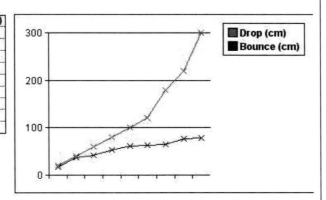

How close was your prediction? Explain the results you obtained.
Then print your worksheet. After checking it, remove your data for
the next experimentor and save it before closing this file.

Figure 4-11

Another form of an electronic task card can be produced by integrating different functions of a works package such as AppleWorks or Microsoft Works. This science activity uses a spreadsheet imported into a drawing program. The spreadsheet adjusts accordingly as students enter their own data. After completing their predictions and conclusions, students print out the sheet.

Workstations

Using a workstation approach is one of the best ways to ensure maximum use of the available equipment and software.
Workstations should

- easily fit into the room,
- take into account the stages of development of individuals in the class,
- lend themselves to the extension of skills, and
- incorporate all the resources available.

The type of workstations will, of course, depend on the age of your students, the topic, the resources available, and the learning experiences your plan includes. Thus workstations will vary from unit to unit. Each of your classroom computers could be used as a workstation, or students might move to a computer, VCR, videodisc player, camera, or tape recorder as required.

Figure 4-12

Most equipment in a technology-integrated classroom is designed for individual, partner, or small-group work. The complexity of the tracking sheet you design will reflect the level and abilities of your students.

My name is _____

Week of _____

 **Art**	Paint an animal. Show its home.
 **Listening**	Listen to the story "Is This My Home?"
 **Writing**	Tell where 5 animals live. (A _____ lives in a _____.)
 **Puzzles and Games**	Play "Animal Bingo" with your friend.
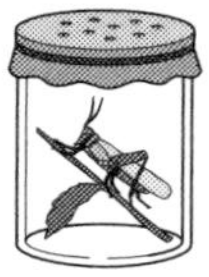 **Science**	Make a home for an insect.
 **Reading**	Read on the computer: "A Home for Harry."
 **Viewing**	Watch the video "Animal Homes."

Weather Web Activity #1
Cloud Types

1. With your partner, choose a type of cloud to study.

2. Prepare a report:
   - describe how the cloud looks
   - explain how the cloud is formed
   - explain what it tells meteorologists about the weather

3. Use cotton batting on a blue background to make a picture of your cloud.

4. Present your picture and report to the class.

Don't forget to cite your Internet sources!

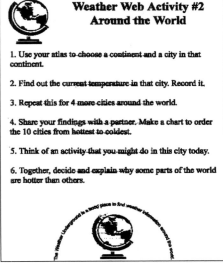

Weather Web Activity #2
Around the World

1. Use your atlas to choose a continent and a city in that continent.

2. Find out the current temperature in that city. Record it.

3. Repeat this for 4 more cities around the world.

4. Share your findings with a partner. Make a chart to order the 10 cities from hottest to coldest.

5. Think of an activity that you might do in this city today.

6. Together, decide and explain why some parts of the world are hotter than others.

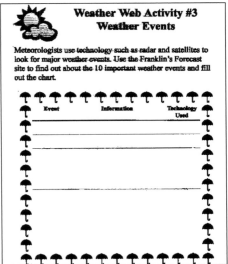

Weather Web Activity #3
Weather Events

Meteorologists use technology such as radar and satellites to look for major weather events. Use the Franklin's Forecast site to find out about the 10 important weather events and fill out the chart.

Event	Information	Technology Used

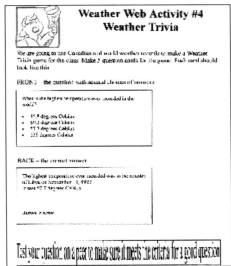

Weather Web Activity #4
Weather Trivia

We are going to use Canadian and world weather records to make a Weather Trivia game for the class. Make 5 question cards for the game. Each card should look like this:

FRONT – the question with several choices of answers

Where is the highest temperature ever recorded in the world?

- 15.8 degrees Celsius
- 94.3 degrees Celsius
- 57.7 degrees Celsius
- 135 degrees Celsius

BACK – the correct answer

The highest temperature ever recorded was in the country of Libya on September 1, 1922. It was 57.7 degrees Celsius.

Answer source

Test your question on a peer to make sure it meets the criteria for a good question

Figure 4-13

In this weather unit, four computers are used as different workstations. Students are provided with task cards to guide them as they use the Internet to access weather information and complete a follow-up activity.

Student Groupings

In most schools, there is not enough equipment to allow every individual student the time to complete technology-intensive projects. The use of partners and cooperative groups is a logical response to this situation as well as being a sound pedagogical strategy. Grouping students takes careful planning. Some groupings may be random, others must be intentional. There is a variety of strategies for grouping students. Although best friends often work well together, you may prefer to select students who will complement each other in their abilities. For instance, a student who is a good communicator but not a skilled technology user might be matched best with a student who needs to develop better communication skills but is a proficient technology user. Cross-gender pairs can be problematic, as girls and boys often approach computer tasks differently. Although it may at first seem logical, it is dangerous to pair a student with very strong computer skills with one whose skills are extremely weak. The consequence of doing so is likely to be that both are frustrated. Instead, try pairing a strong student with one whose skills are medium, and medium with weak.

In order to avoid the possibility that the more motivated students will do the lion's share of the work, assign roles to each partner or group member. The use of roles is one of the defining features of true cooperative learning.

Figure 4-14

In this learning experience plan, students work in groups of four to form their own production company, which will "manage" a famous composer and create a concert tour.[11]

Public relations manager
Your role:
- advertise the concerts
- promote the artist
- create a flyer and newspaper ad
Your electronic tools:
- desktop publishing and graphics

Biographer
Your role:
- write the composer's life story
Your electronic tools:
- Internet for research
- word processor

Schedule manager
Your role:
- prepare the itinerary of places, dates, and times of concerts
- book accomodation and transportation
Your electronic tools:
- Internet for research
- database

Music reviewer
Your role:
- write a newspaper review of the concert
Your electronic tools:
- desktop publishing and graphics

Step 6: *Plan Student Training for the Technology*

Your students will have a wide variety of technology skills. Those who have home computers, whose parents are technology users, and who have a natural interest in using computers for leisure activities will be more literate and confident. Before expecting students to use ICT to accomplish a task on which they will be assessed, you must establish a level playing field by ensuring that all students have the opportunity to develop the required skills. Carefully identify the prerequisite skills students will require for the learning experience upon which you are about to embark. For example, before beginning an activity in which students are required to gather photographic evidence of signs of spring and write about them, you might identify these prerequisite skills:

Creating a Class Anthology Book

What will your role be?

Task 1: Editing
The EDITOR will act as both organizer and leader. He/she is responsible for making sure all the pieces are proof read and ready for print. Using the word processor, he/she will be responsible for typing each of the pieces and readying them for the next stage. EDITORS must not only be competent writers, but possess keen organizational skills and be willing to offer assistance to all other members of the publishing team.

Task 2: Designing
The DESIGNER will be responsible for the overall aesthetic of the published work. He/she will not only design the cover but will also work with the other team members on title design and illustrations to accompany submissions. The images can come from a variety of sources, including original art scanned into the computer, clip art, or downloaded images from the Internet. Please check with the teacher regarding copyright. DESIGNERS must possess a strong visual sense and be willing to learn graphic editing software such as Corel Photopaint and Adobe Photoshop.

Task 3: Publishing
The PUBLISHER will be responsible for integrating all the elements into one seamless desktop package. He/she will not only assemble the materials, but will organize them into a cohesive booklet design. The various literary pieces will dictate the kind of desktop publishing required. PUBLISHERS must have high organizational skills, and work closely with the DESIGNER to enhance the visual aesthetic of the finished work.

Figure 4-15
In this learning experience appropriate for older students, class members work in groups of three to create anthologies of original literary pieces.[12]

- ability to operate the digital camera;
- ability to compose a photo;
- ability to save an image as a jpeg file;
- ability to import digital photgraphs into a word-processed document; and
- ability to place and re-size an image in a document.

Plan time and access that will allow for direct instruction, free and/or guided exploration, and practice with the hardware and software to be used. Chapter 6: Getting Started provides more detailed suggestions for teaching students how to use technology tools.

Step 7: *Timetable*

The next step is to sequence the selected learning experiences to suit the available instructional time and to provide logical concept development. Students need large blocks of time to engage in small-group and individual activities. Subject integration or interdisciplinary instruction is one way to organize the school day into large blocks of time. The best approach is to present curricular material within wholistic or real-world contexts rather than segmenting it into separate disciplines. Some teachers prefer to spend a longer amount of time working with the whole group before moving into cooperative learning groups and individual pursuits. If you are just beginning the transition to a more student-centered approach that accommodates the integration of technology, this may be a good way to begin. If you are experienced with using a variety of teaching and learning styles, you may choose to provide this variety within a day, and from day to day.

Sample Daily Plan for a Measurement Unit			
Day	**Activity**	**Type of Activity**	**Technology**
Monday	Review measurement vocabulary Review addition and multiplication	Whole group Individual	Overhead
Tuesday	Measure students' height and graph	Whole group	
Wednesday	View videotape on perimeter Estimate perimeters of objects and check by measuring	Whole group Small groups	Videotape
Thursday	Workstations: perimeter	Individual	Computers, videotapes, audiotapes
Friday	Workstations: perimeter	Individual	Computers, videotapes, audiotapes
Monday	View videotape on area Estimate areas of objects and check by measuring	Whole group Small groups	Videotape
Tuesday	Draw polygons and exchange to calculate area	Small groups	
Wednesday	Workstations: perimeter and area	Individual	Computers, videotapes, audiotapes
Thursday	Workstations: perimeter and area	Individual	Computers, videotapes, audiotapes
Friday	View videotape on volume Use centicubes to make objects with given volume	Whole group Individual	Videotape
Monday	Build a cubic meter Make buildings from centicubes and find volume	Whole group Small groups	
Tuesday	Workstations: perimeter, area, and volume	Individual	Computers, videotapes, audiotapes
Wednesday	Workstations: perimeter, area, and volume	Individual	Computers, videotapes, audiotapes
Thursday	Workstations: perimeter, area, and volume	Individual	Computers, videotapes, audiotapes
Friday	View videotape on capacity Measure in L and mL	Whole group Small groups	Videotape
Monday	Workstations: perimeter, area, volume, and capacity	Individual	Computers, videotapes, audiotapes, CD-ROM
Tuesday	Workstations: perimeter, area, volume, and capacity	Individual	Computers, videotapes, audiotapes, CD-ROM
Wednesday	Workstations: perimeter, area, volume, and capacity	Individual	Computers, videotapes, audiotapes, CD-ROM

Figure 4-16

Laying out a unit on a day-to-day basis helps to establish and maintain timelines. This example illustrates an ideal way to vary whole-group, cooperative learning and individual work at workstations within a unit.

When students are using ICT, strict timelines are more difficult to establish. Unforeseen events such as lack of access to a particular piece of equipment or Web site exactly when required, technical problems, and time required to become proficient with hardware and software create a need for flexibility of time allotments. It's frustrating for anyone to get organized for a specific task and then discover there's not enough time to complete it. In technology-integrated classrooms, set-up time can be greater than that required to pull out a pencil and paper. For example, it might take five or ten minutes for a student to log on to the computer network, locate and load the desired program, become reacquainted with the program's procedures, and, finally, begin to work. A small group of students might need five or ten minutes to move their chairs and materials to a viewing station, negotiate space for everyone, select a video to watch, plug in their headphones, adjust volume controls, and begin the assignment. Setting up a science lab might take longer still, depending on its complexity. You must take set-up procedures into account when planning blocks of time for student work. Set-up time is not wasted time. Students learn valuable organizational skills and planning strategies that will one day transfer to a work environment.

> **"Your job is to teach. Using technology does take some time away from content, but I've found it generates far more interest; the kids are learning better. They're getting something that can be used in other courses. I'm constantly reassured every time I put them on the computers. They're so excited and they get so much done. The attitude towards the entire class changes. They respect me because I'm giving them something useful."**[13]

There may be times when you do not wish to create rigid time boundaries. The open-ended nature of the challenge may be such that you are not sure of exactly what product students will create or how long it will take. By observing carefully, you can identify students who are using their time wisely and those who are having difficulty. Keep a watchful eye on all the groups to avoid some falling behind, thus creating a waiting line for other students to use the classroom technology. Once this backlog starts, more and more groups begin falling behind, and you have a frustrating scenario to deal with. Some students require assistance in developing better organizational skills and on-task behavior. Strategies to help these students might include breaking the assignment down into shorter, more specific tasks and providing extra help from a teacher, teacher's aide, or parent helper.

Step 8: *Reconsider*

Although this step-by-step approach to planning a technology-integrated curriculum unit may appear at first to be very linear, all the steps are interrelated and interdependent. Cohesive planning is achieved by constantly referring back to earlier decisions. As you lay out your completed plan, stop and reconsider. Is there a sound purpose behind each workstation? Is each selected learning experience consistent with the learning objectives and outcomes for the topic? Does your planned evaluation adequately reflect those same learning objectives? Have you achieved your goal of integrating technology into the curriculum? If you answer yes to all these questions, you are ready to get started!

Summing Up

The chapter you have just read places technology in the curriculum context, where it belongs. A recent newspaper report suggested, and we agree, that teachers should be able to answer these questions:

- What are the students expected to learn?
- In what ways will you structure appropriate learning experiences?
- How is what you are doing now in the classroom different from what you were doing ten years ago?
- How do you know when the students have achieved the expected outcomes?
- How do parents know what their children have learned?

GETTING
STARTED

five

"Teachers are like authors. Their primary interest and focus is on the content and the end result — empowering young people to learn. Technology is simply a tool to help enhance and extend what teachers are already doing. Don't forget we've been using 'multimedia' for generations: a pencil with an eraser on paper with words and pictures and crayons."[1]

For a classroom teacher, the opportunity exists to make technology as much a part of students' experience at school as it already is in their daily life outside of school. Making careful and strategic decisions at the classroom level will enhance your students' performance and will streamline the implementation of your technology-integrated program. Living with technology must become as little a chore as possible. Teachers are too busy with the job of teaching to be spending time tinkering with technology glitches. By carefully thinking about your unique classroom situation(s), you can establish some simple routines that will help enormously. Proceed slowly. Students will not become self-motivated, self-directed, and technology-literate overnight. You are likely to find, however, that many students adapt more quickly to the use of technology than you do. Use this natural adaptability to the advantage of all by allowing these students to demonstrate the use of hardware and software to the class and encouraging them to act as resource persons for others who are less experienced. By showing that you are also a learner, you establish a positive classroom learning environment, model authentic problem-solving strategies, and move into the role of a facilitator of learning.

When all students have their own personal portable computers, collaboration and interaction increases among students and between students and teachers. How can that be?

> Because learning becomes project based. Portable computers enable the formation of workgroups. Teamwork expands because of the ability to collaborate online and after school. The word processor, spreadsheet, presentation program, database, and other applications are blank slates waiting for students and teachers to create together.... Teachers and students work side by side, helping one another to exploit the technology to explore the questions of learning. Students love to help one another — and their teachers — master new and more powerful ways to use the computers. Students also take the computers home and share them and their lessons with parents, siblings, and friends, further expanding the circles of collaboration."[2]

Teachers often wonder about how to establish a classroom environment that promotes respect and a sense of shared responsibility for the care of the technology. This chapter contains many simple and practical strategies for achieving this goal. As schools are increasingly used as community centers and to provide recreational and meeting facilities, security of equipment becomes more important. Safety is also paramount in the technological classroom, particularly with younger students. Consider not only electrical safety and safe movement around a crowded classroom, but also physical safety — proper positioning and posture for students who spend long periods of time sitting at computer screens. In this chapter, we provide some ideas to help keep your classroom organized, safe, and secure.

Organizing Space

Activity-based learning requires particular spaces, configurations, and easy-to-reach storage facilities and resources. However, space is often a rare commodity. Nonetheless, ingenuity on the part of teachers and students has led to well-equipped, well-designed workstations, even within the confines of a single, small classroom! When planning the physical layout, consider the type of learning environment you want to create. An ideal environment
- stimulates active learning,
- allows flexibility in work modes as a member of a group, with a partner, or individually, and
- provides easy access to resources and equipment.

Positioning Computers: For Student Use

The equipment that takes up the most space, usually computers, should be set up first. Positioning computers is governed by several factors:
- the location of the cable that connects the computer(s) to the school network and/or the Internet
- the location of power outlets
- the location of doorways leading into the classroom
- the location of windows — too much direct light makes it difficult to see the computer screen and is also distracting
- the location of blackboards — computers and chalk dust don't mix well, so some schools are substituting whiteboards

Most classrooms have only two or three power outlets so the location options are immediately limited. However, power bars enable several computers to operate from one power outlet. Be sure to check with your school or school system's safety officer regarding fire and electrical regulations. Wires should never pass across floor space where students walk, and running extension cords across doorways violates electrical codes. More safety considerations are discussed later in this chapter.

In arranging tables for computers, several choices are possible. Positioning computers along the wall is an economical use of space. Such an arrangement makes it easy to observe students at work, but in some classrooms it might restrict access to bulletin boards or display space. The screens are not distracting to other students as long as the students are engaged in a different task.

Allow as much space as you can for students to place notebooks and papers between computers, along with easy movement of the mouse on a mouse pad. If you cannot get enough space between them for a notebook or activity card, perhaps you can find a paper holder that clips to the side of the monitor.

If the computers are all stand-alone, rather than networked, they don't necessarily have to be grouped together and the choice of locations is limited only by the availability of power outlets. Because there will often be two chairs at each computer, allow enough space for other students to pass by without disturbing the concentration of those working on screen. If you do not have a data projector, it's a good idea to position at least one computer facing into the classroom for occasions when you, or a student, wish to demonstrate something to the whole group. If you have a printer and/or scanner, they must be easily accessible to students.

Positioning Computers: For Teacher Use

If you have a computer for your own use, consider how you plan to use it and position it accordingly for
- personal communication, lesson preparation, and record keeping;
- whole-class teaching; and
- individual student demonstrations.

Placement of TV/VCR

Once you've set up the computers, you can arrange the other equipment requiring power outlets. A TV/VCR is susceptible to interference from bright sunlight and is thus best positioned in a corner where students can gather around for viewing. If the primary use of the TV/VCR is individual or small-group viewing, invite younger students to sit on a carpet.

Older students may prefer to pull their chairs closely around the TV/VCR so that individual headphones can reach it. Five or six sets of headphones reserved for use at the TV/VCR will usually suffice in a class of 30 students. Encourage students to cooperate in getting organized. One student could be in charge of operating the equipment.

When placing the unit in a permanent location, consider that you may occasionally need it for whole-group viewing. Though the screen may be smaller than that of a regular TV, you might position it in such a way that a large group of students could gather around it. To facilitate this option, ensure that the screen is facing into the main area of the classroom. Students can then turn or move their chairs closer for viewing. A large monitor is more appropriate for large-group viewing, of course, but may not always be available. Students may wish to sit at a desk or table so they can write while viewing.

An audiovisual cart supporting the TV/VCR is ideal for both small-group and large-group viewing. It's also easy to move, should you wish to connect it to a computer for multimedia work.

Audio Equipment

Speaking and listening equipment also requires power outlets, with the exception of hand-held tape recorders operating on rechargeable batteries. In addition to computers with audio input capabilities, a large tape recorder and several small ones are a practical combination. It's also useful to have at least one external microphone that can connect to your computers for higher quality recording than the usual built-in microphones.

A large tape recorder with headphones enables a small group of students to listen to the same selection. Follow-up assignments can vary according to the needs of individual students in the group. Students preparing audio selections for inclusion in multimedia presentations may also need to listen as a small group. Small hand-held tape recorders are ideal for individual audio work.

Other Learning Areas

The positioning of the technology is interdependent with all the other components of a successfully laid-out classroom. When you decide to set up workstations for art, science, manipulative mathematics, or design and technology, subjects that involve more than just pencil and paper activities, strategic layout is also important. An art workstation should be located near a sink, storage shelves, and supply cupboards. A workstation for concrete, hands-on experiences in science or manipulative mathematics activities also requires storage areas nearby. A design and technology workstation might require ready access to a computer for robotics, programming, or control activities. Some teachers put all the learning materials for a specific workstation into a large box and designate a student as "Materials Manager" to bring the box to and from the workstation. Sometimes students select the floor as the most appropriate place to set up an activity. As in every work environment, space must be negotiated among all the users and respected by all. By involving students in the organization of the classroom, the teacher encourages them to participate in making the limited space function as well as possible. It might also be a good idea to invite input from the school custodian!

Floor Plans

A floor plan that works well in one technology-integrated classroom may be hopeless in another. Nevertheless, it helps to study sample plans and to borrow or adapt a feature or features that might suit your classroom.

In arranging the classroom, you will always have to compromise. An ideal arrangement for cooperative learning groups may require that some students will have to turn their chairs around for whole-group lessons. A floor plan that allows all students to have an unobstructed view of the chalkboard may necessitate turning around some desks each time you ask the students to work in groups. Some teachers are comfortable with adjusting the spaces in the classroom to meet the needs of the moment. To a certain extent, your flexibility in this regard is governed by the age of your students and the type of furniture in your classroom. Visit the publisher's Web site to see some sample floor plans.

Classroom Furniture

Ideally, every technology-integrated classroom would have an adequate number of carts, computer tables, printer stands, audio and videotape racks, CD holders, and individual carrels for private study. In Chapter 3, What About Equipment, we suggested several alternatives in specialized furniture for computers and printers. In reality, however, many classrooms have only student desks and a few assorted tables. But a lack of specialized furniture needn't thwart the goal of integrating technology into your program.

Support computers, printers, scanners, videodisc players, and TV/VCRs on strong tables, preferably ones that have a shelf underneath so you can keep wires out of the way. In a technological classroom, additional tables are required for the larger equipment. You'll need an appropriate number of chairs so students can work at these tables.

Tables, with or without shelves, are probably the most adaptable alternative for student seating. Desks with attached chairs are least desirable because they are inflexible and take up a lot of space. Wheelchair access is a must; a physically or mentally challenged student may need a specific working space that accommodates a personal computer, a communications board, or a walking apparatus. Again, adjustable tables rather than single desks are more likely to suit special-needs students.

Establishing Equipment Care and Protection Routines

The better care you take of the equipment entrusted to you, the longer it will last and the better it will work. Just like caring for a car, computers require some simple ongoing care. It is time consuming and frustrating to have computers that regularly need attention from a technician. Whenever students are required to share equipment, materials, and space, routines are necessary to facilitate this sharing. Classes will vary in the extent to which care and respect for the equipment needs to be taught. Even with the most responsible students, however, begin the year with a discussion about care and respect. In order for students to feel ownership for "their" equipment, they should be the ones to develop the guidelines for its care and use. Have small groups of students brainstorm lists of do's and don'ts for the various pieces of equipment in the classroom. A "take care of our computers chart," for example, might include some of the following ideas:

- Do not bring food or drinks near the computers.
- Hands off the keyboard except when you are working on it.
- Tap the keys — do not bang them.

- Do not just turn off the computer — exit gracefully from programs by closing files in sequence.
- Do not mix water, paint, and computers.
- Move carefully around the computer tables.
- Be patient — tap the ENTER key only once, then wait.
- Never use anyone else's login.

Turn all your equipment on and off by the main switch on the power bar, if possible. From a technical point of view, it saves wear and tear on the switches. From a classroom management point of view, this is more important with younger children who may not be able to remember the sequence of switches. If the order of turning on pieces of equipment is critical to their operation (e.g., scanner must be turned on before computer), you may need to post a sign to this effect in an appropriate spot.

Discuss, modify, add to, agree upon, and post these rules in the classroom. Discussing and posting guidelines for care and respect doesn't mean that they will always be adhered to, however, and you will undoubtedly be called upon to review, reinforce, and apply logical consequences with students who habitually show disrespect for school property. Verbal pressure from teachers and peers is often enough to deter a student who has difficulty following established routines. The final consequence for the student who continually abuses equipment is loss of the privilege of using it for a given length of time.

Cleanliness

Care of equipment also includes cleanliness. Wires that drag on the ground are traps for dust and dirt. You can bundle them up and attach them to table legs using fasteners, twist-ties, or tape, though tape doesn't usually last very long. Dust is the enemy of all electronic equipment, and classrooms are notoriously dusty places due to the sheer number of feet that move in, out, and around them daily. This dust collects in computer keyboards and the switches and buttons of other equipment. Not only does this make them unpleasant to use, but it also leads to mechanical problems over a period of time. Also, allergies to dust mites are increasingly common. Keep small equipment in plastic bags when not in use. An ambitious parent group could undertake the task of sewing some simple computer covers for you if the school can't buy them. An old bed sheet draped over the computers at night will be good enough to help protect them from the dust and dirt that is stirred up when the classroom is swept. A student should be given the job of covering and uncovering them, and students can also take responsibility for dusting the computers, especially the screens, on a weekly basis or as required. The more students are involved in the responsibilities of ownership of the equipment, the more respect they will have for it. Avoid dust bunnies and keep the custodian as your friend.

Figure 5-1
Classroom Computer Rules

Do not bring food or drink near the computers.

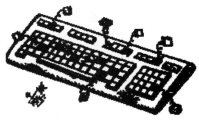

Tap the keys — do not bang them.

Do not just turn off the computer — exit from programs by closing files in sequence.

Hands off the keyboard except when you are working on it.

Do not mix water, paint, and computers.

Move carefully around the computer tables.

Be patient — tap the ENTER key only once, then wait.

Never use anyone else's login.

Tips for Taking Care of Your Computers
- **Clean the screen by spraying a small amount of window-cleaning fluid or water onto a cloth and drying with paper towels.**
- **Clean the mouse by removing the ring to free the ball, revealing two small rollers — make sure they are free of grime.**
- **Clean keyboards with a small pastry brush.**
- **Wipe cases and the rubber ear pads on headphones with a squirt of a mild commercial cleaner, on a soft cloth.**
- **Clean CDs by wiping them with a soft cloth.**

Care of Laptops

Laptops are portable, which means they can be taken everywhere — even into the mud and the rain. Thus they require some special consideration above and beyond desktop models. For younger classes, adult chaperones can be responsible for equipment. Older students should be responsible themselves for each piece of equipment used. Make all students aware of the following guidelines.

- Keep the laptop dry and clean.
- Pack the laptop carefully, including all components and cables.
- Use a backpack that includes an area that is correctly padded for a laptop.
- If you are using a laptop where it is wet or muddy, put the keyboard in a clear plastic bag and air-dry all equipment at the end of the activity.

Storage of Equipment

Organized and efficient techniques for the storage of equipment help students take care of it and also make it more accessible. Large equipment such as computers, large tape recorders, and VCRs are not a problem, as they are generally placed on a table and counter and simply remain there. The smaller items, such as hand-held tape recorders, batteries, calculators, computer discs, CDs, audio and video tapes, headphones, and videodiscs require carefully thought-out storage solutions. When several students are in the process of getting set up for an activity, they need to be able to get the required materials without interfering with one another, without arguments, and without a great deal of noise and fuss. They need to return materials easily and neatly, leaving them ready for use by someone else. You can help them achieve these goals by using a few simple strategies.

Small Tape Recorders

Keep hand-held tape recorders in individual plastic bags. Each bag might also contain a set of headphones and an adapter for plugging the unit in to the wall outlet. This way, the student has everything required without moving around and can get set up quickly for the task at hand.

Audiotapes

Plastic cases protect audiotapes and keep them clean but the cases are often quite brittle and will not stand up to rough treatment. If they are loose in a bin, students have to root through them to find the one they want. This action soon breaks cases and ultimately damages the tapes themselves. An alternative is to purchase an inexpensive audiocassette holder, which allows the tapes to be held in grooves and also has the advantage of exposing the labels for readability. A cheaper but shorter term solution is to mount adhesive-backed book pockets on a sheet of cardboard or bulletin board and label each with the name of the tape which it contains.

Videotapes

Videotapes tend to have more durable cases than audiotapes, so you may be content to put them into a box or bin. Be sure to label each case on the outside so students do not have to waste time opening and closing cases to find the video they need. There are a variety of inexpensive video racks on the market, or maybe a parent has one that could be donated.

Headphones

Headphones can be a nuisance if the cords are always getting tangled. Younger students often delight in pulling and stretching them to make them pop free. Teach students to wind the cords around the headphone before putting them away into a box or bin or hang each set of headphones from a wall hook and let the cords hang free. Our favorite storage idea for headphones is to suspend a large hoop from the ceiling. The headphones are easy to hang on it and they remain tangle-free.

CDs, DVDs, and Videodiscs

CD-ROMs, DVDs, computer discs, and videodiscs usually come in folders or cases of some kind. It is worth investing some time in training your students to handle these items with care and to replace them in their containers after use. Once again, an inexpensive rack is often the best storage solution and clear labeling is important. It is desirable to minimize the amount of direct handling of these items. If the students are using only one CD-ROM during a unit of study, it may be best to leave that disc inside the player at all times. It is safe and ready to use, and it stays clean. In some schools this is not a problem, as the CD-ROM capabilities are managed through towers located centrally, usually in the library. A librarian or library technician is responsible for loading and unloading and the CD is accessed in the classroom by way of a network.

Calculators

Most calculators are quite durable but even so, it is better to tuck them into individual pockets than to simply toss them into a bin. If students bring their own calculators, of course, they can keep them in their own cubbyholes, bins, or desks.

Batteries

If you have equipment that requires batteries (e.g., language/Spellmaster, digital camera), you will need to introduce a system for not only storing those batteries, but for keeping them sorted as to whether they are charged or not charged. One system is to label two small plastic bins or bags as "charged" and "needs charging." This way, when a student removes dead batteries from a piece of equipment, he or she can simply drop them into the "needs charging" bin and insert new ones from the "charged" bin. You need enough extra batteries that the "charged" bin does not run out on any given day. A student can be given the task of placing the "needs charging" batteries into the battery charger at the end of the day and taking them out the following morning for deposit into the "charged" bin. Once this routine is established, it will continue smoothly and batteries won't become a source of frustration. Do keep in mind that some rechargeable batteries should never be charged until they have *completely* run down.

Security of Equipment

You cannot afford to take any risks regarding security. Chances are that, if something is lost or stolen, it may not be replaced for a long time. Without equipment, the program suffers. If you decide to move on to another class or school, you will surely be asked for an accounting of all the technology that has been provided.

Large Equipment

Large equipment such as VCRs, computers, and videodisc players should be secured in a permanent way. Most schools use cables and locks for this purpose. If the piece of equipment has nothing for the cable to go through, a U-bolt may have to be attached for this purpose. A professional thief would be able to remove these locks and cables, but they will serve to discourage vandals or others who may be in the school after hours for assorted reasons. All equipment should be engraved with the school name and an identification number. It is essential to keep an updated record of all serial numbers. Since a serial number can be easily eradicated, the police may advise making some kind of identifying mark either inside the machine or outside in an inconspicuous spot. A description of this identifying mark will serve as proof that the machine belongs to you should the police reclaim it after a theft.

Equipment that is highly visible is bound to be a temptation to thieves. Always close the curtains and blinds at the end of the working day. If the school is often used for evening activities, lock classrooms not in use. During the long summer holidays when various strangers are in and out of schools, it is wise to take all the expensive equipment out of the classroom and lock it away in a secure storage room. In some schools, all large equipment is kept on trolleys or movable tables and moving it from classroom to storage and back is a daily event.

Laptops

Some laptops are used in sets and fit in racks, which serve as recharging stations and/or wireless hubs. In this case they can be easily rolled away into a secure storage area. In other cases, students move around throughout the day with their laptops and security must be given serious consideration. A set of student and teacher rules might include the following:

- Identify your laptop in a permanent way.
- Never leave your laptop unattended.
- Lock your laptop when not in use.
- Use your locker for temporary storage on occasions such as lunch and assembly.

Insurance for laptops that students take home is usually provided by the parents' home insurance policy. In some communities, parents have even organized safety brigades to escort students carrying computers from the school bus to their home. [3]

Small Equipment

It is the small equipment that most frequently disappears. A calculator, small tape recorder, or CD is very easy to slip into a pocket or schoolbag. Short of searching students as they leave the room daily, what can you do about this problem? One of the keys to security of small equipment is a storage system that allows you to check with a glance and see that the correct number of items are visible. This might take the form of numbered pockets or bags hung on hooks. Select a simple strategy and a system that works for you. One of the end-of-day routines can then involve a student checking to see that all equipment is in place.

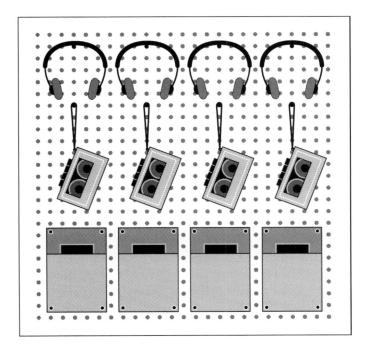

Figure 5-2

A great idea once suggested to us by a principal is to mount a pegboard with hooks and templates to show the location of each piece of small equipment. This is the method used for organization of tools in many workshops.

If there are assorted small items left lying around the room at the end of the day, such as CDs or a Spellmaster, try to develop the habit of tucking them into a file cabinet or desk drawer. This way they are not immediately visible to anyone passing by the door to the classroom. It only takes a moment and it is time well spent.

Safety in the Classroom

As you are responsible for the safety of each student who enters your classroom, don't hesitate to approach an appropriate person in your school if you are unsure about the safety of any of the equipment. This person might be a school administrator, the health and safety officer, or perhaps the custodian. Where electrical safety is concerned, here are some very basic things to look for:

- Electrical circuits should not be overloaded by the use of more than one power bar.
- One power bar should not connect to another.
- Extension cords should not run across doorways or any other areas where students walk.
- Extension cords should not run around sinks or water fountains.
- Cords running around the perimeter of walls should be hooked or taped securely in place.
- Cords should not dangle down where students' feet are likely to tangle in them.
- Electrical cords should not run under carpets.
- Cords should be checked regularly for signs of wear or fraying.

Review electrical safety rules with your students. The younger the students, the more time will be required. You may wish to cooperatively develop some electrical safety rules for the classroom, which might include the following:

- Never poke around inside any electrical machine.
- Keep liquids away from electrical equipment.
- Do not touch a plug, a switch, or any electrical machine with wet hands.
- Never touch an electrical plug or cord that is broken or frayed.
- Never place anything into an electrical outlet except a plug.
- When plugging in or unplugging a piece of equipment from an outlet, hold the plug carefully. Do not pull it out by the cord.

Once they are alerted to be aware of electrical safety, students need only periodic reminders. They will be quick to tell you if they notice any potentially dangerous situations or behaviors.

Student behavior is particularly important in a classroom in which technology limits the amount of space. While moving around the room, students have to negotiate through assorted groupings of tables and student chairs placed at equipment. Take advantage of any available space outside of the classroom to expand your work area. The safety of students and equipment alike can be threatened by rough play or pushing. It's easy for a student to trip, fall, or get bumped in a classroom that is crowded. An active learning environment requires movement, but the confined space within which this movement must take place necessitates certain guidelines. Through open discussions and problem solving with students, these guidelines can be established, maintained, and changed as required. Courtesy and politeness are essential skills in the technological classroom. Respect for others is a social goal that you can develop and encourage through classroom lessons, conflict resolution strategies, and cooperative learning activities.

Safety in Cyberspace

Parents and teachers are understandably concerned about the appropriateness of some of the material available on-line. The media have made us well aware of on-line pornography, violence, and racism. Schools that are now on-line have taken precautions to keep inappropriate material out of the school setting. Those with broad Internet access usually require more procedures than those that have a single modem access in the school library. Some use special hardware and/or software to limit student access, some allow students to visit only approved sites, while others rely on strict acceptable-use policies and close adult supervision. Regardless of the method chosen by the school, wise teachers use good "cyber street proofing" lessons before allowing students to use the Internet. Commercially available programs such as Internet Drivers License (Classroom Connect — http://www.connectedteacher.com) and The Three Little Cyber Pigs (Media Awareness Network — http://www.media-awareness.ca) are designed for this purpose. It's also important to keep in mind that students who are fully engaged in creative learning activities will have neither the time nor the interest to seek out forbidden areas of the Internet. In contrast, students who are turned loose with inadequate forethought, preparation, and supervision are likely to find other ways to amuse themselves on-line.

Software That Limits Access to Inappropriate Sites

NetNanny, SurfWatch, and CYBERsitter are examples of software designed to protect children on the Internet, often referred to as filtering software or Internet content screening tools. At the discretion of parents and schools, they monitor and block inappropriate sites and subject matter. In addition to preventing access to pornography, hate literature, and bomb- and drug-making formulas, you can prevent addresses, phone numbers, and credit card numbers from being sent out on the Internet. There are two types of screening tools available today. Client-based systems are designed for end-users, thus the individual software must be installed on each machine. Server solutions reside on a single machine to which all client machines are attached. Students cannot circumvent the screening mechanism as the server is under sole control of the system administrator.

These software babysitters screen and block both incoming and outgoing commands and content in two different ways. Keyword blocking involves blocking Internet sites that contain certain words. For example, if you enter the word "bomb" in your filtering software dictionary and someone sends the latest pipe bomb recipe via e-mail, the terminal will shut down when the file is accessed. While this allows for good coverage, it also assumes that because one word at the site is objectionable, the entire site contains undesirable content. If a student tries to access http://www.playboy.com, a colorful "Blocked by ..." dialogue box appears. However, while keeping students out of the Playboy site with the keyword "breast," you may also deny them access to sites about cancer research. Even though filtering software uses knowbots and spiders to dig up and then filter any site that includes the use of various words, spelling can be changed and other words substituted.

A better way to block undesirable content is by reference to a database of undesirable material. Typically, a database is created, updated on a regular basis, and maintained by the software publisher, listing sites that fall into several categories that you can selectively turn on and off. A good system will offer daily automatic updates, a large database, and the ability to customize the database yourself.

For more information about filtering software, visit these Web sites by going the publisher's Web site and following the links: CyberSitter, NetNanny, Safe Surf, SurfWatch, Web Doggie, Web Sense

The ongoing costs of filtering software are high, usually requiring an initial investment plus a monthly update, money that might be better spent on learning-related software. Filtering software may also create a false sense of security, and schools that claim they can keep students completely safe from controversial material may find themselves more at risk legally than others who make no such claims. Diverse family values and community values must also be considered, along with students' civil liberties. Some parents may question the school's right to restrict student access to information.

KidSafe Sites

Some schools post a list of sites known to be safe for the appropriate age of the students, and these are the only sites that students are allowed to visit at school. This strategy is used with young students; older students can surf and search within the guidelines of a good acceptable-use policy, as described in the next section. Obviously, close supervision is always required. You'll find a list of sites for very young children at the publisher's Web site.

Another approach is to identify curricular and developmentally appropriate sites in advance for each grade level or theme and make these available as "pages" on the Web server. Students are told they must stay at those sites: no searching, no surfing. Violators suffer loss of Internet privileges or other appropriate consequence. While some teachers may be uncomfortable with this approach, time constraints make it appealing since pointing students toward worthwhile sites saves them time and effort.

You can use your browser software to set up your selected bookmarks as the home page where students begin their explorations. For example, students exploring whales as a class activity open the home page to see a list of approved sites. Alternatively, you can develop a simple Web page of sites using Claris HomePage.

The most likely time that students are apt to stumble across unacceptable sites is when they use a search engine. For this reason, we sometimes limit our younger students to the use of "KidSafe search engines," such as those we've listed on our Web site. These search engines are designed for student use and their databases contain only sites that have been screened.

Acceptable-Use Policies

A balanced approach to using the Internet in schools emphasizes guidance rather than censorship. The strategies we use to teach children about risks in daily life work equally well with the risks associated with the Internet. By establishing clear rules and setting boundaries, we teach young children not to run in the school halls, not to talk to strangers, and not to use violence. We make judgments about how much supervision children require at various ages, and when the risk is extremely high, we keep them in sight or we employ some kind of structure such as a fence or a lock. As children mature, we teach them to respect boundaries and values without being physically blocked from entry. We expect our students to begin exercising judgment and restraint as they move toward adult life.

It is important that schools develop clear policies to guide students' use of the Internet and establish rules and consequences for breaking them. Additionally, schools should consider integrating issues concerning technology and ethics into the curriculum. To protect the school and to reassure parents, most schools have developed and implemented an acceptable-use policy (frequently referred to as AUPs). An AUP is an agreement signed by students, their parents, and the teacher. It outlines the terms and conditions of Internet use. Some school boards or districts institute AUPs. Others are school or even classroom specific. Find out if your school has an Internet AUP. If not, get together with interested colleagues and parents to develop one before allowing your students to access the Internet.

A thorough AUP contains the following:
- a description of what the Internet is
- an explanation of how students will access the Internet at school
- examples of how the Internet will be used to enhance student learning
- a list of student responsibilities while on-line, which might address such issues as
  - privacy
  - morals and ethics
  - freedom of expression
  - legal constraints
  - safety
  - harassment
  - plagiarism
  - resource utilization
  - expected behaviors/etiquette
  - security issues
- the consequences of violating the AUP
- a place for student, parent, and teacher signatures

Rather than simply send an AUP home for signatures, consider beginning the school year with a "cyberspace evening" to introduce the community to the Internet. Have students demonstrate some exciting Internet resources and projects. Talk to parents about how you plan to use the Internet in your classroom or school, and explain your AUP in detail. Stress that, with the privilege to use the Internet, students must accept the responsibility for acceptable use. Some schools adopt a "zero tolerance" attitude while others issue a warning letter after the first violation.

> "**E**ducation is the key. We give a unit of Net Etiquette to each student and staff on the responsible use of the Internet account."[4]

Sample Acceptable-Use Policies:

Take a look at the sample AUP in Appendix 2. Sample AUPs are also available on the Internet. You might start your search for AUPs at http://www.pitsco.inter.net/p/accept.html which is Pitsco's launch to acceptable-use policies or by following the links at the publisher's Web site.

> **E**ncourage parents who have Internet access at home to develop their own **AUP** with their children. A home **AUP** might include rules such as the following:
> - I will not access areas my family and I have decided are off limits.
> - I will not join an on-line service without checking first with an adult family member.
> - I will not give out any information on-line about my home, family, or friends without asking.
> - I will tell an adult if I don't feel right about something I see or read on-line.
> - I will not download files without asking an adult in my family.
> - I will tell an adult if someone I meet on-line suggests that we meet in person.
> - I will tell an adult if someone I meet on-line pesters or insults me, or says things that bother me.[5]

Scheduling Computer Use

The schedule for your school's computer lab may be either fixed, flexible, or a combination of the two. A fixed schedule designates a set time, usually once a week, for each class or teacher. Although this is the type of scheduling used most often in schools, it tends to make computer use into a special event and makes it difficult to integrate the use of the computer as a useful daily tool. With a flexible schedule, a blank timetable is posted on which teachers can sign up for blocks of time as needed. This allows teachers to book the lab for specific projects and to use it for a longer period of time when required. Some schools schedule some fixed blocks of time and leave others flexible.

Teachers sign up weekly or monthly for the flexible blocks.

In your classroom, you have more control over scheduling computer use. Whether you have one computer or five, you will want students to be taking maximum advantage of the technology. Having students work in pairs at the computer(s) is a good way to gain more hands-on time and has been shown to be effective for problem solving and sharing of expertise.

Tips for pairs on the computer
- **Do not pair the strongest computer user with the weakest, as this can lead to mutual frustration.**
- **Friendship pairs work well.**
- **Like-gender pairs work well.**
- **Set an egg timer for five minutes; students switch control of the keyboard and mouse when it rings.**
- **For assessment purposes, demand a product from each student rather than a joint product.**

Use a visual method of displaying who has had a turn at the computer in order to ensure equitable access for all students. Figures 5-3, 5-4, and 5-5 demonstrate various ways of organizing a classroom computer schedule.

Computer Schedule

Week of Jan 21 – 25

	Book report	Space research	Story final draft	Math drills
Gianni	✓	✓	✓	
Sudipta	✓	✓	✓	
Allison	✓	✓		
Federico	✓	✓		
Janie	✓	✓		
Suzanna	✓	✓		
Mike	✓	✓		
Shareen	✓	✓		

Figure 5-3

When students finish their assigned task, they check off their names and tell the next person on the list to take their place at the computer.

Figure 5-4

This type of schedule allows you to designate a task for the day, closing the computers at certain times when you might need all students with you for a special event, an introductory lesson, or class discussion.

Computer Schedule

Monday, Jan 21
Today's task:
Peer edit and produce final draft of space fantasy

9:00 to 10:15	Suzanna & Elaine
	Federico & James
	Mike & Sudipta
	Allison & Janie
10:30 to 11:45	Carrie & Jesse
	Glenn & Sean
	Gary & Scott
	Amy & Valerie
12:45 to 2:00	Sherwyn & David
	1:15 N/A gym time
2:15 to 3:30	Sherwyn & David
	Teague & Rhys
	Cyndi & Jenna
	Shareen & Gianni

Figure 5-5

You might want to designate some blocks of time for student priorities, such as catching up on a missed assignment, preparing a poster for the school drama club, or accessing a mentor by e-mail. Students sign up for a particular reason and must estimate the time they will need.

Computer Schedule

Week of Jan 21 – 25

	Mon	Tues	Wed	Thurs	Fri
9:00 to 10:15	Suzanna book report 20 mins	Elaine & Allison story edit	X	X	
10:30 to 11:45	James math drills 30 mins	Glenn & Sean story edit	Mike math drills 30 mins		
12:45 to 2:00	Sudipta book report	X		Amy & Valerie story edit	
2:15 to 3:30	Cyndi & Jenna poster 1 hour	X		Janie book report 15 mins	X

Tip for teachers of young children:
Get a couple of computer mice that no longer work. Cut their "tails" short and draw a mouse face on the front. Each morning, place the mice on the desks of the first students to use the computer. After their turn, they quietly pass on the mouse to the students whose names are next on the list.

Involve your students in planning a computer schedule that is fair, appropriate for the activity, and understood by all. For some units, the technology component might be a group activity. In others, students may need to move freely to and from the computers for short, specific tasks. Use different scheduling strategies to suit different learning activities.

Although gender issues surrounding computer use are becoming less of a problem as time goes on, there are still indications of boys gravitating to computer use more frequently than girls. Teachers understand the importance of encouraging girls to excel in math, science, and technology. Consider the following strategies that inspire and educate girls and young women to aspire to careers in ICT.

- Ensure female role modeling in the use of school and classroom ICT.
- Encourage girls to get involved in school tech-support teams and help desks.
- Provide opportunities for all-girl settings such as groups or clubs.
- Highlight the many ways in which ICT is used in the real world.
- Invite female mentors from business and industry to speak at career days.
- Employ cooperative learning strategies and use interactive software and Web sites.
- Use creative tools such as publishing, graphics, and Web page creation.
- If necessary, structure equal access to hardware and software for boys and girls by timetabling or reserving equipment accordingly.

The WTN Foundation, funded by the Women's Television Network, is dedicated to encouraging girls and women to embrace emerging opportunities in broadcast and new media technology. You can find tips, contacts, and information for teachers and parents at http://www.wtn.ca/foundation.

Keyboarding Skills

The starting point for using computers effectively comes down to basic keyboarding. Without keyboarding skills, students might be better off using a pencil and paper for their writing. Students who are not given direct instruction in keyboarding develop their own habits and techniques that may limit future speed and accuracy. You either take the time to teach keyboarding or forfeit the time as your students hunt and peck their way through assignments.

Because teachers are more interested in having students use computers to learn than learn to use computers, they may overlook good keyboarding instruction, as noted by this teacher candidate:

> **"I had such a varied functioning group of grade fours that I really had to stay with the basics. Some of the students were actually very nervous around the computer. This is understandable, as it was their first time around one. I know that feeling! The most difficult part during these activities was the almost nonexistent skills of keyboarding. If I were to redo anything, I would have started with basic keyboarding skills first. I believe if the students had some additional knowledge as well as practice in this area there would have been less time wasted."[6]**

The main goals of keyboarding are confidence and typing accuracy. Keyboarding is learned through drill and practice. Most teachers use typing tutor software with sequenced lessons and built-in motivation, but you can also teach keyboarding using word processing software and your own lessons.

Examples of keyboarding software:
- **All the Right Type (Ingenuity Works)**
- **UltraKey (Bytes of Learning)**
- **Mavis Beacon Teaches Typing (Mindscape/ The Learning Company)**
- **JumpStart Typing (Knowledge Adventure)**
- **Typing Tutor (Davidson/Simon & Schuster)**
- **Slam Dunk Typing (The Learning Company)**
- **Stickybear Typing (Optimum Resources)**

Formal keyboarding instruction may begin at about the age of 9 or 10 when students' hands are large enough to span the keyboard. Most teachers report that 15 to 20 minutes per day, three or four days per week for about two months is adequate. Some teachers begin each computer lab session with 5 or 10 minutes of keyboarding practice. You may be fortunate enough to have a set of inexpensive electronic keyboards such as Alpha Smart or Keyboard Wizard available for practice, thus easing the constraint of available computer time.

Prekeyboarding activities, beginning as early as kindergarten, help young children learn to use two hands, type with the ends of the fingers, and know the relative location of keys on a keyboard. Here are some sample prekeyboarding strategies:

1. Color-code specific computer keys using nail polish, fabric paint, or self-adhesive dots.
2. Photocopy a keyboard such as the one provided in Figure 5-6, laminate the copies, and use them for games and short practice sessions. Make an overhead transparency for demonstration.
3. Draw a large keyboard and use it for team games.
4. Paint a large keyboard on the school playground and use it for outdoor games.
5. Name the rows after animals; for example, the top row is the rabbit row because your fingers hop up, the bottom row is the mole row because your fingers dip down.

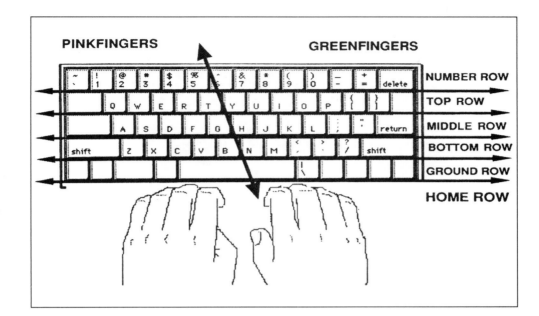

Figure 5-6
Have students color the keys on the left side of the diagonal line red and the other side green. Teach them to use one hand on each side.

Ergonomics

In the days of the typewriter, typing classes included instruction about correct posture and placing equipment at an appropriate height. As evidence mounts about health problems associated with computer use, teachers and students need to be reminded that good keyboarding posture and positioning are necessary to avoid the possibility of serious injury. Teach and model correct posture, and follow these guidelines in placing keyboards and monitors:

- When keyboarding, students' arms should be at about a right angle, level, with flat wrists.
- Wrists shouldn't rest on the keyboard or table.
- Position screens at eye level and an arm's length away.

With students of such varying sizes in one classroom, how can correct positioning be achieved for all? One solution is to have adjustable chairs and/or tables, but these are expensive. It might be more feasible to have cushions of varying shapes and sizes available. Making them might be a worthwhile project for a parent group or senior life skills/home economics class.

Strategies for Training Students to Use Technology

To benefit fully from all that technology offers, students need both direct instruction and freedom to explore. No school or school system can afford the repair bills that result from improper or careless use of equipment. Learning to use a new piece of hardware or software is a hands-on experience requiring time to experiment, or "play" with the technology. This exploration time varies with the complexity of both the hardware and software. Only after both direct instruction and a period of exploration should students be expected to use a technology to accomplish a particular task.

Figure 5-7

It's a good idea to display a poster reminding students of correct posture near the computers.

Copyright © 2001 Trifolium Books. Permission granted to reproduce this page for class use.

A lab setting is an efficient way to introduce computers to beginners and to introduce new software to users at all levels. Lab instruction can work well for large groups if you design learning tasks that allow for the different levels and rates of learning of your students. Many teachers find that when students work with a partner in the lab, as opposed to working alone after whole-group instruction, they are more inclined to experiment, to discover, and to learn.

Demonstration

If your school does not have a data projector or means of connecting a computer to a large screen TV, students can gather around a single monitor as you demonstrate a program or a function. Keep demonstrations brief and focused. Concentrate on the specific features that students will need to perform the task at hand, rather than trying to show all the things the software can do in one session. Take three to five minutes each day for a mini-lesson in which you, or a student, share a tip or new feature of one of the pieces of software currently being used.

"When a new piece of software comes in, I assign a particular student to researching how it works, then providing a demonstration to the rest of the class — including me!"[7]

Ten-minute mini-lessons at regular intervals can be very effective. For example, to practice using spell-check, give students a paragraph such as the following and have them find and correct the spelling mistakes.

Our teacher, Mr Kim, was upset with the class.
"Your making too many spelling mistake!" he said loudly. "Dontcha know now to use the spell check on the computer?"
I lookked down at my storey. There, rite in the centre, was a mistake that seemed to jump off the paige.
"Oh, goodness", I whispered to myself, "I thought I had spell-checked my work".

As a whole group, compare their findings to the findings of the computer spell-check. The following points will arise for discussion:

* *Mistake* is not selected because it is a word, though incorrect in this sentence.
* *Your, storey,* and *rite* are not selected because they are homonyms.
* *Centre* is selected because it is an English spelling, whereas the spell-check may be set to use American spellings.

If the software you are using also has grammar-check, note that it will pick up some of the spelling mistakes.

My Computer Log

Name _____

Date	Project	Software used	Something new that I learned	Something I'd like to find out

Figure 5-8
You can find out what skills students need help with by having them keep a computer log. Glancing over the logs at regular intervals will provide the information you need to plan and group students for tutorials or brief demonstrations.

Free Exploration

Most experienced computer users will tell you that the way they learn new hardware and software is by trial and error. You may be uncomfortable with this method if you have not had many opportunities to learn this way yourself, but it is very effective with technology. Set aside time periods for students to freely explore new hardware and software. Again, pairing students for this activity often leads to better problem solving.

Figure 5-9

A checklist of skills related to a particular type of hardware or software helps students and teachers to keep track of their progress and plan for future learning. This checklist is for word-processing skills.

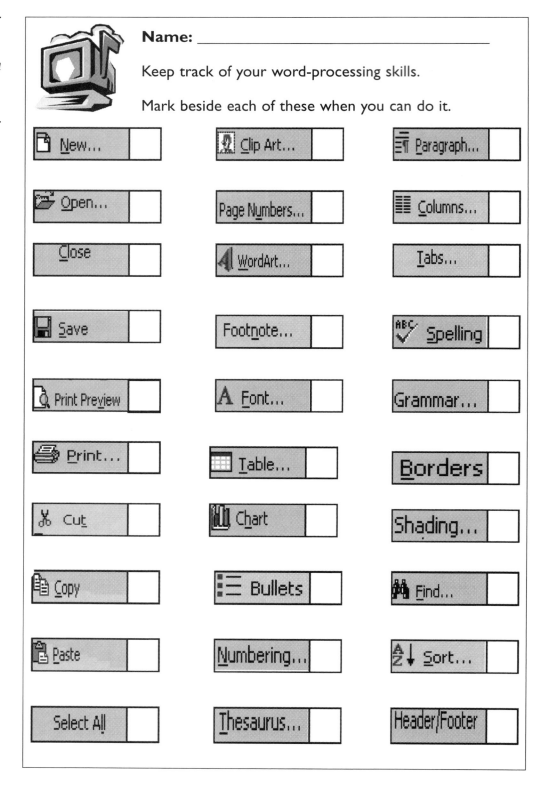

Name: _____

Keep track of your word-processing skills.

Mark beside each of these when you can do it.

New...

Open...

Close

Save

Print Preview

Print...

Cut

Copy

Paste

Select All

Clip Art...

Page Numbers...

WordArt...

Footnote...

Font...

Table...

Chart

Bullets

Numbering...

Thesaurus...

Paragraph...

Columns...

Tabs...

Spelling

Grammar...

Borders

Shading...

Find...

Sort...

Header/Footer

Can you do the Kid Pix Challenge?

Name: _____

1   Make a rainbow colored rectangle.
2   Stamp a bus. Double its size. Quadruple it.
3   Move something from one part of the screen to another.
4   Make a perfect circle.
5   Make something disappear without erasing it.
6   Make snowflakes. Make raindrops.
7   Change the view of your picture.
8   Type your name in 3 different types of letters.
9   Make a word in a word bubble.
10   Pick and then discover a hidden picture.
11   Choose a color me and fill it in with your favorite colors.
12   Give yourself some stars for being such a good learner!

Figure 5-10
You may wish to provide students with a challenge that will focus their explorations somewhat and allow them to demonstrate their proficiency.

Guided Exploration

You can provide step-by-step instructions for using software or equipment such as a camera or scanner. By rotating students according to a schedule, you can then give everyone practice time using this software or equipment. You'll need to set aside several days and plan carefully in order to integrate new hardware and software on a shared basis.

Peer Tutoring

It can be a challenge to keep students on track in a lab setting, but you do not have time in your busy day to introduce a new computer program to every student individually. Therefore, teachers who are familiar with using computers in their classrooms are finding a variety of alternative methods. Recognizing the different learning styles of students and providing alternatives is one of the keys to training students how to use technology. Here are a few ideas you can try:

1. Train one student and have that student instruct others, one at a time, how to use the technology. Choose a different student for each new item and soon you will have a network of experts in your class. Post the names of these experts together with their areas of expertise. This is time consuming if you have only one computer and one expert, but it is effective.
2. Train one student who in turn trains another: "each one teach one." Continue until every student has been both a student and a teacher.

Figure 5-11

Instead of or in addition to exploration, you may wish to structure an activity that will guide students in learning the different capabilities of the hardware and software.

Saving an Image

By the end of this lesson, you will be able to cut and paste a graphic picture from the Internet

Step One:
Go to the following website:
www.rom.on.ca/ontario/risk.html

Step Two:
Select an image you would like to use in your report.

Step Three:
Use the right mouse button to click on the image. A menu will appear. Select "Save Image As…" and give a file name to this image. Choose where you want to save your image.

Step Four:
You can put the image wherever you want in your report, but don't forget to credit it's source.

Remember you must include at least 5 graphic images in your project or on the title page. At least 3 of them must be created by You!

Again, this is time consuming, but every student will try to learn it well knowing that they have to teach another. The risk is that the training will get "watered down" or start to include errors as it is passed from one student to another.

3. Team up younger students with older as computer pals or mentors. In a high school setting, course credits can be given to students who work as mentors for a specified number of hours. Provide specific skills that must be taught and tasks to be accomplished. Both parties benefit from this approach.

> **"A** recent visit to [L'Ouverture Computer Technology Magnet Elementary School, Wichita, Kansas] found students helping each other with software or the Internet in almost every class at almost every moment. Unlike in many schools where children immediately call for the teacher when they get stuck, students here often look first to their peers in their small groups.

> "'I teach them to do that,' says second-grade teacher Rhonda Willome. She says she tells the children, 'Don't interrupt me while I'm teaching.'
>
> "'You learn which kids can help the other kids,' adds Jane Farris, a fourth grade teacher. 'The teacher just can't be everywhere at one time.' "[8]

Tutorials

You can find tutorials within software, in books, and on-line. If these are not at an appropriate difficulty level for your students, you can make your own, though it is a tedious and time-consuming process. As more teachers in the school develop learning guides for pieces of software and hardware, however, you will develop a bank of shared resources.

Instructional Videos

These can be useful, though they are often produced at an adult level. You might choose to show just one short segment highlighting a special aspect of the technology to be used.

Volunteer Helpers

Particularly with younger students, an adult at the computer center or as a lab helper can be a real blessing. Many parents, co-op students, and student teachers are happy to share their computer skills.

Class Experts

In every class, one, two, or more students may stand out as having greater technological expertise. You could assign these students the roles of helpers, advisers, or troubleshooters. Sometimes these more practically minded students are not high academic achievers. Assigning them special tasks and responsibilities is an excellent opportunity to help build their self-esteem and self-confidence.

> "When we begin working with a new piece of hardware or software, everybody in the group, including the teacher, designates themselves as a novice, apprentice, practitioner or expert. This creates the culture of a community of learners and guides the teacher's preparation of task cards and composition of learning groups. Plus, we all know who to ask for help."[9]

School Computer Coaches

Students increasingly are being assigned tasks such as installing computers, building and maintaining Web sites, running help desks, and training teachers. Those in favor of this approach say the experience benefits the students by providing them with marketable technical skills, increasing their self-confidence, and helping them learn to accept responsibility. Opponents argue that schools should not use children to make up for their failure to allocate money to professional development and technical support.

Judy Lindholm, the technology director at Marshalltown, started a curriculum path called Computer Consultants, which students begin in middle school and follow through high school. For every hour of instructional time, the students log an hour of service. Each of the program's 30 middle-schoolers and 24 high school students are assigned to one of the district's nine buildings. The classes meet in the morning before school starts. Students serve as the tech experts for their schools, available to answer questions from teachers, install software, repair hardware, and perform other tasks. The main concern at the start of the program was security, Lindholm says. But giving these students access and responsibility, she says, makes it less likely that they'll try to hack into areas they shouldn't. "The kids aren't going in wildly making changes," says Lindholm. "These kids are the sheriffs, not the bad guys."[10]

Here Are Some Tips for Student Expert Programs:
- Award students class or internship credits for their work.
- Allow students to work only during scheduled times.
- Supervise and mentor students.
- Do not pressure students so much that they let their grades and other activities slip.
- Keep an eye on security. School networks contain confidential documents.
- Inform parents so they do not perceive that students are being used as cheap labor.

Generation www.Y — Kids at the Head of the Class The "Generation Y" (or Gen Y for short) model teaches students the skills necessary to introduce technology into the curriculum, pairing one student with one teacher to create partnerships. Teacher and student cooperatively develop a technology-integrated lesson and use it in the classroom. Thousands of completed activities are catalogued on the Gen Y Web site (http://genwhy.wednet.edu). The Gen Y training course is 18 weeks in length for middle and secondary students and 30 weeks for elementary students. Student training materials are available from ISTE.

Equipment Operators and Instruction Sheets

Although most students know how to use a TV/VCR and a CD player, provide step-by-step instruction for all. Point out the controls and any special features that your students might use. When a group of students shares such equipment, designate one student the "Equipment Operator" who will load and unload tapes and adjust controls for brightness and clarity. This method will prevent arguments among group members while safeguarding the equipment from excessive handling.

An instruction sheet posted near a piece of equipment serves as an instant reference guide for users. It also gives students practice reading and following directions. Reading technical instructions is a valuable skill to develop, one that will help students to pursue lifelong learning in increasingly technological environments.

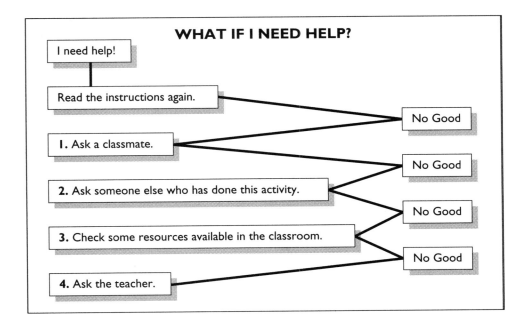

WHAT IF I NEED HELP?

I need help!

Read the instructions again. → No Good

1. Ask a classmate. → No Good

2. Ask someone else who has done this activity. → No Good

3. Check some resources available in the classroom. → No Good

4. Ask the teacher.

Figure 5-12
Good problem-solving skills are complementary to effective technology use. Teach these skills and post a reminder for students. By using cooperatively developed problem-solving strategies, students realize that they are capable of solving many of their own problems. They begin to accept more responsibility for their own learning and your role can evolve into that of facilitator for individualized learning.

More tips for technology training:
- **Have software/hardware manuals or guides readily accessible.**
- **Post a quick reference sheet for basic routines and/or tasks at the computer(s).**
- **Collect Web site addresses where on-line training is available. We list specific software sites in Chapter 9. You can also find a good list at http://www.monroe.k12.la.us/mcs/training.**
- **Use the rule "Ask 3 before Me" so that students get in the habit of consulting class experts.**

The introduction of classroom technology makes routines all the more important. These routines, though initiated by the teacher, have been developed in consultation with the students. When students play a role in establishing routines, they enjoy a sense of ownership and responsibility. When one analyzes what actually transpires in a child-centered classroom, it soon becomes obvious that the apparent lack of structure is based on well-established, well-learned, and well-practiced classroom routines.

"In this situation I become more of the facilitator as opposed to the teacher. They go through a routine of asking other students. If they have difficulty, the other students become the resources for information, for help on the computer, or for the CD-ROM. They usually find out what students in the class know about that program and ask them before they come to me."[11]

Troubleshooting Tips

When first working with computers, we found that there were many little things that could go wrong. These hints for new "techies" might make your life easier and help to avoid some frustration. It's a good idea to share these kinds of simple tips with your students so that they can do some trouble-shooting before calling you for help.

1. If a machine doesn't work at all, first ascertain that every piece of equipment and any required power bars are turned on. Next, check the cables to see if they're all connected. Wiggle the wires to see if you are experiencing a poor connection.
2. If you change cabling or electrical connections, turn the computer(s) off to make the change. Try to isolate a problem by changing only one thing at a time.
3. If a disk doesn't work, be sure that the disk you are using is for the type of computer you are using and that it is not write-protected.
4. If a program doesn't load or run correctly, turn everything off and start all over again.
5. If you are not able to access all the features of a program, check to see that you have the correct version for the amount of memory the computer has available.
6. Before you print, always save your material onto a disk or the hard drive of the computer.
7. To protect your work, make a back-up copy.
8. To prevent someone else from writing onto your disks, use write-protect tabs. Check to make sure the tabs are securely fastened so they do not jam or come off in the disk drive.
9. To protect your disks and computers, do not put magnets or magnetized objects near them. The magnetization could damage the contents.
10. To ensure that disks retain their usefulness, do not leave them in direct sunlight or very hot or cold places for long periods of time.

More excellent troubleshooting tips and checklists can be found in recent technology-related journal articles.

wWw

For more help with troubleshooting your PC, visit PCHell.

Preparing Parents for Technological Change

Some parents experience anxiety when they see a shift away from traditional modes of learning. Understandably, parents want their children to receive the best education possible. The anxiety provoked by change is often rooted in a lack of understanding about the reasons for the change and the precise nature of the change.

Well-articulated goals and strategies, clearly presented to parents at the beginning of the school year, are the best ways to allay this anxiety. Parents also need to be consulted on an on-going basis during the change process and provided with opportunities to learn about the details of technology-integrated programs. In a first-term evening meeting with parents, you can demonstrate your specific classroom strategies and give parents time to absorb and discuss the implications of these strategies. An "open house," later in the year when students are comfortable with the equipment, can give them an opportunity to demonstrate their proficiency and their parents a chance to try out the equipment in the classroom for themselves. An open-door policy that invites parents to drop in, watch students at work, interact with them, and get involved in their learning will do much to alleviate parental concerns. Ongoing communication is the key.

Parents need to receive the distinct message that we are preparing students for a different world, one in which they must continue to learn throughout their lives in order to adapt to technologically oriented working and living environments.

Typical Parent Questions

From our experience in conducting a large number of meetings and discussions with parents and other community members, we can predict many of the questions you may be asked. It's helpful to think about some of these issues in advance, so here are some commonly asked questions along with some helpful hints for composing answers.

Q. With what technology will my child work?

A. Be well informed as to the manufacturer, model, and capabilities of the technology because today's parents are very knowledgeable; however, do not be afraid to admit that your knowledge has limits and that you rely on experts in the field to provide you with information.

Q. What computer system are you using?

A. Answer in a direct way without voicing support for one brand of computer over another, because the moment you praise the superiority of one particular computer, there will surely be someone who disagrees with you. You don't want your discussion to turn into a technical argument about computer platforms. It's more important to stress the general benefits that computers bring to education and the fact that the opportunity for students to work with any computer will make the transition to other makes and models easier. Also talk about educational needs of students and how the programs were selected to meet these needs.

Q. What research has been done on incorporating technology into the classroom?

A. Be able to support what you are doing with current educational research. This proves that you have done your homework and instills confidence in you as an educator. Some parents might appreciate receiving a current article or reading list.

Q. What skills are being taught?

A. With the emphasis today on accountability and learning outcomes, parents will want to know what subject-specific skills are being taught, so be ready with a list or a scope and sequence chart. This is also an ideal opportunity to emphasize the value of cooperative learning skills, thinking skills and, of course, technology-related skills.

Q. How much does it cost?

A. As parents and taxpayers they have the right to know; however, the process is not always as simple as citing an amount. Be sure to include the grant process involved and any special business-educational partnerships. Members of your audience may be able to assist you in financing your innovation or may know someone else who can help.

Q. What does the teacher do?

A. Some people see the teacher eventually being replaced by technology. Highlight the changing role of the teacher in the technological classroom. The job is not becoming simpler but more complex.

Q. How do you individualize my child's program?

A. If you have referred to individualizing the student's program, be prepared to explain in detail how this occurs.

Q. My child has special needs. How are they addressed in this classroom?

A. Parents of special-needs students are frequently concerned that their child is receiving the required support. You might wish to outline some general ways that technology can help students with special needs. The individual needs, however, are usually so specific that you may wish to speak to these parents in detail in a less public forum.

Q. What if my child needs help using the technology?

A. Be ready to explain the classroom routines that are in place to address the immediate concerns that students may have. Again, highlight the variety of roles of the teacher in a technology-oriented classroom and the opportunities for one-to-one interaction.

Q. Are the arts being neglected in a technology-enhanced program?

A. Be prepared to show evidence of the balance between mathematics, science and technology, language arts, and the fine arts in your daily program. Music, art, and drama are not at risk because of the introduction of technology into the classroom; in fact, the teaching of each can be enhanced through the use of technology. Professionals in these fields also rely on technology for many aspects of their jobs.

Q Is my child at a disadvantage in not having a computer at home?

A. Be very sensitive to the fact that not all parents have the financial resources to purchase a home computer. Stress instead the important point that the student has access to computer technology at school. If your school has noon-hour or after-school programs in which students can access computers, this is the time to draw parents' attention to these opportunities.

Q. What kind of computer should I buy?

A. This question is a difficult one. Ideally, the student's home computer would be compatible with the school's system so that work can be transferred. However, many different family members may wish to use the computer for a variety of purposes, so each situation is unique. The family should consider all the proposed uses for the computer and buy something that fills their needs.

Q. What software should I buy?

A. For parents, selecting a piece of software can mean considering a number of factors such as price, ease of access, flashy graphics, packaging, or even what the neighbor has chosen. It's not necessary to talk in specifics here unless there are some pieces of software that you really wish a student to use at home to complete or complement in-school assignments. You may have seen a particular program that you can recommend or you may wish to prepare a list of some general guidelines for the selection of software such as the following.

- Is it age appropriate?
- Does it begin at a level that is realistic for your child's present grade level?
- Does it have enough scope to last your child through several more grade levels?
- Does it provide a wide variety of activities?
- Is it easy for the child to use?
- Does it have visual appeal? (and auditory if your equipment allows for it)
- Are skills introduced in a logical and sequential manner?
- Are feedback and/or rewards given to the child for success along the way?
- Is the child required to think and use problem-solving skills?
- Can you customize the program to meet specific needs?

Suggest that parents take part in using computer programs with their children, just as they would when reading a book.

> **" 'I think it's important that parents do not use the computer as an alternative to TV,' said Ronald Ragdale, a professor in the department of measurement, evaluation, and computer application at the Ontario Institute for Studies in Education in Toronto. 'If parents approach this with the idea that I'm going to get something to teach my children so that I don't have to teach my children, they will be disappointed.' "**[12]

Summing Up

When you involve your students in making choices and decisions about their own learning, they become accountable and responsible. In this chapter, we have provided some strategies that assist in creating a student-centered classroom, with the rules and routines that provide the structure necessary for this type of active learning environment. Internet-based curriculum projects have the potential to further enhance your technology-integrated program — we'll take a look at some of these important issues next.

INTERNET-BASED CURRICULUM PROJECTS

six

"The use of new technologies promotes cooperation among students in the same class and among students or classes in different schools, near or far, for the purpose of making them more aware of other realities, accessing relevant knowledge not strictly defined in advance, and executing projects with a genuine relevance for the students themselves, and possibly for other people."[1]

The value of the Internet as a source of information for traditional research projects is well established. Teachers and students recognize the Internet as a powerful research tool, along with books, magazines, newspapers, audiovisual materials, artifacts, and people. In this chapter we examine the copyright issues that are especially important when students use the Internet as a research source. Because the ability to critically evaluate Web sites is also an essential skill for both students and teachers, this chapter contains advice to help you sort out the wheat from the chaff in cyberspace. Virtual field trips and publishing on the Internet are other easy ways for beginners to get involved in on-line learning. We highlight some of the best starting points for these activities in this chapter.

Using the Internet is but one strategy of the many that teachers know to be effective under the right conditions. The decision to involve students in an Internet-based curriculum project may be based on many factors, but the single most important is the "why" factor.

"I suggest that, keeping in mind a specific, feasible educational use of the Internet, and in terms of both content and processes that students need/want to learn, we consider the honest answers to two questions:

1. **Will this use of the Internet enable students to do something that they COULDN'T do before?**
2. **Will this use of the Internet enable students to do something that they COULD do before, but better?**
   If the honest answer to both of these questions is 'no,' there is no reason to use Internet tools or resources in the way that we are considering. Our time, effort, and resources would be better used in another way."[2]

Students used to searching the Internet for learning resources are discovering the freedom that comes with choosing information sources, communicating with others with similar interests or facing similar difficulties, and working collaboratively on projects. Collaborative Internet-based curriculum projects incorporate many features of traditional project-based learning, but they also include participation of people outside the classroom. The digital age classroom expands beyond the confines of the school walls. In a typical collaborative project, students in different locations conduct activities that require the exchange of information. They may gather data, research and experiment in their own settings, question experts, and learn from one another. Quite sophisticated collaborative Internet-based curriculum projects can be conducted with fairly simple tools; many exemplary projects have been managed with nothing more than a computer, modem, printer, and e-mail. Most teachers report that students are interested and eager participants in these projects because they connect with an authentic audience.

Judi Harris describes 18 types of activity structures for Internet-based collaborative student projects. They fall into three broad categories:
1. interpersonal exchange
2. information collection and analysis
3. problem solving [3]

Imagine the active, engaged learning that can take place in such projects. This chapter will provide you with some excellent sites for finding collaborative projects as well as guidelines for designing your own projects. We also address the challenge of overcoming obstacles that may arise during your Internet-based curriculum projects.

Many projects are facilitated through a school or class Web site, so we include some advice about establishing and maintaining such a site.

Copyright Issues in the Classroom

With so much material easily downloadable from the Internet, you need to be sure that you and your students are knowledgeable about copyright. As a general rule, teachers are permitted to make "fair use" of material for instructional purposes. This usually means limited use, for classroom purposes only, and also pertains to text and images available on the Internet. Most Internet documents contain a copyright statement; thus students should be expected to provide the same level of care with respect to citing Internet sources as they would use when referencing print resources in a bibliography. In addition to providing information about authorship, title, and location of a Web resource, a citation should include the date the material was available at that site. The exact format for citing on-line sources can vary depending on the reference you consult and the publication characteristics of the item you wish to cite.

One basic format for citing a Web site is the following:

Author Last Name, First Name (if available). "Title of item." Date on the document or date of last revision (if available). [On-line] Available: URL, Day Month Year.

Example: Kronk, Gary. "Comets and Meteors: The Differences." 1997. [On-line] Available: http://medicine.wustl.edu/~kronkg/index.html, 30/01/00.

One basic format for citing an e-mail message is the following:

Sender Last Name, First Name. "Subject line from posting". [On-line posting] Available e-mail: to@address from from@address, Day Month Year that the message was sent.

Example: Anders, Mary. "Hale-Bopp" [On-line posting] Available e-mail: student 114@brooklinehs.ca.us from andersm@aol.com, 04/06/99.[4]

If your references are listed in their order of appearance rather than alphabetically, there's no need to put the author's surname first.

Three good guides for citing on-line sources are the following:
- **Classroom Connect**
- **MLA Citation Guide**
- **Media Awareness Network**

Evaluating Web Sites

While the Internet is an increasingly important tool for student research and collaboration, as most teachers are aware, not all of the information is valid. The Internet is a lot like an information free-for-all. Although this may seem a fact to be lamented, it does provide an excellent teaching opportunity.

"Any teacher who has used the Internet in a classroom setting can tell you how troubling it is to see children taking World Wide Web pages at face value, without the evaluative skills to place them in context. In that sense, the Internet can, in the wrong hands, become a tool of propaganda. You could consider the Internet as a wire service, at least on a superficial level. But — and this is a big but — unlike a wire service, its content has not been chosen by professionals who can distance themselves from the motives of the creators of the news. The Internet is like a raw data stream, an open microphone for every interest group, corporation, fan club, professional organization, or fanatic that wants to use it. And if you've ever been near a karaoke club, you know how painful an open microphone can be."[5]

Students need to learn to critically evaluate everything they read, including traditional sources. Take some time to consider the important criteria of accuracy, quality, coverage, relevancy, bias, and currency of information on the Web. Teach students the important skills they require to become media literate and provide opportunities for them to practice these skills. You can access some examples of sites to compare at The Good, the Bad, and the Ugly (http://lib.nmsu.edu/instruction/evalexpl.html).

Figure 6-1

Even a simple evaluation checklist can get students thinking critically about Web resources and provide a starting point for discussion.[6]

Web Site Evaluation Checklist

1. What topic are you researching?

   _____

2. What is the URL of the Web source you are evaluating?

   _____

3. What is the name of the site?

   _____

4. What is the main purpose for this site?

   _____

5. What group or individual is responsible for this site?

   _____

6. Do you feel that the group/individual responsible for this site is a good authority on the subject you are researching?   **Yes/No**

7. Are pages at this site easy to load and navigate?   **Yes/No**

8. Is the information presented in an interesting way?   **Yes/No**

9. Does the site seem to provide enough information about your topic? **Yes/No**

10. Is the information easy to understand?   **Yes/No**

11. Is the information on this page up-to-date?   **Yes/No**

12. Does this page lead you to other useful resources for your topic?   **Yes/No**

13. Is there anything you particularly like about this site?   **Yes/No**
    Describe _____

14. Is there anything you particularly dislike about this site?   **Yes/No**
    Describe _____

15. Would you recommend this site to another student wanting to learn about your topic?   **Yes/No**

Kathy Schrock is the District Technology Department Head for the Dennis-Yarmouth Regional School District in Cape Cod, Maine, and the author of books about the Internet. You can find her excellent critical evaluation surveys as well as lots of useful links to critical evaluation information by others at Kathy Schrock's Guide for Educators site.

Virtual Field Trips

A virtual field trip is a Web-based teaching tool that presents mulitmedia content appropriate for whole group teaching or small group or individual learning. There is a variety of starting points for locating electronic field trips, from commercially sponsored sites to school-hosted databases. As you might expect, many have a cost associated with them and are supported by learning materials of all sorts. Here is a good starting point.

- Global School House Field Trips
  http://gsh.lightspan.com/project/fieldtrips/index.html

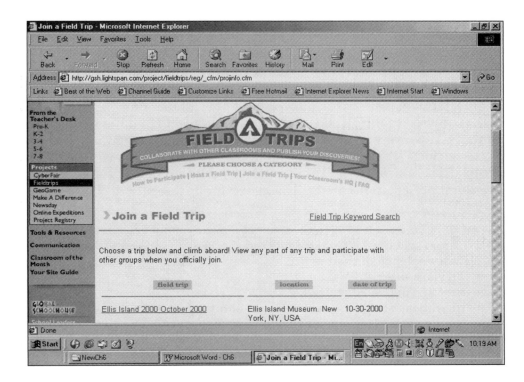

Figure 6-2
Through Global Schoolhouse, you can join a field trip or host one of your own.

At oz-TeacherNet (http://rite.ed.qut.edu.au/oz-teachernet/index.html), a virtual field trip is considered to be a partnership between two or more classes. One class acts as the local host for the field trip and the other class is the remote partner for the field trip. The host class gathers data, answers questions, and reports their findings to the remote class using e-mail. The host class may use a local point of interest near to the school or a site being visited during a school excursion. Digital photographs, video clips, or captured sound can either be attached to e-mail or published on Web pages to add to the exchanges between the students. Students may also use live events during a virtual field trip by using Internet Relay Chat, Microsoft NetMeeting or ICQ chat.

- The Virtual Field Trips' Site http://www.field-guides.com/
  The *Virtual Field Trips Web site* is devoted to providing on-line guided field trips. They include the following special features:
  1. *Specific-Focus Field Trips:* Each covers a single topic such as salt marshes or volcanoes.
  2. *Subject Matter Experts:* Experts on the subject of the field trip have selected the best sites on the Web.
  3. *A Story:* The sites have been arranged in sequential order to build a story for you to follow.
  4. *Stops:* The experts have written a series of "trail markers" or stops that describe each site on the field trip to guide learning.
  5. *Teacher's Resources:* Every field trip has a set of prepared documents that you can print out for each person on the trip.

Try out the virtual field trip links from Vicki Blackwell's Internet Guide for Educators. Visit the publisher's Web site for links to lots more virtual field trips.

Publishing on the Web

Teachers are always looking for authentic ways to publish student work. Donating student products to the school library, publishing books for younger students or peers, reading original work to seniors, and displaying work in shopping malls, banks, and other public places are popular methods. Now we can add to this list the possibility of publishing on the Internet, an idea that is often very motivating to students. Student products published on the Web include art works, stories and poems, digital images, Web pages, and multimedia productions of various sorts. Hyperstudio, Kid Pix and PowerPoint presentations are easily adapted for the Web.

> **"I**n a landmark 1989 article, telecomputing pioneers Margaret Riel and Moshe Cohen reported that when students write for a distant audience of their peers,
> * they are more fluent,
> * they are better organized,
> * their ideas are more clearly stated and supported,
> * their content is more substantial and their thesis is better supported, and
> * they consider the needs of their audience."[7]

Look for on-line magazines and educational organizations that publish original student work, such as the following:
Writer's Window http://english.unitecnology.ac.nz/writers/home.html

Figure 6-3

Writers' Window is a friendly site for student publishing.

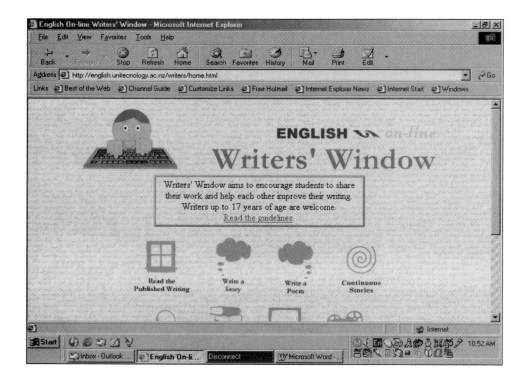

Midlink Magazine http://longwood.cs.ucf.edu/~MidLink/

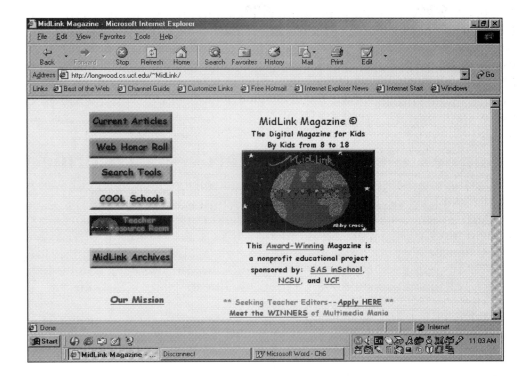

LDOnline http://www.ldonline.org/kidzone/kidzone.html

Every week LD OnLine chooses an artist of the week and a writer of the week whose work will be displayed on the home page of LD OnLine. Any student between the ages of 5 and 18 who has a learning disability can enter, with parent permission.

WebQuests

Bernie Dodge first developed the WebQuest model with Tom March in 1995. Since that time, WebQuests have been extensively used in courses and staff development around the world. A WebQuest is "an inquiry-oriented activity in which most or all of the information used by learners is drawn from the Web. WebQuests are designed to use learners' time well, to focus on using information rather than looking for it, and to support learners' thinking at the level of analysis, synthesis and evaluation." A WebQuest uses on-line resources, selected in advance by the teacher, to challenge students in their critical examination of a given issue, event, or topic drawn from the curriculum. If you are new to the WebQuest concept, begin your orientation at http://edweb.sdsu.edu/webquest/overview.html. A simple search using the keyword WebQuest will turn up thousands of curriculum-related samples; though some are no more than worksheets with embedded URLs, others are well designed according to the WebQuest model and ready to be used in your classroom. Creating your own WebQuest for your students is an engaging, worthwhile activity that ensures your specific curriculum goals will be addressed. You will find guidelines for writing WebQuests at the WebQuest site mentioned above. Bernie Dodge suggests that WebQuest developers use the following five guiding principles to create great WebQuests:

1. Find great sites.
2. Orchestrate your learners and resources.
3. Challenge your learners to think.
4. Use the medium.
5. Scaffold high expectations.[8]

Sample Collaborative Internet-based Projects

A growing number of organizations facilitate collaborative Internet-based curriculum projects. Not only do these organizations provide a forum through which projects can be established and maintained, but many also archive successful past projects at their Web sites. Some of these services have a cost attached, others are non-profit, still others award grants or prizes for outstanding projects. If you are looking for ideas, involvement, connections, management strategies, or helpful hints, try one or more of the following.

Canada's SchoolNet GrassRoots Projects

http://www.schoolnet.ca/grassroots/e/project.centre/search-projects.asp

Figure 6-5

The database of ongoing and completed projects at Canada's SchoolNet's GrassRoots Program provides a gold mine of projects you can join as well as ideas for creating your own project.

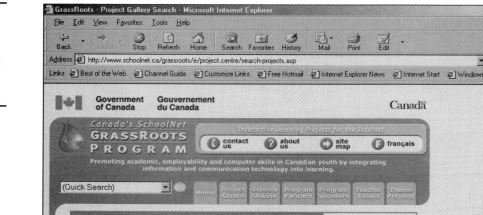

The GrassRoots Program offers funding to schools for the creation of innovative and interactive learning projects on the Internet that
• foster the acquisition of academic, employability, and computer skills in Canadian youth,

- build unique and relevant Canadian content on the Internet,
- integrate information and communication technology into learning, or
- facilitate increased connectivity and training opportunities.

Individual Projects are initiated, designed, and implemented by the teacher and students.

Block Projects are usually developed on a theme or unit of work or subject area, comprise a number of Sub-Projects, and involve several teachers and classes in one or more schools and in one or more school boards. Block Projects require the collaboration and support of all the participating teachers with each teacher and class initiating, designing, and implementing their own Sub-Project as part of the overall Block Project.

Global Schoolhouse
http://www.gsn.org/

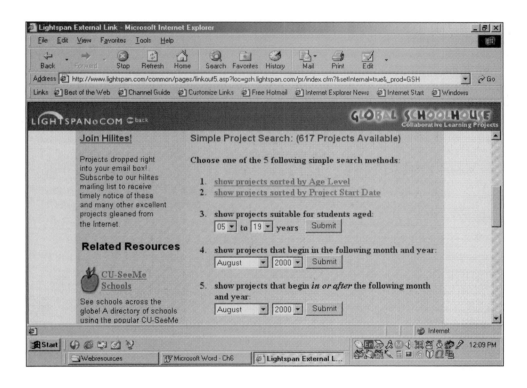

Figure 6-6
GSH's searchable database provides a quick way for teachers to locate a suitable project to address student learning outcomes.

Since 1984, Global Schoolhouse has been a leader in collaborative learning. They continue to provide on-line opportunities for teachers to collaborate, communicate, and celebrate shared learning experiences. Global Schoolhouse's Internet Project Registry displays not only their own projects but also those from organizations such as I*EARN, IECC, NASA, GLOBE, Academy One, TIES, Tenet, and TERC, as well as countless outstanding projects conducted by classroom teachers from all over the world.

Global Grocery List Project
http://landmark-project.com/ggl/

Global Grocery List, now in its 12th year on-line, is a project that generates real, peer-collected data for student computation, analysis, and conclusion-building. Students find and share local grocery prices for items on a common list to build a growing table of data from around the world. This data can then be used for comparisons, finding patterns, and discussion on the factors that control food prices. Useful lesson strategies are also available at the site.

Intercultural E-Mail Classroom Connections
http://www.iecc.org/

IECC is a free service to help teachers link with partners in other countries and cultures for e-mail classroom keypal and project exchanges.

International Education and Resource Network
http://www.iearn.org/

I*EARN enables young people to undertake projects designed to make a meaningful contribution to the health and welfare of the planet and its people. I*EARN is committed to supporting young people in the 60 participating countries in the network to communicate in their native languages. Because of its language diversity as a global network, I*EARN offers an incredible opportunity for students to not only communicate, but also to collaborate on substantive project work, with peers around the world across an incredible span of languages. While the majority of I*EARN projects are multilingual, there are also special on-line conferences for teachers and students to communicate entirely in a particular language. Hundreds of I*EARN projects are described that (1) are currently underway, (2) have been completed over the past 10 years, and (3) are newly proposed. You can search by curriculum area, keywords, student age level, etc. There is also a form to automatically submit your project idea. This database soon will also be able to keep track of project evaluations, list the most popular current projects, and point you to opportunities for meaningful youth action.

Kidlink
http://www.kidlink.org/english/general/index.html

Kidlink is a non-profit organization working to help children be involved in a global dialogue. Since its start on May 25, 1990, over 175,000 kids from 137 countries on all continents have participated. Their primary means of communication is electronic mail (e-mail), but Real-Time Interactions (like "chats"), various types of Web-based dialogues, ordinary mail, fax, video conferencing, and ham radio are also being used. Kidlink is truly multilingual, with activities in Arabic, Danish, English, French, German, Hebrew, Icelandic, Italian, Japanese, Macedonian, Norwegian, Portuguese, Saami, Slovenian, Spanish, and Swedish.

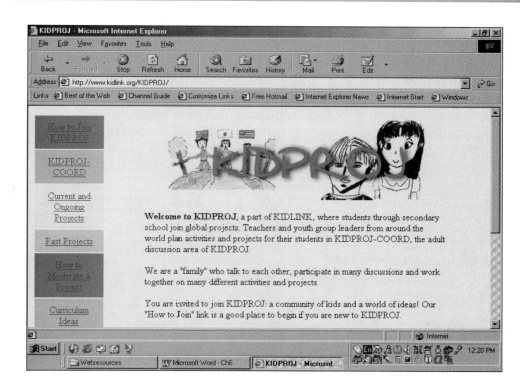

Figure 6-7
*KidProj, the project section
of Kidlink, will help you to
get started on a collaborative
project, whether you have a
specific idea in mind or not.*

NASA Quest

http://quest.arc.nasa.gov/interactive/

At NASA Quest you and your students can meet scientists, engineers, technicians, and other NASA professionals, breaking down the artificial barriers between the school, the wider community, and the world of work. NASA Quest makes it a priority to develop such programs and offer them "out of the box and ready to go" to classrooms around the world.

NASA Quest projects include the following on-line resources:
- biographies of NASA experts and stories about their work days
- several chats per month
- an e-mail service in which individual questions get answered
- audio/video programs over the Internet
- lesson plans and student activities
- collaborative activities in which kids work with one another
- areas for students to publish on NASA's Web site
- background and photo sections
- places where teachers can meet one another

NASA projects run indefinitely, and participants come and go as dictated by their own individual classroom needs.

Online Class

http://www.onlineclass.com/

Online Class has created interdisciplinary, inquiry-based teaching units on a number of topics, which allow you to use the Internet as a communications tool and as a research resource. Each program clusters the following elements around an interactive, collaborative project on-line:

- a collaborative activity among schools
- activities for the classroom
- Web-based reading background
- pre-searched Web links for illustration and student research
- moderated Internet discussion in a "global classroom" of schools
- student work displayed online
- teacher support in how to use the Internet as a classroom tool

Needless to say, these are not free resources, so visit the site to look at the variety of pricing options for your classroom or school.

The Concord Consortium
http://www.concord.org/projects/index.html

The Concord Consortium is a non-profit research and development organization dedicated to a revolution in education through the use of information technologies. They undertake innovative projects in math, science, and technology that move innovations from research into practice through a series of steps. Some projects are at the level of nuts-and-bolts technology, others focus on learners, and some create new structures for learning.

The Electronic Emissary
http://www.ots.utexas.edu/emmissary/index.html

Figure 6-8

To date, the Emissary has supported more than 400 electronic teams of students, teachers, facilitators, and subject matter experts.

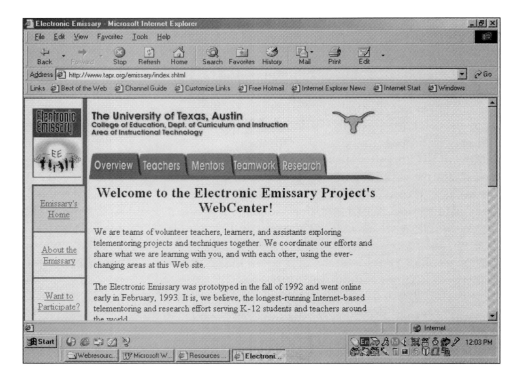

The Emissary is a "matching service" that helps K-12 teachers and students with access to the World Wide Web locate other Internet account-holders who are experts in different disciplines, for purposes of setting up curriculum-based electronic exchanges among the teachers, their students, and the experts. In this way, the interaction that occurs among teachers and students face-to-face in the classroom is supplemented and extended by exchanges that occur among teachers, students, and experts on-line, via electronic mail, text-based chats, Web pages, and desktop teleconferencing.

ThinkQuest

http://www.thinkquest.org

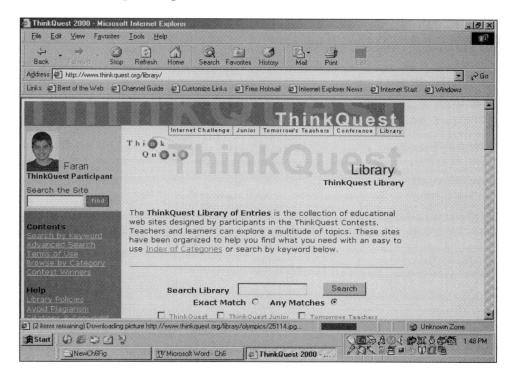

Figure 6-9

One of the most useful ThinkQuest teacher resources is the well-structured library of entries, built by students for students. The library contains a multitude of ideas for teachers to integrate into their classroom curriculum.

The international ThinkQuest program encourages students to use the Internet to create Web-based educational tools and materials. Structured as a contest, ThinkQuest encourages students to form teams to build their educational materials. These teams, typically coached by teachers, collaborate electronically to develop innovative, high-quality educational tools that take advantage of the strengths of the Internet. For example, one entry is a simulation game created by a team of students from Hawaii called Design Paradise. This entry examines the complex interrelationships among industry, environment, and population as students build their own ideal model of a resort community. In the process, students learn about resource management, development, and environmental issues in an exciting, interactive way. ThinkQuest Junior is for younger students and focuses on these students creating materials, called entries, that will help other students of the same age. For example, a team of students might create an entry that will introduce other students to the team's favorite books, or that explores fire as friend and foe.

" **O**ver the years many teachers have reported that when students use telecommunications to engage with real people in another location, they enjoy writing more; are more willing to write, proofread, revise, and edit their work; and are more careful about their spelling, punctuation, grammar, and vocabulary. Combine student projects, Web publishing, and the communications power of the Internet, and teaching is transformed: classroom walls will tumble down. Students interact with real people in the real world using methods and tools people have used for years. Learning becomes authentic and purposeful. Students find new meaning in classroom experiences. You and your students will rediscover and share an excitement to learn."[9]

Planning Your Project

Because many of the steps in planning an Internet-based curriculum project are the same as those for planning any technology-integrated unit of study, we examine in detail only topics that have not already been discussed in Chapter 4: What About Curriculum?

Step 1: ESTABLISH LEARNING OUTCOMES.

Without specific, clearly communicated learning outcomes for Internet-based collaborative projects, students will lack direction and focus, and will be overwhelmed by the sheer quantity of information available to them. Learning outcomes define the criteria by which to measure both student progress and teacher effectiveness in using the Internet as a tool.

Step 2: SET THE CONTEXT FOR LEARNING AND DECIDE HOW STUDENTS WILL DEMONSTRATE THEIR LEARNING.

How will you know when students have achieved the specified outcomes? End your project with a tangible product such as an audiovisual presentation, written report, Web site, video, or student/class portfolio that can be used for summative evaluation purposes. If you are planning to invite others to participate in your project, give it a snappy title that reflects its process or its content goals: "Fast Food Flash," "Great Gourmet Gastronomy," "Taming the Tube." Your students will enjoy creating novel project names.

Step 3: INVESTIGATE OTHER PROJECTS.

Examine other teachers' successful projects and identify the common elements that contributed to their success. Examine the time-lines and number of classes involved. Look for situations that parallel your own in anticipated learning outcomes, student ability, access to computers, time available, and teacher experience. Find a good project that has already been tried, then improve it by customizing it to suit your own needs. You can find many good sites to look for projects in this chapter.

As teachers begin with one project, other projects often begin to emerge from the collaboration among schools. "We began a water habitat project between another Washington State Elementary School and my classes, but as we got to know one another as teachers and the children became acquainted, more ideas of things we could do together online emerged."[10]

Step 4: PLAN ASSESSMENT AND EVALUATION.
How will you evaluate the student learning outcomes you established for your project? How will you evaluate the usefulness of the Internet as a tool, perhaps even the primary medium, for your project? Teacher, peer, and self-evaluation are all appropriate tools in an active, digital age classroom. Develop checklists and rubrics of observable performance indicators to use as assessment criteria. Use observational data, teacher-student conferencing, and a portfolio of work samples for formative evaluation.

> **C**reating guidelines for projects can be time-consuming. This site can help you to make a project checklist for your students. You choose the grade level and type of project you want your students to do. You can choose from writing, presentation, multimedia, or science projects. Then you choose from a list of project guidelines, add your own criteria to personalize your checklist, and create it with the touch of a button!

Step 5: DECIDE THE TYPE OF LEARNING EXPERIENCES AND
       PLAN A TIMETABLE.
Choose the type of learning experience — keypal, information exchange, etc. — and how much time you plan to devote to it, keeping in mind the amount of Internet access time available to your students. Peak use on an educational network is geared to traditional cycles of the school calendar. October through December, February through May, and July (with summer school) are very busy times on the network. However, most of the successful networking activities were planned, and announcements posted, six to eight weeks before the actual project was to begin. Carefully consider the types of teaching and learning strategies that are appropriate for your students and the type and amount of Internet access available in your school and classroom.

Whole-class Learning Experiences
If you're a beginner, consider starting with a teacher-directed whole-class learning experience, especially if you have a limited number of computers with Internet access. Corresponding with another class either locally, nationally, or internationally is a good way to introduce students to the Internet. E-mail can be integrated into just about every subject and grade: reading, writing, social studies, science, business, second-language learning. You can use e-mail as a vehicle for teaching both curriculum-related skills (such as letter-writing, devising questions, or improving punctuation) and Internet-related skills (such as addressing, formatting, and sending e-mail, and on-line etiquette). Once students have mastered electronic messaging in the group setting, they will be able to use it individually as a tool for other assignments.

> **H**ave students working on the same project use the same diskette. Several letters, poems, or reviews can be combined into a single document as pages 2, 3, 4, and so on. This ensures that teachers don't spend unnecessary time getting students' material onto one diskette (or retyping).

You don't have to limit yourself to e-mail. Information gathering related to a particular theme or project can be done by a pair of students, who then report back to the whole class.

Not only is whole-class instruction an effective means to learn the basic skills of Internet use, it is also an appropriate forum for exploring such topics as

- evaluation of Web sites,
- copyright issues,
- citing Internet sources,
- security issues, and
- acceptable use.

Cooperative Learning Experiences

In a well-structured, active learning environment, the Internet can become one of a number of tools that a group of students (or one or two members of each group) can use for a specific purpose. In such a setting, student experts emerge and peer tutoring happens naturally. Most Internet projects involve a great deal of learning off-line. This might involve manipulating graphics or information files that have been gleaned from the Internet, or developing e-mail messages in a word-processing package for uploading later. It can also include posting new findings on a bulletin board or tracking responses to a questionnaire on a graph or map. Each student in the group can play an important role, yet all need not have access to the Internet.

Computer networks allow us to look at cooperative learning in a new way. Students can learn to work in teams in which the members of the team are separated by distance. This reflects the reality of our changing world of work. Before getting involved in a collaborative Internet activity, you can simulate this situation using your school's local area network. For example, while one team member gathers observational data about reptiles in the science lab, another might research the topic in the library, and another might scan drawings and diagrams in the multimedia room. Team members communicate strictly via computer. Following this experience, students will be eager to try collaborating with others in more distant places.

Individual Learning Experiences

You'll need a lot of student access if you expect all students to engage individually in an Internet activity as a mandatory course requirement. However, many schools are fortunate enough to have laptop and/or hand-held computers with wireless Internet access. Clovis Unified School District in California is a participant in Microsoft's Anytime, Anywhere Learning program. "Thanks to the laptops, we actually have children excited about doing their homework," says the assistant superintendent. "If you're looking for a revolution in learning, this is it."[11] To be fair, ensure that all students have mastered the basic skills of Internet use, have attained a certain level of expertise through practice, and can get help when they need it. One of the great strengths of individualization, of course, is that no two students learn in exactly the same way. While one may approach an information search in a step-by-step manner, another may prefer to "surf" through a variety of sites. There is no right or wrong way, as long as the final goal is achieved within the specified timeframe.

If you have a computer with Internet access in your classroom, use it as a learning center that students access as one component of a unit. For example, in a study of whales, allow students an opportunity to find the answers to their questions about whales using the World Wide Web whale-watching site. (http://www.physics.helsinki.fi/whale/)

Students need large blocks of time for Internet use. If you have explored the Internet at all yourself, you know how fast time goes. It is very frustrating to get to the site you've been searching for only to find that there is not enough time left to download the information you want. It is also difficult to predict how long it will take to get to a particular person, or even if you can get there when you want to. Thus, it is inadvisable to create rigid timeframes. Involve your students as much as possible in establishing realistic time limits for the completion of projects, and try to keep your timetable flexible. Don't forget to build in time for sharing the finished products, whatever form they take.

If you teach in a setting where subjects are strictly segregated, team with another teacher. Your two subject areas can complement each other (e.g., language and history; math and science), and students can devote time from both classes to the project.

Step 6: DEFINE ROLES OF PARTICIPANTS.

It's important to decide which staff members will take a leadership role in initiating, managing, and monitoring a collaborative project. The most common method is for the adventurous and innovative teachers to be pioneers and then to encourage others. If you are eager to get involved in a project, brainstorm with interested colleagues and assign tasks according to individual strengths of the team members. For example, classroom teachers might look after overall organization and student groupings; the computer resource teacher might schedule computer use and manage technical problems; selected students might act as Internet researchers or lead communicators; parent volunteers might supervise and assist individual students as they work; and the librarian might display completed projects in the library. Discover your classroom and school student experts and tap into their knowledge by facilitating peer mentorship either in a formal or informal way. In Chapter 5: Getting Started, we describe strategies for establishing peer experts and school computer coaches. If possible, try your project out with a close colleague first, on a small scale. This can help you overcome both technical problems as well as problems with the basic project design. You will find that having a sympathetic colleague available to discuss and solve problems will be a big help.

Step 7: OUTLINE THE DETAILS OF THE PROJECT.

Consider the following guidelines:
- contact person's information (name, school, e-mail, school address, and phone number)
- project title
- grade levels
- curriculum links (list as many as are relevant)
- anticipated student learning outcomes

- number of schools or classes to be involved
- summary of project, including specific timelines
- registration details
- sharing of information at conclusion of project

For a successful Internet-based collaborative project, be clear about your objectives, ensure that all students understand the purpose, plan how you are going to manage the project, and be sure to follow through on your commitments to others.

Step 8: FIND OTHERS TO PARTICIPATE.

You can attract participants from next door or around the world by posting your project description on one of a number of Web sites that store project databases, such as those previously described in this chapter. See the publisher's Web site for more suggestions.[12]

Alternatively, you might send your idea to an educational listserv such as those listed in Chapter 9: Technology Tools for Teachers.

Overcoming Obstacles

Even in the most ideal situations, collaborative Internet-based curriculum projects sometimes fall apart or are not followed through to completion. Interactions between teachers, students, and working professionals can be tricky to establish and maintain despite initial enthusiasm. Why do even closely managed collaborative projects sometimes go unfinished? As more of these projects are initiated, the obstacles and possible strategies for overcoming them are becoming more apparent. The following chart provides a reflection based on some of the recent findings.[13]

Obstacle	Strategies
Lack of support at all administrative levels	Present your proposed project to school administrators, parents, and other stakeholders, ensuring that they understand the project, its timelines, the type of support you will need, and its importance in meeting curriculum goals.
Insufficient computer or Internet access	For most collaborative projects, Internet connections must be available in each participating classroom all day, every day.
Technical problems	Explore the technical requirements of your project carefully with the technology coordinator at your school before beginning. Try to predict the types of difficulties that may arise before they happen. Allow much more time for the project than you think you will need.

Obstacle	Strategies
Emphasis on technological rather than curriculum goals	Frame your project in its curriculum context as History, Science, or English rather than as an e-mail or Web-based activity. Select a title that makes the curriculum context clear.
Misunderstanding or miscommunication of the project plan	Plans should be simple and clearly stated, and include very specific details. Collaboration between participants is time consuming, but some customization at each participating site is often necessary.
Timelines not adhered to	Remind participants when a deadline is approaching. Adjust timelines only when really necessary. Keep in touch through frequent dialogue.

School and Classroom Web Sites

Everyone wants to have a Web site these days. Most schools have their own Web site and many teachers have their own pages, either within the school site or hosted by another service. If your school does not provide Web space, check out the publisher's Web site for links to on-line sources of free Web space, tools, and templates.

Establishing the Purpose of Your Web Site

Begin by brainstorming and listing all the reasons why you want to have a Web site. These might include, but are not limited to
- communicating with parents,
- communicating with students,
- displaying student work,
- showcasing whole class projects, and/or
- providing resources.

Ask yourself what type of information you want on your Web site, such as
- lesson plans,
- scavenger hunts,
- Web-based projects,
- calendar of events, and/or
- photos of student work.

The intended audience of your site will affect its vocabulary and design. Is it primarily for students or parents? What is the level of technology literacy of your audience?

> **"From the beginning, our Web space has been a place where we produce resources, not promote ourselves or even our school. The emphasis has always been and continues to be about what value we are adding to the Internet."**[14]

Building Your Web Site

Educators who develop a school or classroom Web site generally want it to be interesting, engaging, attractive, and useful. The reality is, however, that the quality of some school sites is not equal to the enthusiasm of those who create them simply by virtue of the fact that teachers do not have the time to develop and maintain a high-quality Web site. Fortunately, this problem can be overcome with some of the new tools for creating dynamic Web sites. Today's Web editors make the whole process much easier and faster, allowing you to place text and graphics using WYSIWYG (what-you-see-is-what-you-get) editing. Some of the most popular software applications are described in Chapter 3: Making It Work.

As a time-saver, many teachers use free clip art and animations obtained from Web sites that specialize in this field.

Sites offering free clip art for your Web page:
AAA Clip Art
All Free Clip Art
Art Today
Click Art
Clip Art Collection
Clipper
Corel Office Community
Free Clip Images
FreeCode.com
GIF Art
Mostly Junk
Reallybig
The Mining Company

Sites that specialize in animated GIFs:
AndyArt
Barry's Clip Art
Gemini Graphics
Iconographics Design
Media Builder
Shezam's Animated 3D GIFs
The Animation Factory

For those who like to create their own graphics, new versions of familiar graphics programs such as Adobe Photoshop and Macromedia include tools for image optimizing, resizing, and animation. Any of the graphics applications described in Chapter 3: Making It Work, will also do the job adequately. Adobe LiveMotion and Macromedia Flash use vector graphics for more dynamic multimedia and animation. Flash files require the ShockWave plug-in for viewing.

At the Cyberbee site, you can find step-by-step instructions for making a school home page, a template, design tips, and design tools.

You can also find sites that include tips for the beginner as well as the expert and one that has over 300 pages of tutorials, reference materials, and other free resources to improve your Webmastery skills and perk up your site.

Summing Up

The Internet can be a source of information, a place to publish, and a tool for communication and collaboration. Not too long ago, only teachers who were "techno-wizards" would have considered getting involved in anything on the Internet beyond simply having their students use it for research. Now, as schools become better equipped and acquainted with the power of the Internet and as the technology itself becomes friendlier, more and more teachers are finding that it can turn students on to school in a way that traditional teaching tools usually can't match. Often, they say, it can help cut down on discipline problems, increase attendance, and make students more enthusiastic about learning. The Internet is creating a change in teaching and learning that is so dramatic we can hardly guess how schools will operate in the near future. The exciting thing is that we are here to contribute to the evolution. With a strong sense of educational philosophy and the ability to make wise choices based on student learning outcomes that are worth achieving, educators in digital age classrooms will lead the way.

ASSESSING
STUDENT
PROGRESS

seven

"The primary purpose of assessment and evaluation is to improve student learning."[1]

Why do we assess and evaluate? One of the main reasons is to provide students, parents and guardians, and other educators with important and useful information. This is critical when you are working with a technology-enhanced program that is different from a more traditional approach experienced by parents. However, the most important reason that we assess and evaluate is to improve student performance. Therefore, students need to be part of the whole teaching and learning process, including the assessment and evaluation components.

In the view of D.J. Hargreaves, a professor of education, "Teaching, learning and assessment are inextricably linked and assessment is the most significant motivator for learning."[2] In planning for the technology-integrated classroom teachers identify the desired results, specify the required evidence, and design the learning experiences. This process is advocated in *Understanding by Design* by Grant Wiggins and Jay McTighe.[3] Using this approach, the overall teaching plan is communicated to the class so students can see the big picture and contribute to it. Through their contribution they become part of the plan, resulting in greater involvement and commitment to learning. As technology becomes more and more a part of the classroom, the teacher is not only assessing the educational skills and knowledge defined by the curriculum but also the student's technology skills and competencies. This is no small task, as the required skills in technology grow daily.

Technology-related outcomes are often divided into concepts such as General Technological Awareness, Keyboarding, Using Clip Art, Word Processing, Using Paint or Draw Programs, and Desktop Publishing. Look for resources, such as the Web sites listed in Chapter 5, that provide not only technology skills lists but also accompanying student learning experiences. Appropriate materials will provide enjoyable, instructional time with technology.

Using Paint or Draw Programs

SKILL: Students will select and use the paint and draw tools.   Grade 6
Students will export graphics to another program.   PD 1

TEACHER RESOURCE/REFERENCE

When creating a word processing document using most software packages, graphics from another program can be incorporated into the document. Students and teacher may require time to explore the graphics programs available (i.e., Corel Draw, Print Shop, Publisher) before importing into their document. The tutorial and HELP sections may be helpful (i.e., Corel Draw Tutorial). Use manuals, tutorials, HELP and free exploration to become familiar with programs to be used.

TEACHER PREPARATION:

Become familiar with software packages where modifications and export of graphics is possible (e.g., Corel Draw).

ACTIVITY:

Students use a word processing program to write about their family's Christmas traditions. Save the document.
Do not close the word processing program, instead reduce to the task bar (see icon). 
Students open a graphics program and design a Christmas graphic to accompany their story.
Students may modify the graphic by changing size, colour, orientation, etc.
Students save their modified graphic.
Highlight the graphic (handles), go to Edit menu, and choose copy.
Return to the word processing document by pressing <Alt> <Tab> keys or moving mouse to task bar program and clicking.
Place the cursor where graphic is desired.
Go to the Edit menu, and choose paste.

OTHER ACTIVITIES:

A similar process can be followed to add graphics to any word processing document in any curriculum area.

Reprinted with Permission from the Ottawa-Carleton Catholic School Board

---

Figure 7-1

A technology-related learning experience frequently provides guidance for the teacher as well as step-by-step instructions for the student.

What Is Assessment?

In the past, assessment was understood as being the test or task that was completed at the end of a unit of study. The understanding of assessment has changed significantly in recent years. It is now considered a process of gathering information or data about student progress or a particular program and is based on the following beliefs:

- Assessment promotes learning.
- Students are involved in assessment; they need to know what is being assessed and why it is important.
- Students require more than one opportunity to demonstrate achievement of knowledge and skills.
- Assessment involves a variety of techniques, such as self-assessment, peer assessment, and teacher assessment.
- The methods used in assessment include both product and process.
- Assessment is an on-going part of classroom learning experiences.
- Even though students are involved in the self- and peer assessment, the responsibility for evaluation of the student is the responsibility of the teacher.

The view of assessment and evaluation is changing for a number of reasons. First, our view of learning has changed. There was a time when the learner was viewed as an empty vessel to be filled and the nature of the knowledge imparted required rote learning. Research in learning has shed new light on how we learn. As educators we need to be aware of how learning takes place so that we can adjust our thinking and approach to teaching.

Second, the knowledge, skills, and attitudes required for success have changed. While our students still need to have basic factual information, they will also need to know how to access information. This shift is reflected in the Employability Skills Profile released by the Conference Board of Canada, which highlights not only the importance of academic skills but also personal management and teamwork skills. Some of the academic skills included communication skills (speaking, listening, reading, and writing); thinking skills (the ability to think logically and critically, to solve problems, to use technology and information systems effectively, and to access and apply specialized knowledge); and learning skills with a view to learning as a lifelong process. In addition to academic skills, personal management skills such as a positive attitude and behaviour, a sense of responsibility, and adaptability were seen as important. Today's teachers are looking for demonstrations of a broad range of knowledge, skills, and attitudes.

Third, our students' daily learning experiences are multiple and varied. On a day-to-day basis students are bombarded with images and sounds. If the classroom is to model the real world, then it too must stimulate all the senses. The inclusion of technology in instruction and assessment provides this variety and also assists in addressing different learning styles. The work of Howard Gardiner points out that we all have multiple intelligences that make a difference in our learning and our lives.[4]

In 1994, D. Lazear developed the Multiple Intelligence Assessment Menu which points out various assessment instruments corresponding to the different intelligences. This menu can help you vary the assessments used in your classroom, thus providing greater opportunities for student success.[5]

Figure 7-2

Spotting the Seven Intelligences highlights some of the patterns associated with each type of intelligence.

Spotting the Seven Intelligences

Linguistic Intelligence involves ease in producing language and sensitivity to the nuances, order and rhythm of words. Students who exhibit linguistic intelligence love to read books, write and tell stories. They have good memories for names, places, dates and trivia.

Logical-Mathematical Intelligence relates to the ability to reason deductively or inductively and to recognize and manipulate abstract patterns and relationships. Students who excel at math, have strong problem-solving and reasoning skills and ask questions in a logical manner exhibit this intelligence.

Spatial Intelligence is the ability to create visual-spatial representations of the world and to transfer those representations mentally and concretely. Students who exhibit spatial intelligence need a mental or physical picture to best understand new information; do well with maps, charts and diagrams; and like mazes and puzzles. They can design, draw and create things.

Musical Intelligence includes sensitivity to the pitch, timbre and rhythm of sounds, and responsiveness to the emotional implications of these elements. Students who remember melodies or notice pitch and rhythm exhibit musical intelligence. They tend to be aware of surrounding sounds.

Bodily-Kinesthetic Intelligence involves using the body to solve problems, to create products and convey ideas and emotions. Students who exhibit bodily-kinesthetic intelligence are good at physical activities and have a tendency to move around, touch things and gesture.

Interpersonal Intelligence refers to the ability to work effectively with other people, to understand them; and to notice their goals, motivations, and intentions. Students who thrive on cooperative work, have strong leadership skills, and are skilled at organizing, communicating, meditating, and negotiating exhibit this intelligence.

Intrapersonal Intelligence entails the ability to understand one's own emotion, goals, and intentions. Students who exhibit this intelligence have a strong sense of self, are confident, and often prefer working alone. They also have good instincts about their strengths and abilities.

Reprinted with permission of The Instructor Magazine, July/August, 1992

No one would argue the importance of assessment. Students, teachers, and parents want and need to know the progress being made, but assessment also provides many other benefits.
* It provides an accurate reflection of student progress.
* Assessment can lead to growth in knowledge and skills.
* It can affect teaching and learning strategies used.
* On-going assessment reflects the approach in the real world.
* Assessment can help the teacher to target specific needs.
* On-going assessment can provide motivation for learning.

Fourth, educators and students are hearing and learning about metacognition. Metacognition is knowledge about, awareness of, and control over one's own mind and thinking. Being able to monitor our own learning plays a critical

ASSESSMENT TOOLS FOR THE MULTIPLE INTELLIGENCES

Verbal/Linguistic

Teacher-made tests
Logs and journals
Group projects
Demonstrations
Observation checklists
Interviews
Rubrics
Informal use of standardized tests

Visual/Spatial

Portfolios
Projects
Exhibitions
Logs
Journals
Taped feedback
Interviews

Interpersonal

Observation checklists
Demonstrations
Teacher-made tests
Logs
Journals
Group projects
Interviews

Musical

Checklists
Audio tapes of performances
Video tapes of performances
Anecdotal observation

Logical/Mathematical

Teacher-made tests
Rubrics
Demonstrations
Group projects
Individual projects
Logs
Journals
Interviews
Informal use of standardized tests

Intrapersonal

Logs
Journals
Open-ended questioning
Self-reflection

Bodily/Kinesthetic

Self-reflection
Journals
Observation Checklists
Rubrics

Reprinted with the permission of The Eastern Ontario Catholic Curriculum Cooperative

role in our being able to learn. Whether planning, monitoring, or assessing work, it is important to articulate what we are trying to do, check our progress, and reflect on our learning. Information on the importance of metacognition has led to a greater emphasis on self-assessment.

Types of Assessment

There are a number of different types of assessment methods, and the method used can have a positive or negative effect on student learning. The traditional method of assigning grades to work can lead to feelings of lack of control and involvement on the part of the student. Ramsden believes that "our choice of assessment methods should be conditioned by our goal for student learning" and we should think of assessment "less as a means of getting a single score for comparative purposes, and more as a mean of providing opportunities for students to demonstrate how much they understand."[6]

There are numerous assessment strategies available to teachers.
McTighe, in *Assessing Learning in the Classroom*, categorizes assessment items into

- products such as lab reports, posters, and displays;
- performance such as dramatizations, slide shows, and newscasts; and
- processes such as conferences, discussions, and interviews.[7]

> **"S**tudent assessment procedures should be varied and consistent with the purpose(s) of the assessment(s)."[8]

Authentic Assessment

Regardless of the type of assessment used, it is important that students have an opportunity to participate in authentic assessment. Authentic assessment includes any task that engages students in the real-life application of knowledge and skills. For example, instead of presenting problems about the costs and profits associated with a bake sale, the students would hold a bake sale, track their costs, and calculate their profits.

In authentic assessment there is a link between the methods and tools used during the instruction and those being used during assessment. If a student uses computers during the process, they should also be able to use them during the assessment.

An authentic assessment task can take more than one form. It might be a product, performance, or a process.[9] Regardless of its form, authentic assessments are important because they possess the following characteristics:

- They are multidimensional and complex in nature.
- They incorporate various modalities of learning.
- They demonstrate progress over time.
- They are learned with practice.
- They are built on practice and feedback.
- They are aligned with outcomes and goals.[10]

Performance Assessment

A performance assessment is an active display of learning in which the student demonstrates the knowledge or skills that the teacher wishes to measure. The duration of this assessment may vary significantly and include one or more of a variety of assessment strategies. When the assessment is authentic in nature, the student not only demonstrates the skills, but does so within a real-life context. Most real-life tasks are judged based on a set of criteria and may be judged by more than one person; for example, a panel of experts using well-defined criteria judges competitive skating.

Authentic performance tasks have specific characteristics.
- **The students demonstrate some skill(s) or knowledge.**
- **There are specific expectations of the demonstration.**
- **The nature of the task is meaningful. It should be a real-life problem and context.**
- **Assessment of the task is completed by individuals and may take the form of self-, peer, and/or teacher assessment.**
- **The assessment criteria are available to the students when planning their demonstration of learning.**

Authentic performance tasks may take the form of exhibits, performances, journals, demonstrations, products, or projects and incorporate overall and/or specific skills within a real-world context. When a performance assessment takes place at the end of a block of instruction time or a unit of study, it is often called a culminating performance task. As with any performance task, a rubric typically accompanies the task.

Figure 7-4a

This culminating task asks students to apply their math skills to a real-life situation.

Culminating Performance Task   Recess Games

Strand: Data Management and Probability   **Recommended Grade: I**

Knowledge and Skills:
- Read and discuss data from graphs made with concrete materials and express understanding in a variety of informal ways.
- Organize materials on concrete graphs and pictographs using one-to-one correspondence.
- Pose questions about data gathered.
- Collect first hand data by counting objects, conducting surveys, measuring and performing simple experiments.

Materials:
Clip boards for groups with paper (for surveys), chart paper for final graphs

Task:
The principal has asked that your class provide information on favourite games played at recess. You will need to survey the students and make a graph to present to the students and the principal. The principal would like to purchase new equipment based on the results of your survey.

Procedure:
- A. Explain the task and assessment.
- B. Break into pairs or small groups.
- C. Design the question for your survey.
- D. Teacher assigns classes to survey.
- E. Groups conduct the survey and bring back the results.
- F. Groups use results to make graph.
- G. Groups present results and interpretations.

Assessment Strategies:

Observations: How did they track?
                 What was their question?
                 Did they use numbers?
                 What language did they use? (most, least, etc.)

Product/
Presentation: Use of the rubric to assess the survey/question, graphing or results/presentation and interpretation of data.

Link to Math Journal:
    How did you record your answers?
    Could you record your answer in a different way?
    What did you learn from your information?

Developing Performance Tasks

When launching into the development of performance tasks, the first challenge is to come up with the real-life application. Technology naturally lends itself to performance tasks since it is so much part of our lives. Using technology models the real world and gives the students a chance to demonstrate their technological skills.

Recess Games

Criteria	1	2	3	4
Survey/ Question	■ Inaccurate recording of survey ■ Question not appropriate	■ Conducts tally but results not recorded ■ Question is appropriate	■ Keeps accurate data tally ■ Uses appropriate survey question	■ Can gather data ■ Can keep a record ■ Explains the survey question
Graphing or Results/ Presentation	■ Unable to organize data	■ Data somewhat organized ■ Presentation is not clear	■ Data is organized ■ Presentation could be improved	■ Child organizes and presents data displaying a solid understanding ■ Accurate graph numbers
Interpretation of Data	■ Does not understand the data ■ Lack of understanding concept	■ Unable to interpret results accurately	■ Presents information from graph	■ Child is able to interpret and analyze data

Reprinted with the Permission of the NECTAR Foundation

Figure 7-4b

The teacher selects the expectations to be assessed and develops performance criteria with the students. When developing criteria with students, think of the following questions.

- Are the criteria developed and presented using the student's words?
- Have you provided vocabulary to help the student talk about and think about performance?
- Are the criteria narrow so that the task is manageable in scope and size?
- Are the criteria attainable?
- Have the criteria been posted so that the students can check them?

Culminating Performance Task **Water: Waste Not, Want Not**

Strand: Data Management and Probability **Recommended Grade: 6**

Knowledge and Skills:
- Experiment with a variety of displays of same data using computer applications and select type of graph that best represents the data.
- Construct line, bar and scatter plots both by hand and by using computer applications.
- Connect the possible events and the probability of a particular event in making relevant decisions.

Prerequisite Skills:
- Design surveys, collect data and record results on given spreadsheet or tally chart.
- Display data on graphs (line, bar, pictograph, circle) by using a computer application.
- Construct labeled graphs.
- Use knowledge of probability to pose and solve problems.

Task:
Investigate how much water your home uses in one week and project your water consumption for one year. Report your findings using three types of graphs produced on the computer. Decide which graph best represents your data. Use this graph to draw conclusions on how to reduce your water consumption. Predict how much water your family could save in a year. Contact the municipality to find out the cost of water and estimate how much water your family could save. Display your findings, including your graphs, in poster format.

Procedure:
1. This task can be done individually.
2. The task, skills and assessment are explained. The rubric is examined.
3. The teacher assesses process and product.

Assessment Strategies:
Process: Teacher observation, mathematics journal

Product: Rubric for poster display

Challenge Adjustment:
Include the disposal of used water as well as the access of fresh water.

Materials and Resources:
- Poster paper
- Computer software

Link to Math Journal:
Explain the problems you encountered solving this problem. How did you solve these difficulties? What would you do differently next time?

Link to Career Education:
Invite a resource person from the community and/or municipal government to explain the various careers connected to water availability and disposal in the community.

Reprinted with the permission of The NECTAR Foundation

On-going discussion with the students as to the nature of the task, the expectations, the performance criteria, the materials or resources required, and the assessment will help clarify any questions and produce a better product or performance.

Figure 7-5a

A culminating performance task such as this may also include challenge adjustments and links to math journalizing or career education.

Waste Not, Want Not			Rubric for Water Poster	
Criteria	**1**	**2**	**3**	**4**
Problem Solving	■ requires assistance to understand the activity	■ shows partial understanding requires clarification	■ completely understands the problem	■ understands problem and demonstrates additional insight
	■ little planning evident	■ some plan evident	■ effective plan evident	■ thoroughly planned
Understanding Concepts	■ states hypothesis but does not support it with evidence	■ requires assistance to understand significance of results and to communicate results	■ understands significance of results, clearly communicates results	■ communicates understanding of the significance of results in an insightful manner
	■ conclusion may not fit the evidence; limited suggestion for reducing water consumption	■ requires some assistance to identify ways of reducing water consumption	■ adequate suggestions for reducing water consumption	■ suggestions for reduction of water consumption; demonstrates considerable understanding
	■ incomplete graphs	■ all graphs present but preference not indicated	■ 3 graphs present preference indicated with some explanation	■ 3 graphs present and preference indicated with some explanation
Skills	■ limited skills in use of data collection, organization, use of data and creation of graph	■ some skill in use of data collection, organization, use of data and creation of graph	■ accurate use of data collection, organization, use of data and creation of graph	■ skillful use of data collection, organization, use of data and creation of graph
	■ inaccurate projection of amount of water of one year	■ minor miscalculation of one year's water	■ reasonable projection of one year's water	■ insightful projection of one year's water
Mathematical Language	■ incomplete data presented	■ data presented but disorganized or unclear	■ data presented clearly	■ data presented precisely
	■ inadequately communicates water consumption	■ adequate communication of water consumption	■ communication of water consumption precise	■ thorough communication of water consumption

Reprinted with the permission of The NECTAR Foundation

Figure 7-5b

How do you know if it is a good authentic performance task? Ask yourself these questions.
1. Does the task have a meaningful context?
2. Is the task related to the demonstration of specific knowledge and/or skills?
3. Is there a specific purpose or audience?
4. Is the task role-related?
5. Does the task involve both process and product?
6. Are there accompanying performance criteria?

Figure 7-6a

In this performance task, students design and publish a newsletter to welcome new students in September. They focus on topics such as the layout of the school, extracurricular activities, up-coming events, etc. Note the criteria selected for inclusion in the rubric for this task.

Culminating Performance Task   Newsletter: Welcoming New Students

Strand: Language   **Recommended Grade: 6/7**

Expectations:
- Respect each other as members of the community
- Fulfill a role in cooperative learning
- Use formal and informal language appropriate to context
- Identify purpose and audience for writing
- Use a variety of sentence kinds
- Organize paragraphs
- Use simple and compound sentences
- Use voice appropriate to content and audience
- Use Microsoft Publisher
- Adhere to timelines

Task:
As a member of a production team, you will design and publish a newsletter to welcome new students to your school in September. Using technology, you will present both your process and product to the class.

Suggested Time:
- 8–10 hours

Background Information:
- Expertise in using software programs
- Journalistic background on graphic design of newsletters

Materials and Resources:
- Microsoft Publisher
- Digital camera
- Projection tablet
- Brochures, flyers, magazines

Welcoming New Students		Rubric for Writing of Newsletter	
Element	**Levels1 / 2**	**Level 3**	**Level 4**
Organization Paragraph Structure	■ No topic and/or concluding sentences evident	■ Uses topic, developing and concluding sentences	■ Multi-paragraphs demonstrate coherence
Style Use of simple and compound sentences	■ Uses primarily simple and/or poorly coordinated compound sentences	■ Contains a balance of simple and compound sentences	■ Uses simple and compound sentences effectively
Content Relevance of ideas	■ Contains irrelevant material	■ Uses relevant facts and details	■ Uses relevant ideas and facts effectively
Mechanics Spelling and punctuation	■ Spelling and punctuation errors interfere with communication	■ Spelling and punctuation errors do not interfere with communication	■ Free of spelling and punctuation errors

Reprinted with the permission of The Eastern Ontario Catholic Curriculum Cooperative

Figure 7-6b

The Use of Exemplars

Dr. Grant Wiggins has stated that "if we expect students to do excellent work they have to know what excellent work looks like."[11] An exemplar is an example of the expected product or process. It can be very specific, such as a title page or business letter, or it could be more comprehensive such as a project. For the newsletter task described in Figure 7-6, the exemplar could be a newsletter created by a student the previous year. These exemplars will provide the students with concrete evidence of the desired level of performance but there are also other benefits to using exemplars.

- Exemplars ensure consistency in assessment.
- Exemplars are valuable for self- and peer assessment.
- Exemplars provide parents with an example of the expected product or performance.
- Exemplars help the teacher in determining the level of performance.

By collecting a variety of exemplars, you will have a number of valuable tools to assist in the teaching and learning process.

Working with Rubrics

"To begin with the end in mind means to start with a clear understanding of your destination. It means to know where you are going so that you better understand where you are now so that the steps you take are always in the right direction."[12]

The past decade has seen an increase in use of the rubric in the assessment of student learning. This scoring scale, which consists of achievement criteria and corresponding descriptors of levels, is used not only to assess student work but also to guide student progress. When students possess a rubric outlining the performance criteria and levels of performance prior to completion of the task, they possess their destination and are better equipped for success.

Culminating Performance Task   Go Fish!

Strand: Numeration and Number Sense   Recommended Grade: 6

Knowledge and Skills:
- Add and subtract decimal numbers with 1, 2, 3 decimal places
- Multiply decimals by 3-digit whole numbers
- Add and subtract 5-digit numbers with regrouping (3 addends)
- Multiply a 3-digit number by a 3-digit number
- Multiply a 3-digit number by a 3-digit number
- Divide 5-digit numbers by 2-digit numbers with regrouping

Prerequisite Skills:
- Use decimals numbers to write monetary amounts
- Add and subtract decimal numbers with 2 decimal places
- Add and subtract 5-digit numbers with regrouping (3 addends)
- Multiply a 3-digit number by a 2-digit number
- Divide 3 and 4-digit numbers by a 2-digit number with regrouping

Task: Your school principal wants you to set up an aquarium in the main hall. He has allocated a maximum of $750 to spend in total. Your team is to prepare a plan to submit to the principal for approval. The plan should include:
- Evidence of your knowledge of equipment and supplies
- Description of the fish to stock the aquarium
- Summary of costs
- Diagrams and other graphics to assist your explanation

Procedure:
1. This task should be done in teams of 3–4 students.
2. The task, skills and assessment should be explained to students before they begin. The rubric for the plan should be discussed.
3. Student teams conduct research on setting up an aquarium. They develop their plans and present them to the school principal for comment.
4. Both process and product are assessed.

Assessment Strategies:
Process: 1. Self, peer and/or teacher assessment of cooperative learning and research skills
           2. Teacher observation of problem solving and application of math skills.
Product: The rubric is used to assess the plan.

Challenge Adjustment: A research requirement could be added which necessitates the use of a combination of resources: print, human and computer.

Materials and Resources:
- Access to a variety of resources on setting up an aquarium
- Computer software to input the plan (optional)

Link to Math Journal: Students respond to:
a. What did you learn from this task which would help you to develop an improved plan for another project?
b. How could your team work together more efficiently?

Link to Career Education:
One of the following people could be invited to visit the class to provide information on aquariums. Included could be an explanation of the type of work done by the individual.
- Representative from a science museum
- Pet store owner
- Marine biologist
- Icthyologist

Reprinted with the permission of The NECTAR Foundation   **Figure 7-7a**

Go Fish!

Criteria	1	2	3	4
Content	■ Inadequate description of the equipment and supplies required ■ Not all costs listed ■ Some fish listed but none described	■ Adequate description of the equipment and supplies required ■ Costs listed with minimal detail ■ Fish listed but not described	■ Complete description of the equipment and supplies required ■ Costs listed with necessary detail ■ Fish listed with some description	■ Thorough description of the equipment and supplies required ■ Costs listed with great detail ■ Fish listed and described in detail
Application of Math Skills	■ Many errors in calculations ■ Evidence of ability to demonstrate few of the skills	■ Some errors in calculation ■ Evidence of ability to demonstrate some skills	■ Few errors in calculation ■ Evidence of ability to demonstrate most skills	■ No errors in calculations ■ Evidence of ability to demonstrate all skills
Format	■ Disorganized ■ No use of illustrations, graphs, etc. ■ Material unattractively or haphazardly arranged	■ Some organization evident ■ Minimal use of illustrations, graphics, etc. ■ Neat. Some evidence of arrangement	■ Organization evident through cover, table of contents, use of headlines and page numbers ■ Effective use of illustrations, graphics, etc. ■ Neat and attractively arranged	■ Well organized ■ Creative use of illustrations, graphics, etc. ■ Neat and innovatively arranged

Reprinted with the permission of The NECTAR Foundation

Figure 7-7b

This culminating performance task is accompanied by a rubric. This rubric specifies three criteria (content, application of math skills, format), four levels of achievement, and descriptors sometimes called performance indicators.

Why Should We Use Rubrics?

"Rubrics are not only scoring tools but also, more important instructional illuminators."[13]

1. Rubrics give students a clear understanding of how they are doing, what they need to work on, and the next step in the progression to achievement of specific outcomes.
2. Rubrics make the student part of the assessment process.
3. Ideally rubrics are available to the students before they start the task. The use of rubrics can lead to greater success on the part of the students because the specific nature of rubrics clarifies the task.
4. Rubrics, with their criteria and levels of performance, increase reliability of assessment.
5. Rubrics provide consistency. Each student uses the same rubric to demonstrate knowledge of concepts and skills.
6. Rubrics are valuable for students when they assess their own work and the work of their peers because they pinpoint strengths and weaknesses.
7. Rubrics help students to set personal goals.

Constructing Your Own Rubrics

As you construct a learning task, you identify the criteria for assessment. Sometimes they are very specific and with a narrow focus, such as a rubric for a business letter. Other times the criteria may be broader, such as those used in a culminating performance task. The criteria may be of equal importance or could be weighted differently.

Following the establishment of the criteria, the next step is to identify the performance indicators for each of the levels of performance. A performance indicator is a description of the level of performance of the student. The writing of the performance indicators is the most challenging, because the wording must reflect the level and the nature of the criteria being assessed.

The level at which you begin constructing performance indicators is up to you, but many teachers start with the expected level of performance and work in both directions. When the rubric has been completed, the students require an opportunity to discuss it before starting the task. Initially, you may write the rubric(s) but as your comfort level grows you may wish to involve the students in the process. They bring their experience to the rubric design and they will have a greater sense of ownership because they were involved in the design process.

Descriptive Terms for Rubric Development

Degrees of Quality
- Excellent
- Good
- Fair
- Poor

Degrees of Quantity
- Many
- Some
- Few
- None

Degrees of Frequency
- Always
- Consistently, Usually, Frequently
- Sometimes
- Rarely, Never

Degrees of Effectiveness
- Highly effective
- Effective
- Minimally effective
- Ineffective

Degrees of Understanding
- Thorough, Complete
- Substantial
- Partial, Incomplete
- Misunderstanding, Serious Misconceptions

Figure 7-8

Having key words at hand is always helpful and will speed up the process of rubric creation.

Assessment The activity will be assessed based on the following rubric.

Criteria	Level 1	Level 2	Level 3	Level 4
Time used effectively while doing search	■ Observed that time rarely used appropriately effectively	■ Observed that time usually used appropriately and effectively	■ Observed that time used appropriately and effectively	■ Observed that time usually used very appropriately and effectively
Number of and appropriateness of Web sites located considering time constraints	■ Very few appropriate Web sites located and/or much guidance needed	■ Some appropriate Web sites located and/or some guidance needed	■ Many appropriate Web sites located with little or no guidance required	■ Incredible number of appropriate Web sites located with no guidance required
Spelling, grammar and spacing assignment	■ Poor use of program to correct these types of errors (several errors)	■ Some use of program to correct these types of errors (some errors)	■ Good use of program to correct these types of errors (few errors)	■ Excellent use of program to correct these types of errors (no errors)
Appropriate use of table	■ Table not completed by use of program demonstrating that no understanding of program abilities	■ Table completed by use of program but only satisfactorily demonstrating some understanding abilities	■ Table completed by good use of program, demonstrating good understanding of program abilities	■ Table completed by superior use of program, demonstrating strong understanding of program abilities
Appropriateness of pictures	■ Pictures are ill placed and not relevant to the paper. There are not two pictures present.	■ Pictures are somewhat relevant and placed relatively well. Two pictures are used.	■ Pictures are relevant to overall message and well placed. Two pictures are used.	■ Pictures are very relevant and add greatly to overall message of the paper. They are very well placed. At least two pictures are used.

Figure 7-9

This rubric applies to a learning task in which students search the Web for resources and create a document of their research that includes a table.

During the completion of the task, the rubric provides a valuable function. Students use it to guide their learning. Teachers frequently post the rubric in the classroom so that students can consult it readily. As the task is being completed, the students may use the rubric to set goals for future learning. Upon completion of the task, the rubric is used to assess the product, demonstration, or performance. The student, the student's peers, and/or the

Storyboard Rubric

Stack Creation	Level 1	Level 2	Level 3	Level 4
Storyboard — connections	■ Stack has little or no flow. Lacks correct number of cards	■ Stack does not flow smoothly. Some tools are used. Correct number of cards	■ Stack flows well. Tools are used correctly. Correct number of cards	■ Stack flows well and logically. Extensive use of tools in creative way. Correct number of cards
Text (content)	■ Information is missing; grammar and spelling not checked	■ Information is complete; errors are not corrected	■ Information is complete and well-presented	■ Information is complete, well-presented and creative visually
Button creation	■ No buttons used or buttons used do not show direction	■ Buttons used but direction not clear, no button actions (sounds)	■ Buttons used with directions clear, actions appropriately used (sound)	■ Buttons are functional with actions, direction and more (colour, shape)
Clip-Art graphics	■ No clip-art or graphics in presentation	■ Clip-art included but not relevant to topic	■ Clip-art and graphics included and are relevant to topic	■ Clip-art and graphics are used well with topic. Extra features or clip-art has been added
Digital photo or scanned image *(videoclip as alternative)*	■ No photo or image	■ Photo or image included but not properly placed	■ Photo or image included and properly placed in stack to create visually pleasing effect	■ Photo or image included, properly placed in stack and creatively displayed on card
Overall presentation	■ Presentation is not complete; visuals do not enhance work	■ Presentation does not appear complete; visuals some-what enhance work	■ Presentation is complete and visually enhances work	■ Presentation is complete, visually enhances work, and contains added features to increase interest

Figure 7-10

This rubric is used for a learning task in which students create a storyboard to plan their Hyperstudio stack.[14]

teacher can do this. The availability of the rubric will bring greater reliability to the assessment and focus assessment on the results of the task. A real benefit of the rubric is that it also provides the basis for communication and/or clarification with the student, parent, or other interested parties. See Appendix 3 for frequently asked questions about rubrics.

Assessment Portfolios

"Just as the artist chooses from an array of water-colours to paint his/her picture, the creative teacher chooses from a repertoire of assessment tools to paint his/her picture of the student as a lifelong learner.... The artist's palette serves as an organiser for all the various paints, just as a portfolio serves as an organisational palette for all the authentic assessment tools. The portfolio pulls all the 'loose ends' together to paint a picture of the whole student — not just an isolated or fragmented picture of the student."[15]

Portfolios have the potential to pull a variety of assessment tools together to convey a picture of student progress. Unlike specific assessments, a portfolio can present a comprehensive picture of each student at a given point in time.

> **"T**he portfolio is a form of assessment that is authentic, continuous, multidimensional and interactive."[16]

A portfolio is a representative and purposeful collection of a student's work over a set period of time. In addition, it shows growth over time and provides students with opportunities to critically examine their work, enhancing the student's ability to self-evaluate and reflect on his or her learning. The process is usually accompanied by a set of guidelines that provides the basis for the selection of content as well as the quality criteria to be used.

> **"A** valuable tool in student assessment, portfolios provide students the opportunity to see their progress and tell the stories of their learning."[17]

Portfolios have a number of strengths. First, they are used to collect data and demonstrate achievement. The collection of data focuses on the positive, not the negative, by demonstrating what the student can do. The student wishes to show what has been accomplished and, therefore, it is an excellent basis for discussion with the student and/or parents. The second major strength of the portfolio is the active participation of the students. They are involved in the selection of materials for the portfolio, are engaged in self-assessment and reflection, and also set goals for future learning. Since portfolios reflect individual accomplishments, a third strength of the portfolio is in its respect of the individual learning styles and rates of learning. Fourth, portfolios are an excellent basis for a parent-teacher-student conference for they contain evidence of student learning.

> **"P**ortfolios are as varied as the children who create them and as the classrooms in which they are found."[18]

There are a number of key steps to consider when introducing assessment portfolios.
- Decide on the type of portfolio and its purpose. The age of the students and the subjects you teach and the outcomes or skills that you want to see

demonstrated will affect your decision. At the very beginning explain the portfolio process to the parents and the benefits for their children.

- Explain the purpose of the portfolio to the students.
- Set the criteria for success. This will be teacher-directed with input from the student.
- Establish a rubric or rubrics to be used by the students and teacher in the assessment and evaluation of the portfolio materials.
- Students complete work samples and assess them.
- Teach the students self-reflection. They will need to reflect on their learning with the purpose of setting goals. The teacher usually facilitates this process.
- The contents of the portfolio are reviewed and culled if necessary.
- The portfolio is shared with peers, parents, or others.

Practical Suggestions

For the Teacher:

1. Decide on a specific purpose, a priority.
2. Align the purpose with what will go into the portfolio.
3. Use criteria to document change, growth and/or achievement.
4. Practice self-reflection — the key to student ownership of learning.
5. Start saving student work.
6. Clarify outcomes for students.
7. Increase student control.
8. Encourage student self-reflections.
9. Develop descriptive criteria.
10. Send home the work that has NOT been placed in the student's portfolio.
11. Keep the original work and send home a copy of the work kept in the portfolio. (Or trust your students to return the original work as part of your personal management responsibility program.)
12. Invite parents to peruse the portfolio.
13. Write a letter to parents/guardians to ask for their help and support with the conferences.
14. At conference time, enrich your parent-student-teacher meeting with the addition of the students' portfolios.
15. Celebrate achievements!
16. To set up a flexible portfolio system use legal size file jackets as segments of a storage case. (They are cheap, expandable and leave plenty of room for labels.)
17. Insert 2–3 file folders to go inside the jacket. Label and colour code each file: red for working files; yellow for selected pieces; green for next year's teacher.
18. Encourage the students to put all work in progress in their folder as it is created. Then, periodically, move a few selected pieces to the portfolio folder, a move that should be flexible and purposeful. Students can change their minds as they get new pieces for the working folder which they think are better examples than earlier works. The key is not to let the portfolio get too big.

Reprinted with the permission of The Eastern Ontario Catholic Curriculum Cooperative

Figure 7-11

As teachers and students have implemented portfolio assessment, they have compiled a number of practical suggestions.

Electronic Portfolio Assessment

Several software packages have been developed to help students and teachers create multimedia portfolios. They include the following:

- Electronic Portfolio by Scholastic
- HyperStudio by Roger Wagner
- The Digital Chisel by Pierian Springs
- Kid Pix Studio by Broderdund
- Learner Profile by Sunburst

As an alternative to purchasing software, you might choose to use multipurpose software such as the following:

- ClarisWorks by Apple
- Office by Microsoft
- Kid Works 2 by Broderdund
- Microsoft Works by Microsoft

Regardless of the level of computer expertise of the students and teacher, an exercise such as portfolio assessment will improve student learning, teacher enthusiasm, and parent involvement. The real advantage of the electronic portfolio is that, in addition to printed text and graphics, it can include photographic, video, and audio samples of student performance. Keeping a portfolio from year to year also allows the student, parents, and teachers to visualize and value the student's educational growth and potential.

For information on alternative assessment go to the publisher's Web site for links to the following sites:
- **Portfolio sites that provide additional information and first-hand experience with the use of portfolios.**
- **A site that provides a listing of alternative assessment resources on the Web.**
- **A site that provides links to sites on assessment and is especially useful to principals.**
- **The CRESST Homepage, which provides a variety of performance assessments and scoring rubrics for elementary and high school subjects.**

Evaluation

While assessment is the process of gathering data, evaluation is the process of integrating and interpreting information from many sources. It is the process of judging the quality of student work according to specific knowledge and skills and the assigning of a value to completed work. The teacher has the sole responsibility for evaluation. The form of judgment such as A, B, C, D, 1, 2, 3, 4, or a specific mark will vary from district to district but there are certain common understandings about evaluation.

- Evaluation involves the students. They need to know the data that lead to the evaluation.
- Evaluation takes into consideration the individual student. D. Keystone, author and technology coordinator, believes "it is important to recognise individual differences, rates of personal growth, consistency and independ-

ence which an individual student demonstrates at a particular level. For it is these less tangible but often revealing and insightful constructs of the learning process that give meaning to judgements made about a given student's progress."[19]

- Evaluation supports learning. Evaluation does not signal the end of a process but is part of a cycle that sets goals for further learning.

Examples of Assessment and Evaluation Tools

Diagnostic
- interest inventory
- samples of work
- journals
- miscue analysis

- educational profiles of the students
- stages of development
- cloze exercises
- writing folders
- formal testing

Formative
- samples of work showing growth
- on-going selection and inclusion of activities

- observations
- self-assessment sheets
- peer assessments
- miscue analysis
- recordings
- samples of work at various stages of production
- conference records

Summative
- samples of completed work related to specific learning outcomes

- tests which prove mastery
- completed projects
- writing samples
- self-assessments
- peer assessments
- observations
- recordings
- photos
- conferences

Reprinted with the permission of The Eastern Ontario Catholic Curriculum Cooperative

---

Figure 7-12

Various types of tools and methods are appropriate for different types of assessment and evaluation.

Evaluation may take one of three forms.
1. Diagnostic evaluation is done when you want to know what a student can do before entering into a particular program or a particular spot within a program. It is used to determine the level of achievement or performance throughout the learning process. This form of evaluation is never incorporated on the report card.
2. Formative evaluation provides information on the progress of the student. It provides on-going feedback on a student's performance throughout the learning process.
3. Summative evaluation is the final achievement given to a student at the end of a unit of work, semester, or school year. This is the report card mark.

General information on different types of assessment and evaluation can be found by going to the publisher's Web site and following links.

- Find information on educational assessment, evaluation, and research and methodology. A new on-line journal is available called "Practical Assessment, Research and Evaluation."
- The North Central Regional Educational Laboratory's Critical Issues site provides valuable information on ensuring equity with alternative assessments, rethinking assessment and its role in supporting educational reform, etc.

See Appendix 3 for commonly asked questions about assessment and evaluation.

Using Technology in Assessment and Evaluation

Technology can assist in the demonstrations of learning. Video-taped interviews, multimedia presentations, and Web searches are only a few of the electronic products that can be used by students. Lesley Farmer in "Authentic Assessment of Information Literacy Through Electronic Products" outlines ways of getting started with authentic assessment that incorporates technology.[20]

- Collect examples of authentic assessments of electronic products.
- Build on existing strategies that incorporate electronic products. One method is to videotape a simulation.
- Collaborate with another teacher to design an interdisciplinary unit that weaves in authentic assessment and electronic products.
- Brainstorm with students' ideas for electronic products that would demonstrate deep learning and also apply to daily life.
- Use phrases such as "What does it look like?" (retell), "What do you feel like when …?" (relate), and "How do you know?"(reflect).
- Start with a clear-cut presentation, such as lab procedure or step-by-step demonstration, and develop two rubrics, one that describes competence of the content and another that describes the presentation itself.
- Have students develop electronic portfolios of their work in which they have to choose items that show progress over time and that represent their best efforts. Then have students write reflective letters explaining their choices and assessing their own progress.

Research recounts how various schools and school systems have used technology to assist in the improvement of learning. Software, videos, and videodiscs have been used in a variety of ways to bring about improvement at the school level. They have been used to plan for instruction, to assess curriculum knowledge, to assess social skills, and to allow teachers to communicate and share ideas.

Not only educators but also parents search for assessment tools that will identify the level of performance of students. With this knowledge, instructional plans can be developed and interventions designed. Currently, software exists that focuses on dynamic assessment, which looks at the learning process rather than the product. If the educator knows how the student responds to specific types of instruction, the best teaching and learning strategies can be employed. Computer technology can help with this type of assessment. DynaMath is one example of software designed to provide a dynamic assessment of multi-digit, multiplication facts.[21] Computer-based dynamic assessment has many benefits, including features, such as applying prompting procedures in a standardized way; storing information; producing reports; and generating graphic representations of data.[22]

The acquisition of basic skills is always a concern. A number of software programs exist to assess skill development. Monitoring Basic Skills Progress is a computer-based program that assesses progress in reading, math, spelling, and writing.[23] If you are looking for subject specific software, MathCheck from IPS Publishing allows the teacher to construct custom-designed assessments. In addition, a number of programs assess reading skills and help teachers ensure that students comprehend material and progress appropriately. Some current reading assessment programs include the following:

- CARS by Curriculum Associates
- Online Reader by EBSCO Publishing
- Accelerated Reader by Advantage Learning Systems
- Reading Counts by Scholastic
- Tomorrow's Promise Reading by Jostens
- PassKey by McGraw-Hill Lifetime Learning

In addition to the assessment of subjects, technology can be used to assist in the assessment of social skills. Irvin, Walker, and colleagues write about a videodisc program that allows students to view scenarios and respond to a series of questions that assesses the student's recognition cues.[24] This program can be used to guide the formation of instructional goals and to plan interventions.

Figure 7-13

Regardless of the type of assessment, evaluation, or reporting practice there will always be an opportunity to comment positively on the work of the students. Here are 100 ways to say "Well done." Unfortunately we do not know the author but are grateful for the positive comments.

Summing Up

A Closing Thought

1. You must have been practising!
2. You are doing much better today!
3. Keep working on it, you're getting there.
4. Keep up the good work!
5. You're really improving!
6. That's great!
7. Keep on trying!
8. You're on the right track now!
9. Excellent!
10. Fine!
11. You made it look easy.
12. You're really working hard today!
13. Good thinking!
14. That's the way to go!
15. Wonderful!
16. You haven't missed a thing!
17. You are really learning a lot!
18. You can be proud of that!
19. That's good!
20. Good work!
21. That's coming along nicely!
22. Super!
23. You figured that out fast!
24. Keep it up!
25. You're doing fine!
26. You've got that down pat!
27. That's better!
28. Terrific work!
29. Well done!
30. You've got it now!
31. Terrific!
32. That's very acceptable!
33. Sensational!
34. You certainly did well today!
35. You did that very well!
36. You are very good at that!
37. Superb!
38. You're really going to town!
39. Good job (name)!
40. You remembered!
41. I'm very proud of you!
42. Perfect!
43. That's the right way to do it!
44. Not bad!
45. You outdid yourself today!
46. That's better than ever!
47. That's the way to do it!
48. I'm proud of the way you worked today!
49. Well look at you go!
50. That's not half bad!
51. I like that!
52. Fantastic!
53. Exactly right!
54. Marvelous!
55. Good for you!
56. That's it!
57. Nice going!
58. Amazing work!
59. That's brilliant!
60. Congratulations!
61. Outstanding!
62. You did it that time!
63. You've got your brain in gear today?
64. You are learning fast!
65. That's it!
66. Good going!
67. You have just about mastered it!
68. One more time and you'll have it!
69. You certainly did well!
70. That's great work!
71. Much better!
72. Right on!
73. Magnificent!
74. Now you have the hang of it!
75. Now you've figured it out!
76. Tremendous!
77. That's a pleasant surprise!
78. It's a pleasure when you work like that!
79. That's really nice!
80. That's the best ever!
81. Now you have it!
82. Now that's what I call a good job!
83. That's the best that you have done!
84. You really make my job fun!
85. I'm really pleased with your work!
86. That's quite an improvement!
87. You've just about got it!
88. I've never seen anyone do it better!
89. You're doing a great job!
90. That was good thinking!
91. I couldn't have done it better myself!
92. You're getting better every day!
93. Congratulations, you've got it right!
94. I knew you could do it!
95. That was a first class job!
96. You really did a lot of work today!
97. I'm happy to see you working like that!
98. You're doing beautifully!
99. That kind of work makes me smile!
100. Hurrah! You've got it.

STUDENTS WITH SPECIAL NEEDS

eight

"What I see as the real contribution of digital media to education is the flexibility that could allow every individual to discover their own personal paths to learning. This will make it possible for the dream of every progressive educator to come true: In the learning environment of the future, every learner will be special."[1]

In education today, we find ourselves in an exciting and challenging time of constant change. As educators, it is essential that we adapt and respond to this change keeping in mind students with special needs. Every class is made up of individuals, each with a preferred learning style: some are highly visual learners, others work best through auditory channels, and still others learn well by moving around and manipulating real objects. The inclusive classroom promotes the integration of special needs students and, therefore, presents challenges in determining accommodations and adaptations that need to be implemented to improve student performance. For intellectual, emotional, physical, or social reasons, or a combination of these, some students seem to need something extra to help them work toward their potential. The range may include intellectual differences, sensory handicaps, communication disorders, physical handicaps, behavior disorders, and developmental disabilities, and various combinations of these. With the addition of increasing numbers of students for whom English is a second language, we see a complex puzzle of students with many different needs to be met in one classroom. As we search for ways to meet these varied needs, ICT can provide valuable assistance. Using ICT can provide control and autonomy for special needs students to learn at their own rate. The use of the computer is particularly motivating to the special needs student because it allows the student to feel an increased sense of independence and control. Not only is using technology highly motivating for most students, but it can be used to implement and complement the strategies that we already know are helpful in working with students with special needs. Each exceptionality presents its own uniqueness and thus requires specialized knowledge, techniques, and technologies. Rather than attempting to delve into each exceptionality in detail, we have chosen to examine, in general terms, some strategies that we believe to be useful for many students with a range of special needs.

> **"The computer and related technologies are powerful tools to engage students in new learning and to enhance their ability to access, process and communicate information. But for at risk and exceptional students, computers provide even more. By presenting material orally, they provide my students who struggle with reading written text, the opportunity to move beyond the mechanical decoding of words in order to focus on the content of a passage. The students who become frustrated at their inability to 'keep up' with their peers in the completion of math lessons and assignments can achieve success by using a self-paced, interactive software program that provides frequent feedback and reinforcement."[2]**

Using Technology to Individualize Your Program

Individualizing your program is a necessity. Learning experiences must correspond with the student's needs, abilities, and individual learning styles and will differ in process, product, and evaluation. You will need to adapt your program, that is, adapt the expectations of the curriculum to meet the student's individual strengths and needs. Program modifications include adapting the pacing, repetition, quantity and quality of the instructional process to meet the individual needs of the students. Technology can help you move toward your goal of creating and implementing effective modifications that truly measure what the special needs student knows.

> **"I've used a piece of software such as HyperStudio in a regular classroom setting with gifted, visually impaired, behavioural and communicational exceptionalities. This multi-media project allowed individual learners to work at their own pace and integrate their own previous knowledge and skills, while also providing opportunities for students to showcase their personal strengths. Student experts facilitated various peer tutoring roles such as the use of digital cameras, scanning, editing and technical trouble shooting — a necessity in a room with 30 different learners. This provided creative opportunities for my students, giving them the chance to produce work in an interesting and motivating manner. The children's pride and feeling of success at the end of a project of this nature is immeasurable."[3]**

QUOTES FROM SPECIAL NEEDS STUDENTS AFTER VIDEO INTERVIEW

Quotes from students with special needs during an interview on why they liked using the computer.

"...get to see my words after it's printed."

"...fast access to the Internet."

"...get work done faster."

"...e-mail from your friend."

"...not sloppy."

"...waste time writing on paper."

"...makes my life easier."

"...just use the backspace."

"...do not have to concentrate on the paper and pencil, concentrate on the screen."

"...don't have to get up and get an eraser."[4]

It is important to consider how ICT enhances teaching and learning and improves the performance of the special needs student. Computer technology offers powerful solutions to obstacles faced by students with special needs. In particular, it allows differentiated instruction for the special needs student. You should not select computer software before defining goals for its use. Four basic principles for evaluation of computer software for special needs students are the following:

- Use of computer technology must be appropriate. The computer is not always the best medium.
- Software must be compatible with learner needs and characteristics.
- Software must be compatible with the needs and intentions of the teacher.
- Software must be compatible with curriculum expectations, instructional strategies, and assessment practices.

Resources that can be easily accessed and used with a minimum of assistance are of the greatest benefit. For students with learning difficulties, look for software that incorporates features such as

- reduction of distraction and irrelevant stimuli;
- simplification and repetition of task directions;
- an abundance of practice;
- modelling and demonstrations;
- prompts and cues;
- instruction in small, manageable steps; and
- immediate and frequent reinforcement and feedback.

For intellectually gifted students, look for software that incorporates features such as

- open-ended questions;
- student-controlled choices and levels;
- content introduced in highly stimulating ways; and
- immediate and frequent reinforcement and feedback.

Be aware that not all learners with the same condition will respond in the same way to the same software program — what works with one special student may not work with another. When selecting software for students, carefully consider each student's preferences, interests, abilities, and symptoms. A software selection that has been successful with one student may not fit the learning style or needs of another, even though both students may have the same academic requirement.

Figure 8-1

Use this checklist of questions when selecting software for special needs students.

> ### Quick Checklist of Questions to answer when selecting software for Special Needs Students:
>
> - What do I want the computer experience to do for the student and what do I hope to accomplish?
> - What features does the student need?
> - Can the program be customized for the student's needs?
> - What is the student interested in?
> - Is the program easy to use?
> - How will the student access the program?

Authorable software is of particular interest to teachers of special needs students. Authorable software is a type of software in which data such as individual spelling lists or stories can be entered. This allows you to customize activities for students. These kinds of easy modifications will assist the exceptional student to participate as a fully equal class member and to join with the other students in the regular daily program.

Use technology to do the job of introducing, teaching, or reinforcing skills to one group of students while you work with another group. While students are engaged in tasks using computers, videos, laser discs or audio tapes, you are free to conference and work with individuals on a one-to-one basis. A learning center/workstations approach can be used to make this work well.

> **"A**s a teacher of a regular classroom with four identified students, open-ended software is an excellent tool as it allows everyone to succeed at their own level. It inspires increased self-confidence. Students who struggle with pencil and paper have become experts in the lab, and for the first time find themselves leaders in the classroom."[5]

Planning for Exceptional Students

Planning for the exceptional student often requires an individual educational plan (IEP) that outlines very specific learning goals and curriculum expectations for the student based on strengths and needs. The IEP is a flexible, working document that requires regular updates showing dates, results, and recommendations.

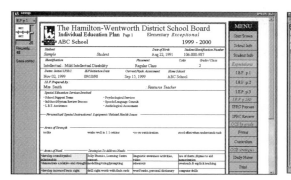

Figure 8-2

An Individual Education Plan can be created using an electronic database. Plans laid out within a set format on the computer are easy to access and can be updated quickly. Teacher comments and observations can be jotted onto the profile quickly and then elaborated upon later when more concentrated time is available.[6]

Electronic database programs have been developed that include a comprehensive collection of layouts that assist in planning and tracking individual educational plans, student profiles, special education forms, and daily notes. An electronic management tool such as this will also often feature a database of curriculum expectations, as well as value lists of needs and strategies geared to the special needs student.

> **"A**n invaluable student information database continues to evolve out of an immediate need to manage individual and group information respective of the educational needs and performance ability of each learner. It permits the user an opportunity by which to facilitate the collection of data for use in writing of individual plans; track program-based performance; monitor the academic, social, emotional, and behavior development of a teacher's client base; and establish best practices to be documented when reporting. It works well both at an individual level and as part of a collaborative process at all levels of education."[7]

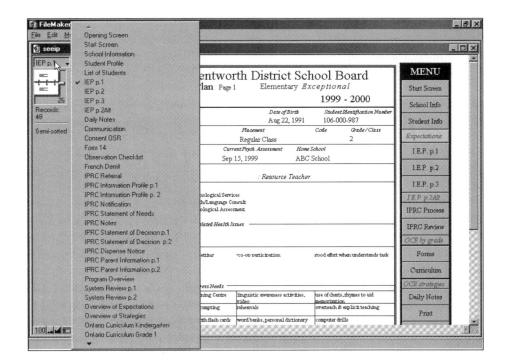

Figure 8-3

This type of electronic management system for record keeping and tracking is a portable, flexible tool that saves time and promotes accurate documentation.[8]

Regardless of the type of goals, they require careful monitoring and tracking. This arduous task is greatly facilitated by using the computer. Select software that can assist in planning and tracking individualized educational programs.

> **"S**ince becoming a Learning Resource Teacher a year ago, I can honestly say that without the SEEIP Program (Special Education Electronic Information Package) my paperwork would be unfathomable. I inherited this position from a superior teacher who kept all records in an accurate, organized fashion; however, the sheer amount of physical space these records take is cumbersome at best. Using the computer I am able to streamline, update at any time, modify, rearrange, correct, re-write, etc., at the touch of a few buttons. What took hours before can now take considerably less time. The documents also look much more professional than the older, handwritten variety, which I feel lends more credibility to Special Education in general. My only regret is that I do not yet own a laptop on which to take notes during important meetings — handwriting scripted notes seems slow and inefficient in contrast to the computer program. Perhaps this piece of equipment will eventually become standard issue for Learning Resource Teachers. I can only hope!"[9]

Technology can also provide evaluation that helps to individualize programs. Many computer programs include an evaluation component. In some programs, students move through modules in which mastery of certain skills or concepts is required before the student can progress to the next module. Because a computer can randomly generate questions based on a common format, students can practice a skill as often as required for mastery. Once you know the computer program thoroughly yourself, you will know exactly what the student must understand in order to successfully complete the lesson or module. When you see evidence of that successful completion, you can be confident that the student knows the skill(s). A computer evaluation may also be diagnostic in nature and used as a basis for designing appropriate follow-up learning experiences, whether or not they are technology oriented.

Figure 8-4

An individualized tracking sheet template for recording results of an informal educational assessment. It can also then be modified to include other assessments or evaluative comments.

Informal Educational Assessment

Student_____ Grade_____ D.O.B. _____

Test	Date	Results/Comments
Letter Knowledge		Visual Stimulus /13 Auditory Stimulus /13
Phonics		Initial Consonants /10 Initial Blends & Diagraphs /10
Blending Sounds / Vowels		End of Word /10 Vowels /10
Phonograms / Blending		Phonograms /10 Blending /10
Graded Word List		Gr.___ independent Gr.___instructional Gr.___frustration /10 /10 /10
Oral Reading		Gr.___ independent Gr.___instructional Gr.___frustration
Silent Reading		Gr.___ independent Gr.___instructional Gr.___frustration
Listening Comprehension		Gr. _____% Gr. ___ ___%
Spelling List		List 1 /32: grade ____ List 2 /32: grade ____
Auditory Analytical Skills		Grade _____
KeyMath		Grade _____
Mathematics Placement		Grade _____
Comments:		

Another approach is for a school or school system to develop a bank of assessment items on a specific topic. These items are then put into a database on computer disk or CD-ROM. When a teacher wishes to test students' understanding of a particular skill, there are many items from which to choose. If a written test is appropriate, the selected items can be printed out. You may not yet have such things in your school, but be alert for them as they come onto the market. Remember that truly authentic assessment includes portfolios of student work, observational data, and performance appraisal. The techniques outlined in Chapter 7: Assessing Student Progress are appropriate for all students, including those with special needs.

Cooperative Learning and Peer Helping

Research supports our experience that the strategy of students working in pairs on the computer is often more effective than students working individually.[10] This is particularly true when the activity is of a problem-solving nature, but does not always apply to drill and practice software, word processing or keyboarding skills.

> "**C**hildren who work together at a computer are routinely observed to correct each other's mistakes, cooperate in the completion of assigned tasks, and discuss the assignments in ways that clarify the task, even when neither partner appears to understand it at the outset....Growing evidence suggests that collaboration at a machine reduces low-level errors and creates support for higher level activities."[11]

For students with special needs, providing a "buddy" often makes it possible for them to participate in the regular activities of the classroom. A buddy can help a physically disadvantaged student manipulate equipment, read for a non-reader, check organization and completeness for a learning disabled classmate, help a distractible partner to stay on task, or communicate in the first language of a non-English–speaking friend. When faced with a particular student whose needs are very specific, the role of a buddy is easy to define. Partnerships and teaming help to foster interpersonal and intrapersonal skills and create an interdependence that assists in "developing social skills and [promotes] effectiveness in increasing learning, recall, and applications.... The world needs people who not only can use the technological tools of the age but who can do so as part of a team."[12]

Cooperative and collaborative learning groups are another way to provide the support the exceptional student often needs. A group of students can watch a video or listen to an audiotape together, or work on an interactive computer program. The teacher's skill in facilitating cooperative learning and the students' teamwork skills are just as important when using computers as in any other cooperative learning experience. Guidelines for group work, developed with the students, will help learning experiences to run smoothly. When roles are carefully assigned to group members, each student gets a chance to contribute in a meaningful way to the final product. For example, the gifted student can be given a more challenging role such as facilitator, recorder, checker, or questioner, whereas a less able student might fare best in a role such as materials manager, time-keeper, or noise monitor. It is not always necessary for all students in a learning group to complete an identical activity. In fact, an assignment can be structured such that some students are expected to do the basics while others include enrichment. The cooperative part of the task is in the helping, editing, and checking. Self-esteem is enhanced and confidence will grow. "The Internet provides another avenue for collaboration — across classrooms!"[13] Students can correspond with keypals, participate in cross-classroom projects, work with a mentor, ask questions of and discuss issues with experts, and publish their own work on the World Wide Web. These five types of collaboration are available on the Internet and allow students to interface with others and solve problems, share knowledge, and learn cooperatively. Gifted students in particular benefit from using the "real world" to pursue their studies through use of the Internet.

Modifying Your Program

It is neither realistic nor desirable to strive for a classroom in which students work on individualized programs or in cooperative learning groups all the time. Whole-class instruction remains an integral part of the learning process, and many students learn very well this way. An eclectic mix of approaches produces the best results. By modifying the process, content, and product of your program, you can enable the exceptional student to function as a competent class member in the whole-group setting.

Process

The process and context in which technology is integrated in the classroom may include modifications, accommodations, and adapations to the instructional setting, as well as to strategies and resources available to the special needs student. In earlier chapters, we have pointed out furniture and space considerations for a physically disabled student or a student requiring specialized equipment. A laptop computer may be the best solution for a student whose mobility is extremely restricted. For a highly distractible student, a single desk or study carrel may be required as a space for concentration when he or she is involved in an individual pursuit. Some simple routines can make life much easier for exceptional students and save a lot of frustration. For example, before expecting students to complete a task individually, try doing one or more similar tasks as a whole group. This modeling could result in sample pages of work in each notebook that remind students of your requirements (e.g., format, titles, organization). Show videos to the whole group and have some discussion before requiring students to look at them again for a specific purpose. When introducing new computer software, demonstrate it briefly to the whole class before letting students explore on their own. These routines will benefit all students and are often life-savers for certain exceptional students. Color coding of different workstations and/or activities is helpful to the learning disabled, non-English–speaking, or mentally handicapped student who may otherwise have difficulty keeping track of movement and organizing work. You may need to break some tasks down into smaller steps or add more visual examples for certain students to be successful in working from written directions. This means considering how and what curriculum is presented, the materials used, the instructional strategies and methods, the sensory modality, the instructional setting, the amount and the pace of the task.

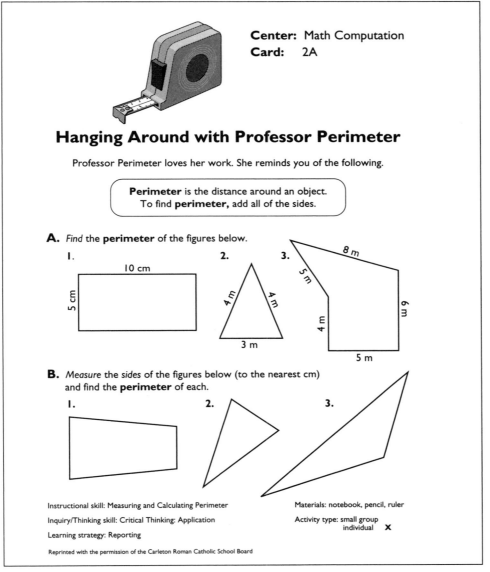

Center: Math Computation
Card: 2A

Hanging Around with Professor Perimeter

Professor Perimeter loves her work. She reminds you of the following.

> **Perimeter** is the distance around an object.
> To find **perimeter**, add all of the sides.

A. *Find* the **perimeter** of the figures below.

1. 10 cm / 5 cm

2. 4 m / 4 m / 3 m

3. 8 m / 5 m / 4 m / 6 m / 5 m

B. *Measure* the *sides* of the figures below (to the nearest cm) and find the **perimeter** of each.

1.

2.

3.

Instructional skill: Measuring and Calculating Perimeter

Inquiry/Thinking skill: Critical Thinking: Application

Learning strategy: Reporting

Materials: notebook, pencil, ruler

Activity type: small group
individual **X**

Reprinted with the permission of the Carleton Roman Catholic School Board

Figure 8-5

Highlighting key words on an activity card can help an exceptional student clearly understand what to do. When you make cards using a word-processing program, simply bold, underline, change the font, or change the size of the most important words.

"Use of the computers proves especially helpful to the children because the computers give them control over their own learning. On the one hand, the computer is very calm and patient with children who need different amounts of time to learn a word, read a sentence, or identify a picture. On the other hand, the computer is tremendously dynamic — the children get very excited by the voices, music and sound effects the computer adds to a story."[14]

Audiotapes of reading selections are often necessary for the student with reading difficulties. They allow the student to listen and read along. Conversely, a written copy of listening activities may be required for a hearing-impaired or non-English–speaking student. When teaching intellectually challenged students to use technology, avoid using highly technical terms, provide visual cues to accompany your auditory presentation, and allow time for lots of hands-on practice. Post a list of operating instructions at each piece of equipment for reference. By providing a relaxed, comfortable learning environment, you enable all your students to feel secure and you encourage risk-taking.

Content

For some exceptional students, the content of your program may present challenges. It is necessary to modify or accommodate the curriculum expectations of your program to the special needs student. This is an area in which technology can be very useful. Look for computer programs that are self-paced, allow the student to work slowly in small steps, and provide instant feedback. There are many software packages available with these features.

> "**T**echnology is integrated when it is used in a seamless manner to support and extend curriculum objectives and to engage students in meaningful learning. It is not something one does separately; it is part of the daily activities taking place in the classroom. Technology enriches the activity and enables students to demonstrate what they know in new and creative ways."[15]

The potential of e-books for exceptional students with a wide range of disabilities is considerable and already being reported by teachers. For students with reading problems, electronic text allows a computer to read the text aloud while highlighting the words on the computer screen. For students with visual disabilities, spoken text is also an obvious advantage. For students who have difficulty opening books and turning pages, e-books provide an independent way to access books. Although these features have long been available on desktop computers, portability and "anytime, anywhere" access is a leap forward.[16]

The multimedia nature of CD-ROM, DVD, and videodisc technology is especially beneficial in the presentation of abstract ideas. Many science concepts that are difficult to explain can be presented in a way that makes them easy to understand through electronic media. Magnetism is a good example. If you have ever tried to explain to students how atoms become aligned with like poles facing the same way in a magnetized needle, you will appreciate the ease with which this can be done on a well-produced videodisc or electronic encyclopedia. Many electronic encyclopedias on CD-ROM also have charts, film clips, and graphics that help students to understand content.

> **"T**he teaching characteristics of multimedia — the integration of video, audio, text and graphics — match the learning needs of students with learning disabilities.
>
> "All learners, not just learning disabled, benefit from the enhanced multi-sensory characteristics of multimedia."[17]

Product

Sometimes you may be expecting a significantly different product from the exceptional student than from the rest of your students because the learning goal for this student is completely different. In many cases, however, exceptional students can use the same materials and produce a final product appropriate for their levels of ability. The following strategies help in setting attainable standards for students with special needs, whether they are engaged with technology or not:

- Reduce the number of workstations, by eliminating those that are inappropriate, on the student's individual tracking sheet.
- Reduce the number of questions given on an assignment card.
- Provide more structure by giving the student a prepared answer sheet or template (e.g., fill in the blanks).
- Allow the student to use a calculator, computer, or concrete materials whenever required.
- Allow the student to respond on audiocassette rather than in writing.
- Ask for pictures or diagrams instead of language.
- Conference with the student to allow for oral responding instead of written.
- Give the student a small amount to do at one time, set a suitable time frame within which you expect it to be done, and provide frequent feedback.
- Provide the student an exemplar of the assignment as reference during task completion.
- Pair the student up with a "buddy" who can offer assistance when needed.

> **"T**he use of technology can provide powerful assistance to students who have much to say but difficulty in saying it. I remember one Grade 6 student, Luis, who had a communicational exceptionality, and as well, an ESL background. His class was researching animal classifications and the processes of life common to all living things. The students were required to present their findings in a form of their own choice. After gathering key information from various resources including books, CD-ROMs and Internet Web sites, Luis decided to use a presentation software program to demonstrate what he had learned. In addition to written text, his slides included hand-drawn and scanned pictures, as well as dubbed-in sound effects and oral descriptions of some of the text on the slides. An oral presentation of a traditional nature would have been a definite challenge for Luis. But the huge smile on his face following his multimedia presentation reinforced the idea that technology can go a long way to support successful student learning."[18]

Hand-held computers can be motivational and help students to organize. Older students often like to organize their own computer desktops and manage applications.

> **"W**hen I started high school, I was looking for a way to keep myself organized and interested. The Palm devices did just that. I started out with a Palm III handheld. I kept notes, homework, and flash card applications on it. Then, I began to add different school programs such as a periodic table, a scientific calculator, etc. … I am now in my junior year of high school, and I keep programs like PalmStats [Statistics Program], a scientific calculator, a graphing calculator, and Flash! [a flash card program]. Recently, I ordered wireless Internet, and now I can do even more work on the go. So far, I have used it to get encyclopedia articles, get definitions to words, and even get answers to questions when they weren't in the book."[19]

The computer is often used as a tool to assist with writing and publishing for students with special needs. Word processing is a terrific benefit for the student who has great difficulty with handwriting. It is a powerful motivator that produces a final product to be proud of — no messy eraser marks. Word processing and desktop publishing activities permit the use of graphics, fonts, spellcheck, and grammarcheck, which assist in increased concentration on the writing process and less focus on fine motor difficulties. Students will often write more and produce better quality written work. Providing students with frequent activities will allow them to move from novice to apprentice to practitioner to expert user of word processing and desktop publishing software.

Figure 8-6

Create task cards that are color-coded to represent novice, apprentice, practitioner, and expert learning experiences. Instructions for the task card are written on one side of the card and an exemplar of the learning experience is on the other side of the card. Provide students the opportunity to complete a task card at a computer workstation. The students choose a task card that they feel is at their ability level. This type of activity promotes choice and reflective practice with their increasing use of technology for learning.

Goldberg Machine

1. Create an absurdly-connected machine that does a very simple task in a complex roundabout way. In other words, a machine that performs a very simple task in a totally convoluted manner.

2. Some ideas: feeding your cat / tying your shoe / an alarm clock / frying an egg

Rube Goldberg, cartoonist, believed that there are two ways to do things, the simple way and the hard way, and that a surprisingly number of people preferred doing things the hard way. Checkout the website: http://www.rube-goldberg.com/bio.htm

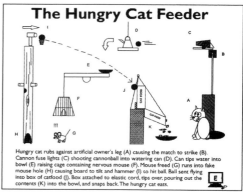

The Hungry Cat Feeder

Hungry cat rubs against artificial owner's leg (A) causing the match to strike (B). Cannon fuse lights (C) shooting cannonball into watering can (D). Can tips water into bowl (E) raising cage containing nervous mouse (F). Mouse freed (G) runs into fake mouse hole (H) causing board to tilt and hammer (I) to hit ball. Ball sent flying into box of catfood (J). Box attached to elastic cord, tips over, pouring out the contents (K) into the bowl, and snaps back. The hungry cat eats.

Create a Toy

1. Create a toy.
2. You must use at least 3 different shapes. ■ ★ ⬣
3. Name your toy.

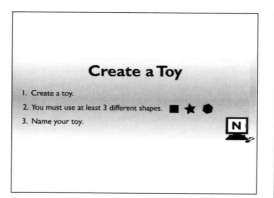

Tag-along Toy

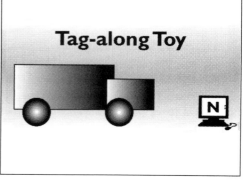

Assistive Technology and Adaptive Devices for Special Students

The potential of technology to assist students with a variety of exceptionalities is virtually unlimited. Assistive technology offers innovative technology solutions for communicating and learning through customizable hardware and software tools. Though it is likely that resource people within your school system (special education teachers, consultants, etc.) and the parents of the child will be the decision makers in this regard, be aware of some of the possibilities that technology allows. Hardware adaptations include alternative keyboards with overlays, and mouse alternatives such as trackballs and trackpads, and portable electronic word processors. Software adaptations to standard operating systems include assisted keyboard features such as mouse keys, sticky keys, repeat keys, and slow keys. It is possible to design an overlay for a keyboard where keys launch a series of multimedia images complete with captions, animation, and recorded sound. Keys can also be programmed to speak and read back words, phrases, or sentences. Dedicated software programs include talking word processors, word prediction programs, and voice-recognition programs. Skill-building software teaches key language and cognitive skills such as phonological awareness, rhyming, and sound discrimination; direction following, working memory, and eye-hand coordination.

Alternative Input Devices

Some students have difficulty inputting or are unable to input into the computer in the traditional manner through the keyboard, trackball, or mouse. Devices presently available to assist these students include
- computers that operate through voice recognition;
- joysticks, paddles, and switches to be operated with the hand, foot, chin, or the raising of an eyebrow;
- keyguards, which are flat boards with finger holes that fit over the standard keyboard to stabilize hands and prevent accidental contact with the keys;
- plastic keyboard overlays that fit over the entire keyboard allowing for temporary labeling or color coding and protecting from spills or drooling;
- miniature keyboards requiring very little movement or force;
- king-sized keyboards that are less sensitive to touch so that students cannot accidentally hit several keys at a time if they have a spasm;
- power pads that are touch sensitive, used instead of a keyboard;
- touch-sensitive programmable membrane boards that can be applied to the monitor to allow it to be used as a touch screen;
- keyboards that have keys representing sounds rather than letters;
- head control devices;
- voice input systems;

- scanners that scan text, visuals, and 3-D objects from outside sources into the computer;
- Braille computers.

These are only some of the wide variety of alternative input devices that allow a special student to participate in regular classroom learning experiences and to optimize individual competencies.

> **"All children will learn: not on the same day; not in the same way."**[21]

Alternative Output Devices

Traditional methods of receiving output from the computer can also be a problem for some students. Again, new developments in technology can assist these students. Some of these include

- magnified video display screens for use with video playback or computer;
- talking word processors for writing and communication;
- speech synthesizers allowing for audio output;
- Braille output devices.

Technology has the potential to help teachers better meet student needs by allowing individual students to learn in their preferred way. As technology advances and school systems find more ways to use technology, the hope is that it will become a tool that can give all students opportunities to succeed not only in school but also in future work and in life itself.

> **"Society is in trouble, but there is hope! Every one of us must serve as models for our children. All it takes is one human being to unconditionally love and support a child, and s/he can be turned around. Children are very flexible!"**[22]

Web-based Resources

The Internet is an incredibly effective communication and learning tool that assists with managing change by permitting you to access educational research and network the sharing of ideas, resources, and information on a global basis. The Internet has virtually limitless uses for teachers, students, and parents. At the publisher's Web site you'll find links to these sites that offer excellent supports for Special Education teachers in the way of resources, links, and current practice.

- Special Needs Opportunity Window
- Council for Exceptional Children
- Internet Resources for Special Children
- Ldonline
- Special Needs Network
- KidsConnect
- Closing the Gap
- Education and Special Education Links
- Sarah's Special Needs Resource Page

There are excellent resources, different perspectives, and a vast amount of support on the Internet that assist in understanding and programming for the exceptional learner. It is rewarding to implement with success an idea, strategy, or lesson from a "net" resource that would have been otherwise not available.

Summing Up

Technology fosters three very important skills: exploring, expressing, and exchanging. These skills contribute to learning that is open-ended, individualized, hands-on, interactive, and collaborative. All students, with their diverse needs and specific strengths and weaknesses, can thrive in such a classroom culture.

> **"The power of technology for learning emerges through the choices it provides students of different abilities, talents, and academic strengths. Every student will have the same access to learning by working with teachers to make informed decisions about how information is found, represented, expressed, and engaged. For example, advances in streaming media will enable students who respond best to visual stimulation watch a book unfold via streaming media delivered over the Web. Innovations in 3-D graphics will allow a student to create a virtual identity and perhaps enter the story as a virtual character in a simulated world. At the same time, developments in voice recognition and voice synthesis will empower students unable to type or use a mouse to interact with technology with nothing more than their voices. Advances in computer vision will add the ability to interact with technology through gestures and even facial expressions. Students with a flare for the artistic can express math concepts through graphic representations while young writers express the same concepts in words. Learning will become more inclusive, engaging students on a personal level tailored to individual needs and interests."[23]**

TECHNOLOGY TOOLS FOR TEACHERS

nine

"We strive to acquire digital tools in order to empower students to accept new roles in their own learning and to expand their possibilities for collaboration and construction of knowledge. Teachers who model effective learning behaviors send a powerful message to their students about the value of learning and gain credibility as co-learners."[1]

It's great to see your students motivated and excited by the power of technology! Now — what about you, the teacher? Just as students using technology are more motivated by tasks and exhibit more care in their final products, so technology has the power to energize teachers, increase their productivity, create pride in their accomplishments, and renew the challenge of teaching. Furthermore, computer use is associated with professionalism in our society — facility in using a computer has become one of the marks of an educated person. For teachers, computer proficiency is essential. As the technology changes and as new theories emerge regarding the role of technology in learning, continuing on-the-job training is important. Most teachers want to use technology and see that technology holds potential for them, but many also need encouragement to invest the time required for the change. They realize that the very opportunities opened by the computer initially make tasks more difficult and time-consuming. Nonetheless, computer literacy for teachers is an investment that will pay off handsomely in the long run.

"All too frequently, technology is still placed only in the hands of students, while teachers are forgotten and the importance of learning by example is ignored."[2]

In Chapter 3: Making It Work, we presented an overview of a variety of applications and their potential uses in the classroom, with a focus on what students can do with each. In this chapter, we change the focus to what *teachers* can do with these tools. Our aim is to point out some ways in which using a computer can make you more productive, more creative, and more flexible in your profession. We examine computer use for lesson planning and presentation, on-line communication, and administrative tasks.

> **"If computer technology is to have an impact on teaching and learning, teachers must be comfortable with computers, seeing them as tools that enhance rather than interfere with their daily teaching."[3]**

Lesson Planning and Presentation

Both long- and short-term planning are best done using a flexible tool that allows easy editing and modification because timetables, unit plans, weekly schedules, and daily plans are all susceptible to interference by unscheduled interruptions and special events.

Any word processor or desktop publishing application will do the job nicely for you. Once you have set up a suitable daily or weekly planning template, you can enter events and learning experiences quickly and make the required changes simply. If you are fortunate enough to have a computer on your desk, there's no need to print out a paper copy. Even if you have to share a computer with your students, it's still more efficient to enter and print out your next day's plans than to write them by hand once you get used to it. Try a variety of formats until you find one that best suits your needs.

Some school districts and departments of education have developed electronic planners specifically designed for implementation of their mandated curriculum. Although their use may require a shift in the type of planning you are used to doing, it's worth trying one out. The advantages of such tools are the rigor and consistency of units developed and the ease of sharing among teachers across the district (see Fig. 9-1).

Some lessons are best presented directly from the computer, for example, using a spreadsheet to demonstrate number patterns in mathematics; a graphics program to demonstrate the effect of color on mood; or a computer-assisted learning module to introduce a new skill. A data projector, or an LCD (liquid crystal display) tablet used on an overhead projector, allows projection from the computer onto a large screen for whole-class lessons. By substituting an LCD tablet or data projector for the blackboard, you can prepare a lesson before class on the computer, store it, and re-use it from class to class or in subsequent years. The quality of the presentation is better than from the blackboard, it is quickly and easily modifiable, and the whole class can share a single computer without crowding around a small monitor.

From formal presentations to the generation of samples of creative writing or math equations, more useful material can be created in a shorter period of time using a computer.

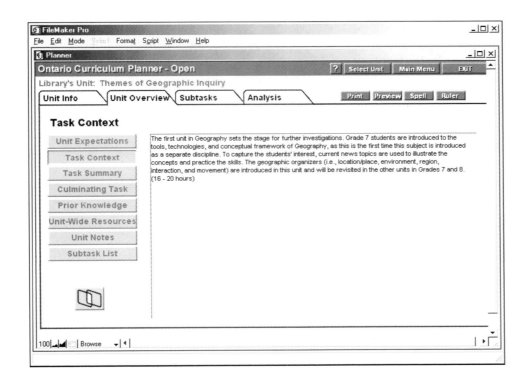

Figure 9-1

This electronic curriculum unit planner allows teachers to create, share, and modify unit plans. The Filemaker Pro database offers timesaving features such as the ability to easily insert learning outcomes, teaching strategies, or assessment tools rather than tediously typing them yourself.

> **❝...once teachers are competent 'productivity tool' users, they frequently search for ways to use these same computer powers to enhance their classroom instruction."[4]**

With the increasing role of digital imagery in our world, teachers are exploring ways to use primary sources in classroom instruction. The University of Virginia's Digital Media Center (http://www.lib.virginia.edu/clemons/RMC/collections-home.html) has assembled links to sites with image resources that can be used in K–12 schools at this time. Other on-line sources at the publisher's Web site include image banks, lesson plans, and integration ideas.[5]

Multimedia is an exciting way to create classroom presentations, and some lessons lend themselves well to the diversity multimedia brings. HyperStudio, PowerPoint, Corel Presentations, and ClarisHomePage are some of the most useful tools for teacher-created multimedia lessons. The process of creating a multimedia lesson is labor-intensive and requires careful planning, but the benefit is that once you have invested the initial time into its creation, you have a product you can use over again many times. A bank of shared lessons quickly emerges when a group of teachers of the same grade each prepares a few.

> **❝Depending on their style, some teachers teach themselves multimedia; others learn it from their fellow teachers or from their students. Teachers who are successful find ways to use multimedia personally to:**
> - **make presentations**
> - **transform textbook materials into a multimedia format**
> - **conduct original research**
> - **bring new life to 'tired' knowledge**
> - **renew their commitment to teaching."[6]**

If you feel ready to tackle the challenge of creating a multimedia lesson presentation, try using the following seven steps as a guideline:

- Identify a specific content area.
- Have a clear understanding of what the students will be able to do at the end of the lesson.
- Develop an outline to organize and sequence content.
- Create a checklist of appropriate media materials for inclusion.
- Consider a variety of presentation methods.
- Create a storyboard.
- Produce the lesson.[7]

For those times when you teach using an overhead projector, you can't beat PowerPoint and Corel Presentations for the design of professional, effective overhead transparencies.

Web-based Lessons

You don't need to develop your own multimedia lessons. With an Internet connection to the computer from which you are projecting, you can teach directly from the Web. Whole-group lessons come alive with dynamic Web sites providing authentic, immediate, multimedia content. You can take your students on a virtual tour of an art gallery, a rain forest, or the inside of a volcano. Try these sites to see what on-line tours offer:

- The Thinker — Unlike many museum sites, which share only a small fragment of their collection on-line, more than 70,000 images are available from this American museum.
- Smithsonian — Offers a rich collection of treasures, including paintings and artifacts.
- Adventures are available at a site where you can choose from canoeing, kayaking, horseback riding, rock climbing, mountain biking, skiing, and more.

Webcams show images captured by a digital camera directly attached to a computer located somewhere in the world. Many aquariums and zoos are using Webcams to make their exhibits available on-line. These sites can provide opportunities for students to observe and collect real data, to make inferences about their observations and test their validity. Take a look at some Webcams by following the links at the publisher's Web site.[8]

Businesses and government agencies place data in on-line data banks, thus providing real data for authentic student investigations. This data can be useful in social sciences, humanities and mathematics explorations. For example, the "Exploring Data" Web site (http://exploringdata.cqu.edu.au/) developed by the Education Services Directorate in Queensland, Australia, provides a wide variety of data sets ranging from air pollution to pottery. Often this data can be transferred from the Web site to your school server and opened in a spreadsheet such as Microsoft Excel. Remember that when data is acquired from the Web, students must be taught how to evaluate the credibility of the source. You can find some on-line databanks by following the links at the publisher's Web site.[9]

Webcasts, as the name suggests, are live broadcasts over the Web. They generally include a presentation from an expert in a certain field and provide an opportunity for students to ask questions. Support materials such as Teachers' Guides, biographies, background information, and archives are often provided. Timing is critical to using Webcasts in the educational setting, as they take place on specific days and times. You might consider making arrangements for students to access a large screen for greater participation and engagement.

Figure 9-2

This NASA Webcast (http://quest.arc.nasa.gov/aero/ events/marsplane/) focuses on planetary flight. The page also has links to the curriculum standards addressed by the activity.

Opportunities for small-group and individual on-line lessons abound on the Web.

Ten time-saving Web tips for teachers:
1. **Collaborate with your colleagues.**
2. **Collect favorite education sites instead of searching anew each time.**
3. **Bookmark favorites and keep your bookmarks organized into folders by category.**
4. **Back up your favorites file on a diskette from time to time.**
5. **Find a search engine you like, get to know it, and stick with it.**
6. **As soon as you see that your search is not turning up what you seek, reconsider your keyword(s).**
7. **If a URL gives you one of those "file not found messages," try shortening it by removing file extensions. (e.g., If www.trifolium.org/pubs/books/techclass/index.htm doesn't work, try www.trifolium.org/pubs/books/techclass/ and then try www.trifolium.org/pubs, etc.)**
8. **Try the least busy times on the Web: early morning and late at night.**
9. **Set aside a small amount of weekly Web time, just for staying up to date and keeping your files organized.**
10. **Use on-line tutorials for learning new technology skills from the comfort of your own home.**

Student Materials

Student handouts and worksheets created on the computer can be cleaner, sharper, and more interesting than those produced by hand. You can easily add graphics that make worksheets more appealing, especially to younger students. A good desktop publishing program makes the creation of student worksheets a creative and efficient task.

Many teachers are now using electronic worksheets instead of paper. These may incorporate active links to Web pages, allowing for quick and easy access to teacher pre-selected Web sites.

Figure 9-3

This electronic worksheet for young students was created in ClarisWorks/AppleWorks 5.0. It incorporates a spreadsheet into a drawing program. Students simply input their data and print.

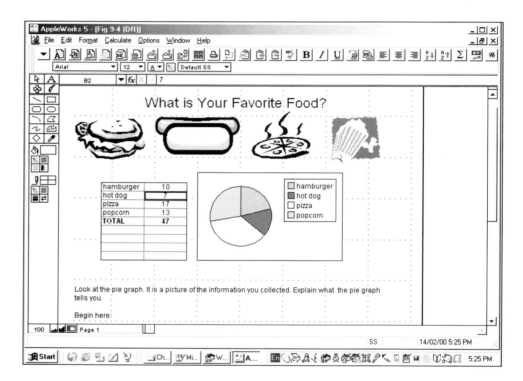

Links to Chapter 3:
What can teachers do with word processing software?
- write, store, and easily revise long-range, unit, and daily lesson plans
- create student worksheets

What can teachers do with desktop publishing software?
- create student worksheets and activity cards
- design and print certificates and awards

What can teachers do with graphics software?
- design posters for clubs and events
- create graphic organizers such as Venn diagrams, concept maps, and flow charts

What can teachers do with multimedia software?
- use Hyperstudio instead of overheads to enhance lessons and help reach visual learners
- share Hyperstudio lessons with colleagues

INTERNET ADDRESSES

1. http://seds.lpl.arizona.edu/nineplanets/nineplanets/nineplanets.html
2. http://www.tcsn.net/afiner/title.htm
3. http://pds.jpl.nasa.gov/planets

RESEARCH QUESTIONS

Name of Planet: _____

Size of Planet: _____

Distance from the Sun:_____

Atmosphere (main gases): _____

Number of Moons: _____

Any Rings? (How many?):_____

Length of Rotation (around own axis): _____

Length of Revolution (around the sun): _____

Temperature:_____

Physical Characteristics/Composition: _____

Gravity: _____

Figure 9-4

This simple electronic worksheet, created in Microsoft Word 97, incorporates active links to space-related Web sites. Most relatively new versions of word processors have the capability to include active links that take students directly to the sites they need.[10]

- make electronic flash cards and quizzes
- create engaging activities as an alternative to reading text
- show student projects and electronic portfolios at interview time

What can teachers do with presentation software?

- create multimedia lessons
- guide students through the main points of a discussion
- support concepts with graphs and charts
- make attractive overhead transparencies

What can teachers do with video technology?

- film student speeches and have students use them for self-evaluation
- play videos of students at work for parents while they wait for their interview with you
- bring back a record of a trip to the forest, museum, or anywhere else
- record a science experiment

Teachers often invite parents to visit their child's classroom. For a high-tech alternative, a Webcam set up in the classroom can broadcast to the school's Web site. This provides an opportunity for parents to peek into the classroom at any time (or certain selected times) for a real-time view of the learning that's going on. Security issues must be addressed by obtaining permission for transmission at the beginning of the school year.

Assorted Teacher Utilities

Software designed specifically to facilitate everyday teacher tasks is now readily available, for example, puzzle-generating software and Web sites. Teachers often use various kinds of puzzles to reinforce vocabulary, practice spelling, or develop thinking skills.

Figure 9-5

With a puzzle generator such as Puzzlemaker (http://puzzlemaker.school. discovery.com/) or Hot Potatoes (http://hotpotatoes.com), crossword puzzles, word searches, cryptograms, math squares, and mazes are quick and easy to develop. Students can also make puzzles for their classmates.

If you have ever tried to create a concept map or web using a publishing or word-processing tool, you know how time consuming it can be. Inspiration, from Inspiration Software, Inc. (http://www.inspiration.com), is the software tool for this task. Using Inspiration, you can create concept maps, diagrams, outlines, and flow charts with ease.

Blackboard.com (http://www.blackboard.com) is a popular Web site for on-line courses. It is much easier to build an on-line course using the Blackboard.com tools than starting from scratch using HTML. Blackboard Course Sites provide templates and other applications for both creating and taking on-line courses. A resources area makes customizable educational content available for educators to incorporate into their courses. The Blackboard Company licences server products on levels, with various different possibilities for installation and maintenance. Large school districts may choose to host their own servers; smaller ones may access a shared server.[11]

The assessment and evaluation tools described in Chapter 7: Assessing Student Progress might also be considered teacher utilities, such as test-generating software, which either provides data banks of items from which to choose or allows you to create your own items. The test can be printed out and duplicated for student use. Some testing packages enable students to take the test on-screen, and, upon completion, the computer marks responses and provides immediate results. These results are then compiled for teacher access — a lot of valuable time is saved. The exciting potential of electronic portfolios is also discussed in Chapter 7: Assessing Student Progress. Multimedia software such as Hyperstudio allows students to document their progress relative to mastery of specific outcomes supported with audio and video evidence.

On-line Communication

Many school administrators use internal e-mail to communicate with teachers and office staff, hopefully decreasing the number of staff and committee meetings. Teachers are required to be e-mail literate as an increasing amount of job-related information is disseminated by this medium. In most cases, e-mail accounts and training are provided by schools or districts, and you can make arrangements to load the appropriate software onto your home computer.

Free electronic mail accounts are available from
- **Yahoo E-mail**
- **American School Directory**
- **RocketMail**
- **Excite**
- **HotMail**
- **Juno 1-800-654-5866**
- **Find out about other free e-mail options using the Free E-mail Guide — follow the link at the publisher's Web site.**

Most e-mail programs will allow you to
- send electronic mail to a specified address
- send one or more carbon copies
- reply to electronic mail sent to you
- forward electronic mail
- set up an address book with "nicknames" for addresses you use frequently
- save messages to a file
- send enclosures or attachments
- automatically include a customized signature
- delete electronic messages
- store messages in folders

None of these tasks are difficult; with a little mentoring and practice, you can quickly and easily become a proficient e-mail user.

Telecommunications can link you to other teachers, to subject experts, and to the many organizations that provide resources and assistance to educators. Joining a listserver (or listserv) is an immediate way to connect with other teachers who are using the Internet. Listservers are special-interest groups available through the Internet. Members post messages, and listserv software redistributes them to all members of a given discussion group. In order to join a listserver, you need only basic knowledge of how to send an e-mail message and specific information on how to subscribe to any given list. To participate, simply send a subscription message ("subscribe <listserver name> <your name>") to the listserver address (e.g., listserv@msu.edu). Once you've subscribed, you will begin receiving messages from the list. You will be able to contribute your ideas and thoughts directly to the group, too, by using the group e-mail address (e.g., edtech@msu.edu). Once you have subscribed to a listserv, you will receive important introductory information from the list owner. Save this message! It may be useful to print the message and keep it in a binder. Whenever you want to suspend your subscription, you will want exact information on how to unsubscribe.

Some discussion groups for educators:
ArtsEdNet Talk
- **Arts education discussion.**
- **Subscribe to artsednet-request@pub.getty.edu**

CREWRT-L
- **Creative writing — how and why creative writing is being taught.**
- **Subscribe to listserv@umcvmb.missouri.edu**

Edtech
- **A discussion group for use of technology in education. An excellent place to begin appreciating the potential of technology.**
- **Subscribe to listserv@msu.edu**

Ednet
- **A discussion group for educational networking.**
- **Subscribe to listserv@lists.umass.edu**

K12-webdev
- **A mailing list for K–12 Web site developers.**
- **Subscribe to list@mail.lr.k12.nj.us**

K12small
- **A forum for education in small or rural schools.**
- **Subscribe to listserv@uafsysb.uark.edu**

Kidlit-L
- **A forum for the discussion of children's literature.**
- **Subscribe to listserv@bingvmb.cc.binghamton.edu**

Kidsphere
- **Extremely popular list for elementary and secondary school teachers. The volume of mail on this list tends to be high, but it is a stimulating place to begin using the Internet as a professional tool.**
- **Subscribe to kidsphere-request@vms.cis.pitt.edu**

LRN-Ed
- **Support and information for K-12 teachers.**
- **Subscribe to listserv@listserv.syr.edu**

SchoolNet
- **General educational focus. One of a number of SchoolNet lists.**
- **Subscribe to listproc@schoolnet.ca**

SNEtalk-L
- **General discussion in the area of special needs education.**
- **Subscribe to listproc@schoolnet.carleton.ca**

TESLK–12
- **Teaching English as a second language in K–12.**

- **Subscribe to listserv@cunyvm.cuny.edu.**

Webtalk
- **For teachers attempting to develop Web sites and make use of the Web in their classrooms.**
- **Subscribe to majordomo@teachers.net**

In addition to listservers, a growing number of discussion groups are published on the Web. These may be called on-line forums, message boards, or on-line conferences. You can review current messages and post replies directly on the Web. The downside to forums is that you need to be on-line to view messages, and posted messages may be quite out of date if a forum is not particularly active. Try these forums:

- Teacher Talk
- Educator's Forum
- TalkCity Education Center
- Teacher-2-Teacher
- Discovery Channel School Forum
- PedagoNet

Picture yourself participating in an on-line conference about using new software, in which you can share your own experiences, read those of others, and "chat" with colleagues in real time. After the conference ends, you can exchange worksheets and lessons. In these days of diminishing resources in education, the ability to conference, consult, collaborate, and share with peers efficiently is increasingly important.

Links to Chapter 3:
What can teachers do with e-mail?
- **correspond with family, friends, and colleagues**
- **ask a question of an expert**
- **collaborate with peers on a common project**

What can teachers do with listservs?
- **learn about the latest in their subject specialty**
- **keep up to date on special events, conferences, etc.**

What can teachers do with newsgroups?
- **pose a discussion question to students**
- **read the opinions of other teachers about educational issues**
- **collaborate with peers on a common project**

What can teachers do with Web conferencing?
- **collaborate with peers on a common project**
- **chat with students or peers**
- **share files such as text, images, and music**

What can teachers do with IRC?
- **collaborate with peers on a common project**
- **chat with students or peers**
- **access information and opinions from outside the classroom**
- **interview an expert**

What can teachers do with Web publishing software?
- **create Web-based lessons**
- **add a distance learning component to a course or unit of study**
- **post assignments, handouts, and homework**

More and more teachers are using the Web to communicate with students and parents. Teachers are developing their own Web pages posted either on their school site, their personal Internet Service Provider's site, or one of the many free spaces available on the Internet, such as http://www.geocities.com. Students will have difficulty keeping their homework assignments secret from their parents once they are easily available on the Web. Many school systems around the world are experimenting with secure, password-protected sites through which parents can access their children's grades, attendance records, assignments, and disciplinary reports. Several free sites offer an on-line environment where teachers can post assignments, publish student work, and send and receive messages from parents.[12]

Administrative Tasks

Computers can expedite administrative tasks, thus giving you more time to teach. Some school districts provide software licensed for teacher use at home. If not, an integrated package or suite is a wise choice of home software to purchase. A typical package might include a word processor, spreadsheet, and graphics program. As an example of how using the computer can make your communications with parents more direct and personal, personalizing letters is easy using the mail-merge feature of a word processor. Simply identify the variable portion of your letter (e.g., name and address), create a list of the variable information, and print out the letters, with the computer changing the variable information each time.

A database is the easiest way to keep track of a variety of student information, such as names, addresses, telephone numbers, birth dates, names of parents or guardians, bus routes, health issues, and emergency information. Your school secretary may already have this information, which could be passed on to you on a disk or by e-mail. If not, it may take a couple of hours for you to enter the data, but the subsequent ability to sort, modify, access, and print specific information as required makes the initial work most worthwhile. You can re-use your database template from year to year.

> **"The important point to be made is the virtually instantaneous retrieval of data and the ability to pass that data on to someone else with a minimum of effort. Once you have such a system [class database]...you will not ever want to go back to the old way."[13]**

A spreadsheet can be used to maintain a budget, whether for classroom supplies, fund-raising events, a milk program, or a class trip. Spreadsheets are commonly used to keep track of marks or grades because they make it easy to total scores and find averages. Commercially available gradebook or marks management software allows you to input marks, assign differential weighting for various tests and assignments, and immediately see the final results. Student information can be sorted, and space is often provided for teacher comments. In some cases, these may be linked to an electronic report card. You can also purchase software for attendance that allows you to record students' names, enter the times absent or late, and then do a variety of searches (e.g., by name, date, homeroom class). Using an integrated package, you can import from your database into various spreadsheets, thus saving time.

		Asmt 1	Weight	%	Asmt 2	Weight	%	Asmt 3	Weight	%	Final%	Mark
Armano	Mari	82	0.4	32.8	95	0.5	47.5	9	I	9.0	89.3	A
Atkinson	Jennifer	87	0.4	34.8	72	0.5	36.0	8	I	8.0	78.8	B+
Beare	Ron	82	0.4	32.8	87	0.5	43.5	7.5	I	7.5	83.8	A-
Chavez	Anita	82	0.4	32.8	72	0.5	36.0	7.5	I	7.5	76.3	B+
Cyr	Guy	72	0.4	28.8	82	0.5	41.0	8.5	I	8.5	78.3	B+
Davis	Shauna	82	0.4	32.8	82	0.5	41.0	9	I	9.0	82.8	A-
Fong	Loy	87	0.4	34.8	82	0.5	41.0	9.5	I	9.5	85.3	A
Hayward	Dayna	82	0.4	32.8	87	0.5	43.5	9	I	9.0	85.3	A

Figure 9-6

To obtain exactly the format you want, you might prefer to design your own spreadsheet for managing marks.

Links to Chapter 3:
What can teachers do with word-processing software?
• write and personalize parent letters
• prepare resumés, job applications, assignments, committee work
What can teachers do with an electronic database?
• record student information so it is easy to access, sort, and update
• maintain collections of curriculum resources or lesson plans
What can teachers do with spreadsheets?
• keep track of student marks
• keep track of book orders, milk money, excursion fees, etc.
• create budgets for special events such as ski trips, bake sales, etc.
• maintain an inventory of items that are out for repair, serial
   numbers of equipment, things borrowed and returned by students
What can teachers do with presentation software?
• introduce curriculum and programs at parents evenings
• present personal lectures for a workshop or conference
What can teachers do with video technology?
• play videos of students at work for parents while they wait for
   their interview with you

"September 28, 1999
SI am a second year band director in the public schools. Last year I had a difficult time keeping track of schedules, appointments, and practices. While I kept an old-style planner, I found that I left it in my office most of the time. When a new appointment was mentioned I had the intention of going back to my office and writing down the new date in my planner. While sometimes I remembered, other times I was interrupted by a student asking for help and put it on the back burner. This year one of my first back-to-school purchases was a PalmPilot™ Professional connected organizer. Because of its compact size, I keep my new planner with me at all

times and write down appointments immediately. Another great point about having this much power is that while I monitor study hall I can also get letters written to administrators, parents, and students. This has increased my productivity and given me more time to plan for my students."[14]

Imagine how effectively you can introduce your program at the initial parent meeting using multimedia presentation software. In the business world, this is how ideas are usually presented; as professionals in education we need to use the same tools. One of the big advantages, which makes it worth investing time in preparation, is the ease of updating your presentation from year to year.

Figure 9-7

Use presentation software such as PowerPoint or Corel Presentations to showcase your classroom learning experiences and plans to parents, administrators, and colleagues.

Training

A common response from teachers with whom we work, upon hearing of all these possibilities, is "This sounds great, but where, when, and how do I go about learning to do all these things?" Start by examining the opportunities in your locale. Once you are committed to becoming a lifelong learner with technology, look for mentors among your colleagues and courses at local high schools, software companies, community colleges, universities, and on the Internet. Training in specific software is often available in the form of daylong seminars or evening classes of short duration.

Sometimes the most efficient way to learn a piece of software is to first have an experienced user walk you through it, devote some time to personal experimentation, and practice, and then meet again with the "expert" for clarification and problem solving. There's no substitute for hands-on time when learning new software; jump in and tackle a task, keep the help menu handy as a reference tool, and be prepared to experience some frustration.

Some school districts and businesses now require job applicants to submit their resumés as Web pages. Though this may at first seem daunting, it is easier than you think. Claris HomePage, for example, includes a template for exactly this occasion. Just fill in your own information and e-mail your page as an attached file.

The strategies for teaching students to use technology detailed in Chapter 6 are the same strategies we can use:
- **demonstration**
- **free exploration**
- **guided exploration**
- **peer tutoring**
- **tutorials**

You can find lots of software training on the Internet. Begin by looking at the home page of the company who makes the software or try conducting a search for the specific software using its name plus the word "tutorial" or "training" as your keywords. Many school districts provide links to sites for software training to assist their employees in keeping their skills up to date.

On the Internet, you will also find lesson plans specifically designed to integrate technology, tips from teachers currently working with technology, and advice from experts in the field. Try some of these examples:

- How to Use the Internet in Your Classroom
  A combination of video, discussion, and Web activities.
- Tammy's Tech Tips
  Really practical classroom strategies.
- Kathy Schrock's Guide for Educators
  Teaching students how to evaluate Web sites.
- Multimedia Classrooms Inc; Classrooms without Walls
  Everything you want to know about using multimedia in the classroom.
- ThinkQuest
  Look at examples of student-created Web sites.

SchoolKiT is Microsoft's curriculum integration Web site. A free membership to SchoolKiT (http://www.schoolkit.com/) gives you access to the SchoolKiT REX software and some student activities at no cost. SchoolKiT GOLD is the paid subscription service, which gives you access to all of the libraries and new content and modules as they are released. Each SchoolKiT activity presents a curriculum-based challenge and launches the student into a Microsoft Office application. REX, the Resource Explorer, is the piece of software provided to install and keeps track of the SchoolKiT resources that you download to your computer.

Be on the lookout for on-line conferences; they provide outstanding professional development in your own home on your own schedule.

If integration of technology into the curriculum is a goal in your school system, you can expect that some training and support may be offered to teachers. You may also have an opportunity for input into the selection of offerings. Think of asking for workshops such as the following:

- Software solutions: technology resources for teachers
- Effective teaching and learning strategies with technology
- How to integrate technology into the curriculum
- Classroom computer and lab management strategies
- Databases and spreadsheets
- Digital camera, scanner, and working with photos
- Multimedia authoring
- Presentation tools
- Web page creation
- Internet issues in the classroom
- Collaborative Internet applications
- Internet-based student activities, e.g., WebQuests, Internet worksheets
- Grade/marks management software
- Tips from the field: experienced teachers present successful classroom strategies
- Sharing session: growing through shared experiences with peers
- Meeting the needs of exceptional learners with technology

If you are a person who works with teachers and technology, see *Learning and Leading with Technology*, November 1999. This issue is devoted to models for Professional Development. Also see *Secrets of Success: Professional Development that Works* by Jamie McKenzie in *From NowOn* (http://www.fromnowon.org) or *eSchool News*, March 1998.

Look for this type of practical assistance wherever you can find it. Conferences such as the International Society for Technology in Education (ISTE), the National Education Computing Conference (NECC), and the Educational Computing Organization of Ontario (ECOO) offer a variety of sessions for both beginners and experienced technology users. Both the workshops and resource displays at these conferences are very useful. Educational journals are also great for keeping in touch with the latest technologies and teaching ideas. Encourage your principal or librarian to invest in a school subscription to magazines like *Learning and Leading with Technology*, *Electronic Learning*, and *From Now On Online*. Of course, all these suggestions require a time commitment, so first explore the professional development opportunities in your school or school system. Quite often, money is set aside to free teachers from classroom duties for professional growth.

If you're a novice, keep these tips in mind as you go through the learning process:
- **It can be done.**
- **It's exciting, fun, and easy to use a computer.**
- **Don't be afraid to break it.**
- **Learning to use new hardware or new software can be difficult and frustrating at first, but it's always worth the trouble.**
- **Hang in there — the best is yet to come.**
- **No one is an expert.**
- **You can't learn it all in one day.**
- **You will never know it all.**[15]

If your school or school system administration is not helpful in the move to integrate technology, you can still pursue your personal goals. Contact colleagues in other schools and districts to find a support group. Try expressing your interest in educational technology on-line: you will meet a "virtual community" of people with a common interest. Utilize parent help, both for working with students and helping you to learn new software. Look for conference funding through professional associations and service organizations, and actively pursue assistance from the local business community through connections such as friends and parents. By sharing your enthusiasm with others, you will be part of a movement capable of creating change.

In Chapter 1: Why Integrate Technology, we cited lifelong learning as an essential skill in today's world. Lifelong learning means staying up to date by whatever means available.

> **C**ontinuous personal and professional development is the minimum requirement for success today... If you're not adding to your store of knowledge aggressively and continuously, you're actually falling behind."[16]

By assessing the contemporary information and communication technology skills required and consciously directing your natural abilities toward the development of these skills, you can become a technology-using teacher. Set a realistic personal technology goal, such as learning to use one new piece of software each term, and be prepared to use some evenings, a few hours each weekend, and/or holiday time to accomplish it. Remember to document your personal growth as you go along so your resumé will reflect the personal initiative you have demonstrated.

> **E**ach person is the president of their own career. As the president of ME Inc., you have to set up your own training department."[17]

Teacher Technology Competencies

A variety of instruments are being developed in an attempt to measure teacher competencies with technology, primarily computers. These instruments are generally used for anonymous self-assessment. Teachers may use them to assess their personal skills and plan their training accordingly. Districts can judge the effectiveness of their staff development programs. Some of the rubrics focus more on technical skills; others on integration of technology with teaching. The International Society for Technology in Education has developed national educational technology standards for teacher preparation (http://cnets.iste.org/index3.html).

You can find other examples of teacher competency frameworks at the following Web sites:
- Massachusetts State ABE Technology Plan (1999)
- Community Learning Network
- Wisconsin Educational Technology Conference
- The Virginia Board of Education
- Milken Exchange on Education Technology

If you are in a leadership position, you may be interested in reviewing "Rubrics for Leadership: What Technologically Literate Superintendents, Principals and Directors Should Know and Be Able to Do with Information Technologies" at http://www.isd77.k12.mn.us/resources/dougwri/rublead.html (January 1999 draft).

Summing Up

The stories of teachers who have embraced technology, sometimes from a very shaky beginning, are inspiring. Some report that technology has revitalized their teaching, some that they are engaged by the creative power of the computer, and others that they are so much more productive and organized.

As information and communication technology multiplies the possibilities for individualized, hands-on, collaborative learning, teachers are finding more opportunities to apply the compelling educational principles of Dewey (learning by doing), Piaget (knowledge construction). Active learning in the digital age classroom is something teachers do in collaboration with their students. As John Cotton Dana, an important figure in the nineteenth-century public library movement, proclaimed, "Who dares to teach, must never cease to learn."

BIBLIOGRAPHIC NOTES

Chapter 1 Notes

1. H. Daniels, M. Kaufman, G. Meo, J. Naylor, and E. Whelihan. "Planning for technology: Circa 1992." *SIGTC Connections*, Vol. 8, No. 4, 1992, p. 29.
2. W.R. Daggett. "Tech Trends." http://38.202.153.15/tech.trends.html.
3. Kathy Foley. "Internet 2: The Sequel." The International Center for Leadership in Education. January 10, 2000. http://www.nua.ie/surveys/analysis/weekly_editorial/archives/2000/issue1no108. html
4. Foley, ibid.
5. Foley, ibid.
6. S. Carton. "The revolution is coming." *The International Center for Leadership in Education.* January 12, 2000.
7. "Connecting to the Internet." *Education Week: The Internet.* p.1.
8. J. O'Neil. "Using technology to support 'authentic' learning." *ASCD Update*, Vol. 35, No.8, October 1993, p. 4.
9. B. Hedney. "The professional development of teachers in an information technology era." *Output*, p. 7q.
10. P. Cox. "Cyberdegrees." *The Wall Street Journal*, November 17, 1997, p. R26.
11. G. Smith. "Focus on computer literacy." *Output*, Vol. 26, No. 2, 1995, p. 38.
12. O'Neil. p. 5.
13. O'Neil, p. 4.
14. Ibid.
15. Ibid.
16. Center for Applied Special Technology. "The role of on-line communications in schools: a national study." Peabody, Mass.: CAST, 1996. www.cast.org/stsstudy.html.
17. N. Bennett. "Habits of mind." *Learning and Leading With Technology,* March 1997, p. 18.
18. Ibid.

19. J. O'Neil. "On technology schools: A conversation with Chris Dede." *Learning and Leading With Technology*, March 1997, p. 6.
20. J. Kosakowski. "The benefits of information technology." *ECOO Output*, Vol. 21, No. 2, p. 15.
21. H. Gardner, *Frames of Mind.* New York: Basic Books Inc., 1989.
22. FDLRS/Tech and FDLRS/East. Florida Diagnostic and Learning Resources System Network. "An exploration in matching software to Gardner's seven types of intelligence." (a paper completed by the Florida Diagnostic and Learning Resources System Network)
23. K.L. Peck and D. Dorricott. "Why use technology?" *Educational Leadership*, April 1994, p. 14.
24. D. Dwyer. "Apple classrooms of tomorrow: What we've learned." *Educational Leadership*, Vol. 51, No. 7, p. 4.
25. E.R. Bialo and J. Sivin-Kach. *The effectiveness of technology in schools: A summary of recent research.* Washington, D.C: Software Publishers Association, 1996.
26. Peck and Dorricott, p. 14.
27. J. Brennan. "We must compute." *The Ottawa Citizen*, October 18, 1992, p. B1.
28. The Conference Board of Canada. "Employability Skills 2000+". http://www2.conferenceboard.ca/nbec/pdf/esp2000.pdf.
29. The U.S. Department of Labor. "SCANS Secretary's Commission on Achieving Necessary Skills," 1991 and 1992. http://www.academicinnovations.com/report.html.
30. S. Rockman. "Workforce Preparedness." The Leader's Guide to Education Technology. http://www.edvancenet.org/res_guide_work2.shtml.
31. Kosakowski, p. 17.
32. A. Zehr. "Business group calls for more technology training." *Education Week on the Web*, March 3, 1999, p. 1.
33. Ibid.
34. W.M. Bulkeley. "Technology: Hard lessons." *The Wall Street Journal Reports*, November 17, 1997, p. R1.
35. H. Clopton. "Nobody believes it's the quick-fix for America's K–12 ills. Linda Roberts on the role of technology in the classroom." http://www_4teachers_org KeyNotes Nobody believes it's the quick-fix.html.
36. Bulkeley, pp. R4 and R6.
37. T. Peters. *The Pursuit of WOW!* New York: Vintage Books, 1994, p. 324.
38. S. Durkin and D. Neils (1996). The HP e-mail Mentor Program. http://mentor.external.hp.com/.
39. C.R. Pool. "A new digital literacy: A conversation with Paul Gilster." *Educational Leadership*, November 1997, p. 11.
40. Zehr, p. 1.
41. F. Robert. "The Model." Technology: What We've Learned. *The Wall Street Journal*, November 17, 1997, p. R18.
42. T.K. Glenna and A. Melmed. "Fostering the use of educational technology: Elements of a national strategy. A Rand Report." Santa Monica, California: Rand, 1996. www.rand.org/publications/MR/MR682/contents.html.
43. Clopton, p. 3. http://www_4teachers_org KeyNotes Nobody believes it's the quick-fix.html.

Chapter 2 Notes

1. T. Peters and N. Austin. *A Passion for Excellence*. New York: Warner Books, 1985, p. 486.
2. C.D. Maddux, D.L. Johnson, and J.N. Willis. *Educational Computing: Learning with Tomorrow's Technologies*. Boston: Allyn & Bacon, 1992.
3. Jim Rogers. Teacher, Ottawa Carleton Catholic District School Board, Ottawa, Ontario, "The Media Integrated Classroom" (video), Carleton Roman Catholic School Board, 1991.
4. Debra Killen. Teacher, Chelsea School, Chelsea, Quebec, quoted in Ann Heide and Linda Stilborne, *The Teacher's Complete and Easy Guide to the Internet*. Toronto: Trifolium Books Inc. 1999, p. 248.
5. B.M. Green. *Great Workshops*. Watertown, Massachusetts: Tom Snyder Productions, 1990, p. 43.
6. Microsoft's Anywhere, Anytime Learning program, http://www.microsoft.com/education/instruction/articles/aal_clovis.asp, June 2001.
7. A. Stone. "Action for Equity." *The Computing Teacher*, Vol. 14, No. 3, p. 54.
8. R. Skolnick, A. Larson, and C. Smith. "The power of multimedia." The Electronic School, September 1993, p. A7.
9. Jeffrey Branzburg. "How Well Is It Working? Customizing Your Technology Assessment." *Technology and Learning*, February 2001, pp. 24–35.
10. M. Fullan. "Change processes and strategies at the local level." *The Elementary School Journal*, Vol. 85, No. 3, 1985, pp. 391–420. "Curriculum implementation." *The International Encyclopedia of Educational Technology*. New York: Pergamon Press, 1989, pp. 485–491. *The Meaning of Educational Change*. Toronto: OISE Press and Teachers College Press, 1982. K.A. Leithwood and D. J. Montgomery. *A Framework for Planned Educational Change: Application to the Assessment of Program Implementation*. Toronto: The Ontario Institute for Studies in Education, 1981. R. Wright. "A contextual model of curriculum implementation" Thesis (Ph.D.), University of Ottawa, Ottawa, 1982.
11. Wright, ibid.
12. The CEO Forum School Technology and Readiness Report, Year 3, June 2000. http://www.ceoforum.org, June 2001.
13. Betsy Norris, sixth-grade teacher and technology coordinator, http://www.4teachers.org/testimony/norris, December, 1999.
14. *Roger Schenk, "Engines for Education," 1994 http://www.ils.nwu.edu/~e_for_e/nodes/NODE-43-pg.html, May 1999.*
15. K. Ryba and B. Anderson. *Learning with Computers: Effective Teaching Strategies*. Eugene, Oregon: The International Society for Technology in Education, 1990, p. 71.
16. http://www.wired.com/news/culture/0,1284,37263,00.html
17. Toshiba Laptop Learning Challenge, http://www.nsta.org/programs/laptop/teach/rationale.htm May 2001.
18. Kim Carter. "Laptop Lessons." *Technology and Learning*, May 2001, pp. 39–49.
19. Microsoft's Anytime, Anywhere Learning program, http://www.microsoft.com/education/aal/research3.asp, June 2001.
20. Jennifer C. Patterson. "Kids on the Run: Mobile Technology." *Technology and Learning*, January 2001, pp. 44–47.

21. Eamonn O'Donovan. "Small Wonders." *Technology and Learning*, October 2000, pp. 15–19.

22. Jennifer C. Patterson. "Kids on the Run: Mobile Technology." *Technology and Learning*, January 2001, pp. 44–47.

23. Jean Shields. "Wireless Networks Come of Age." *Technology and Learning*, March 2001, pp. 9–11.

24. Eamonn O'Donovan. "Dealing with Information Overload." *Technology and Learning*, January 2001, pp. 9–11. Craig Nansen. "The Intranet Solution." *Technology and Learning*, November 2000, pp. 38–39.

25. R. Knee, A. Musgrove, and J. Musgrove. "Lights, Camera, Action!" *Learning and Leading with Technology*, ISTE, November 2000, pp. 51–53.

26. Steve Bosak. "Electronic School," September 1999 http://www.electronic-school.com/199909/0999toolsofthetrade.html, May 1999.

27. *K. Kearns. "The forgotten medium — Are we too visually dependent?"* NASSP Bulletin, *Vol. 69, No. 480, 1985, pp. 45–49.*

28. Margaret Johnson. New Roles for Educators. "Electronic School," September 1999. http://www.electronic-school.com/2000/01/0100f1part1.html.

29. The Education Forum, Conference Board of Canada, "Ethical guidelines for business–education partnerships." 1995. http://www.conference-board.ca/nbec/template2000/pubs.htm, January 3, 2001.

30. T. L. Tolbert. "Industry access to university technology: Prospects and problems," in E. J. Friese (ed.), *The Private Sector/University Technology Alliance: Making It Work.* Proceeding of a conference of the National Council of University Research Administrators, Dallas, Texas, September 1984, pp. 24–28.

31. C. Murray. "Eight Great Steps to Getting Corporate Sponsors," June 1994. gopher://cwis.usc.edu:70/00/Librar...chers/Corporate_Funding/8steps.txt.

32. Margaret Johnson. New roles for educators. "Electronic School," 1999. http://www.electronic-school.com/2000/01/0100f1part1.html.

Chapter 3 Notes

1. http://ceris.schoolnet.ca/e/tech8.html, September 10, 2000.

2. Taylor, in R. Logan, *The Fifth Language: Learning and Living in the Computing Age.* Toronto: Stoddart Publishing, 1996.

3. P. Reynolds, with Gary Stager. *The North Star Guide to Technology Planning.* [United States]: FableVision Press, 2000. http://www.fablevision.com/northstar/techplan/index.html.

4. P.K. Komoski. "Educational computing: the burden of ensuring quality." *Phi Delta Kappan*, December 1984, pp. 244–248.

5. Dan Bennett. *Exploring Geometry with The Geometer's Sketchpad.* Emeryville, California: Key Curriculum Press, 1999, p. viii.

6. http://www.edweek.org/sreports/tc98/cs/cs3.htm, July 22, 2000.

7. Kendall Hartley. "Online Simulations." *Learning and Leading with Technology*, ISTE, November 2000, pp. 32–35.

8. Melanie Fernandez. "Electronic versus paper." *Learning & Leading with Technology*, Vol. 26, No. 8, May 1999.

9. Amy Poftak. "Getting a Read on E-Books." *Technology and Learning*, April 2001, pp. 22–34.

10. Robin Dunbar. Faculty of Education, University of Ottawa, 1999.
11. Colleen Cooley. Faculty of Education, University of Ottawa, 1999.
12. David Way. Faculty of Education, University of Ottawa, 1999.
13. Jesse Everett. Faculty of Education, University of Ottawa, 1999.
14. Tay Vaughn. *Multimedia: Making It Work*. Berkeley, California: Osborne/McGraw-Hill, 1994, p. 6.
15. Paulina Aquilera. Faculty of Education, University of Ottawa, 1999.
16. Renee Schwartz. "Hyperstudio User Stories." Roger Wagner Publishing. http://www.hyperstudio.com/hsstory/stories.html December 12, 1999.
17. F. D'Ignazio. "Student multimedia book talks: Illuminating on a shoe-string." *The Computing Teacher*, Vol. 21, No. 3, 1993, p. 32.
18. Amy Hynick. Faculty of Education, University of Ottawa, 1999.
19. Susan Brownlee. Faculty of Education, University of Ottawa, 1999.
20. K. Ryba and Bill Anderson. *Learning with Computers: Effective Teaching Strategies*. Eugene, Oregon: ISTE, 1990.
21. Jason Lloyd. Faculty of Education, University of Ottawa, 1999.
22. Merima Romijn. Faculty of Education, University of Ottawa, 1999.
23. http://www.edweek.org/sreports/tc98/cs/cs8.htm, July 22, 2000.
24. Caroline McCullen. "You Ought to Be in Pictures." *Technology and Learning*, November 2000, pp. 40–44.
25. A. Doyle. Technology Coordinator, Polytechnic Preparatory Country Day School, Brooklyn, N.Y.: http://www.ascd.org/pubs/el/feb99/extdoyle.html December 19, 1999.
26. The Blake School Home Page http://bear.blake.pvt.k12.mn.us/campus/projects/lower/lego/pulley97/index.html
27. Don Sleeth. The Kids and Computers Web Site, http://www.kidsandcomputers.com/dosversion1/micro.htm January 31, 2000.
28. Nicole Sleeth. Kids Can Program. http://www.hvac.cc/kidscanprogram/main/PluginProjects/Nicole/race.htm January 31, 2000.
29. "Top 10 key factors for choosing software identified by recent educator survey." *ISTE Update*, Vol. 11, No 6, April 1999, p. 5.
30. D. Dockterman. *Great Teaching and the VCR*. Watertown, Massachusetts: Tom Snyder Productions, 1993, p. 5.

Chapter 4 Notes

1. Jamieson A. McKenzie. *How Teachers Learn Technology Best*. Bellingham, Washington: FNO Press Inc., 1999. pp. 76, 81.
2. International Society for Technology in Education, NETS Project, *National Educational Technology Standards for Students*, June 1998.
3. Ibid.
4. Fred D'Ignazio. "After the Internet...the Encyclopedia?" *Learning and Leading with Technology*, May 1999, p. 57.
5. G. A. Caissy. "Planning for computer use in the classroom." *Computers in Education*, March, 1988, p. 10.
6. W. Glasser. *Control Theory in the Classroom*. New York: Harper & Row, 1986.
7. McKenzie, ibid., p. 29.
8. From an activity created by Val Robinson. Faculty of Education, University of Ottawa, 1999.

9. From an activity created by Maureen Langsford. Faculty of Education, University of Ottawa, 1999.
10. Adapted from an activity created by Shannon O'Grady, Faculty of Education, University of Ottawa, 1999.
11. From an activity created by Cathie Churchill. Faculty of Education, University of Ottawa, 1999.
12. Adapted from an activity created by Rob Perry, Faculty of Education, University of Ottawa, 1998.
13. Bart Hays, teacher, Morse High School http://www.benton.org/Practice/Edu/, August 22, 2000.

Chapter 5 Notes

1. Mary O'Haver, teacher, Fairland Elementary School http://www.benton.org/Practice/Edu/, August 22, 2000.
2. Microsoft's Anywhere, Anytime Learning program, http://www.microsoft.com/education/aal/reality.asp, June 2001.
3. Toshiba Laptop Learning Challenge http://www.nsta.org/programs/laptop/teach/mgmt.htm, May 2001.
4. Peg Szady. Teacher, Monta Vista High School, California, quoted in Ann Heide and Linda Stilborne, *The Teacher's Complete and Easy Guide to the Internet*, Toronto: Trifolium Books Inc. 1999, p. 73.
5. Dyanne Rivers. "Peep shows and predators inhabit cyberspace too: Streetproofing kids for the info highway." *Home and School*, May 1995, pp. 23–25.
6. From an observation report produced by Priti Thaker. Faculty of Education, University of Ottawa, 1999.
7. Patricia Weeg, teacher, Delmar Elementary School, http://www.benton.org/Practice/Edu/, August 22, 2000.
8. http://www.edweek.org/sreports/tc98/cs/cs3.htm, August 22, 2000.
9. Lisa Neale, special education teacher, Hamilton-Wentworth District School Board, Hamilton, Ontario.
10. Kathleen Vail. Electronic School, June 1999 http://www.electronic-school.com/199906/0699sbot.html.
11. From a video by Jim Rogers, teacher, Ottawa-Carleton Catholic District School Board, Ottawa, Ontario. *The Media Integrated Classroom*, Carleton Roman Catholic School Board, 1991.
12. E. Church. "Shopping for educational software." *The Globe and Mail*, April 15, 1993, p. C1.

Chapter 6 Notes

1. [Online] Available: http://ceris.schoolnet.ca/e/tech7.html, September 10, 2000.
2. J. Harris. "Wetware: Why use activity structures?" *Learning and Leading with Technology*, ISTE, 25(4), 1997–98, pp. 13–17.
3. J. Harris. *Virtual Architecture: Designing and Directing Curriculum-Based Telecomputing*. Eugene, Oregon: ISTE, 1998.
4. A. Heide and L. Stilborne. *The Teacher's Complete and Easy Guide to the Internet, 2nd Ed*. Toronto: Trifolium Books Inc., 1999, pp. 134–35.

5. P. Gilster. *A Primer on Digital Literacy*, adapted from the book *Digital Literacy*, Somerset, New Jersey: John Wiley & Sons, 1997. [Online] Available: http://www.ibiblio.org/cisco/noc/primer.html.

6. Heide and Stilborne, p. 128.

7. Moshe Cohen and Margaret Riel. "The effect of distant audiences on students' writing," *AERA Journal*, Summer 1989, pp. 132–59.

8. Bernie Dodge. "Five Rules for Writing a Great WebQuest." *Learning and Leading with Technology*, ISTE, May 2001, pp. 6–9.

9. [Online] Available: http://www.lightspan.com/teacher/pages/pd/finding.asp?_prod=LS&_nav=T3_TOOLS_PROFDEV, September 10, 2000.

10. Kristi Rennebohm Franz, [Online] Available: http://www.benton.org/Practice/Edu/, September 10, 2000.

11. Microsoft's Anytime, Anywhere Learning program, http://www.microsoft.com/education/instruction/articles/aal_clovis.asp, June 2001.

12. Judi Harris. "Telecollaborators Wanted." *Learning and Leading with Technology*, ISTE, May 2001, pp. 46–49.

13. J. Harris. "Taboo topic no longer: Why telecollaborative projects sometimes fail," *Learning and Leading with Technology*, ISTE, 27(5), February 2000.

14. Mary O'Haver, Fairland Elementary School, [Online] Available: http://www.benton.org/Practice/Edu/, September 22, 2000.

Chapter 7 Notes

1. The Ontario Ministry of Education and Training. *The Ontario Curriculum Grade 9 & 10, Program Planning and Assessment*, 1999, p. 9.

2. D.J. Hargreaves. "Student learning and assessment are inextricably linked." *European Journal of Engineering Education*, Vol. 22, Issue 4, December 1997, p. 401.

3. G. Wiggins, J. McTighe. *Understanding By Design*. Alexandria, Virginia; ASCD, 1999.

4. H. Gardiner. *Frames of Mind: The Theory of Multiple Intelligence*. New York: Basic Books, 1984.

5. D. Lazear. *Multiple Intelligence Approaches to Assessment: Solving the Assessment Conundrum*. Tucson, Arizona; Zephyr Press, 1994.

6. P. Ramsden. *Learning to Teach in Higher Education*. London: Routledge, 1992.

7. J. McTighe. *Assessing Learning in the Classroom*. National Education Association, 1998.

8. D. Midwood, K. O'Connor and M. Simpson. *Assess for Success*. Toronto, Ontario: Educational Services Committee, 1994 (revised), p. 33.

9. McTighe, ibid.

10. L. Farmer. "Authentic assessment of information literacy through electronic products." *Book Report*, Sept./Oct. 1997, Vol. 16, Issue 2, p. 11.

11. G. Wiggins. "A true test: Toward more authentic and equitable assessment." *Phi Delta Kappan*, 70(9), p. 703.

12. S. Covey. *Seven Habits of Highly Effective People*. New York: Simon & Schuster, 1989.

13. W.J. Popham. "What's wrong and what's right with rubrics." *Educational Leadership*, October 1997.

14. Erin Beacom. Faculty of Education, University of Ottawa, 1999.

15. K. Burke, R. Fogarty and S. Belgrad. *The Mindful School: The Portfolio Connection*. Palatine, Illinois: IRI/Skylight Publishing Inc., 1994. p. vii.

16. S. Valencia. "A portfolio approach to classroom reading assessment: The whys, whats, and hows." *The Reading Teacher*, 43(4), p. 333.

17. E.A. Hebert. and L. Schultz. "The power of portfolios." *Educational Leadership*, April 1996, p. 70.

18. F.L. Paulson, P.R. Paulson and C.A. Meyer. "What makes a portfolio a portfolio?" *Educational Leadership*, February, 1991, p. 60.

19. D. Keystone. "Assessment of technology." *Primary Educator*, 1998, Vol. 4, Issue 4.

20. Lesley Farmer. "Authentic assessment of information literacy through electronic products." *Book Report*, Sept/Oct. 1997, Vol. 16, Issue 2, p. 5.

21. M.M. Gerber, D.S. Semmel and M.I. Semmel. "Computer-based dynamic assessment of multidigit multiplication." *Exceptional Children*, 61, p. 114.

22. M.W. Bahr and C.M. Bahr. "Educational assessment in the next millennium: Contributions of technology." *Preventing School Failure*, 41(2), p. 90.

23. L.S. Fuchs, C.L. Hamlett, and D. Fuchs. "Monitoring basic skills progress (computer program)". Austin, Texas: Pro-Ed, 1990.

24. L.K. Irvin, H. M. Walker, J. Noell, G.H.S. Singer, A.B. Irvin, K. Marquez and B. Britz. "Measuring children's social skills using micro-computer-based videodisc assessment." *Behavior Modification*, 16, p. 475.

Chapter 8 Notes

1. Seymour Papert. *The Connected Family: Bridging the Generation Gap*. Atlanta, Georgia: Longstreet Press, 1966, p. 47.

2. Marilyn Legault. Information Technology Consultant, Hamilton-Wentworth District School Board.

3. John Highley. Teacher, Mohawk Gardens Public School, Hamilton-Wentworth District School Board

4. *Students with Special Needs*. 1998.

5. Bert Neale. Teacher, Pauline Johnson School, Hamilton-Wentworth District School Board.

6. Courtesy of Hamilton-Wentworth District School Board.

7. Gene Bucci. Learning Resource Teacher, Highview Middle School, Hamilton-Wentworth District School Board.

8. Courtesy of Hamilton-Wentworth District School Board.

9. Trish Adam. Learning Resource Teacher, Sherwood Heights School, Hamilton-Wentworth District School Board.

10. W. Constanza. *The Electronic Text: Learning to Read, Write and Reason with Computers*. Englewood Cliffs, New Jersey: Educational Technology Publications, 1989. K. A. Krendl and D.A. Lieberman. "Computers and learning: a review of recent research." *Journal of Educational Computing Research*, Vol. 4, No. 4, 1988, pp. 367–89. G. Fisher. "The social effects of computers in education." *Electronic Learning*, March 1984, pp. 26–28.

11. J. Watson. "Cooperative learning and computers in education." *Electronic Learning*, March, 1984, p. 5.

12. Richard Goldsworthy. "Collaborative classrooms." *Learning and Leading with Technology*, Vol. 27, No. 4, December/January 1999–2000, p. 2.

13. Ibid.
14. *Becoming Partners. A guide to starting and sustaining successful partnerships between education and business.* Cuperetino, California: Apple Computer Inc., p. A45.
15. Laurie B. Dias. "Integrating technology: Some things you should know." *Learning and Leading with Technology*, Vol. 27, No. 3, September 1999.
16. Amy Poftak. "Getting a Read on E-Books." *Technology and Learning*, April 2001, pp. 22–34.
17. M.L. Special and L. M. LaFrance. "Multimedia students with learning disabilities: The road to success." *The Computing Teacher*, Vol. 20, No. 3, 1992, p. 31.
18. Legault.
19. Brian Robbins. http://www.palm.com/community/stories/brobbins.html, May 2001.
20. Don Tapscott. *Growing Up Digital*. New York: McGraw-Hill, 1999.
21. Witchita, Kansas, Public School Board motto, 1993.
22. C. Norris. "Computing and the Classroom: Teaching the At-Risk Student." *The Computing Teacher*, Vol. 21, No. 5, 1994, p. 12
23. Microsoft's Anywhere Anytime Learning project. http://www.microsoft.com/education/vision/sch/pg4sb.asp, June 2001.

Chapter 9 Notes

1. Margaret Johnson. "New roles for educators." *Electronic School*, 1999. http://www.electronic-school.com/2000/01/0100f1part1.html
2. A. November and D. Thornburg. "Telecom: The good, the bad and the ugly." *Electronic Learning*, Vol. 12, No. 7, 1993, pp. 16–17.
3. *Power On! New Tools for Teaching and Learning*. Washington, D.C.: Congress of the United States, Office of Technology Assessment, 1998, p. 89.
4. J. F. Beaver. "Using computer power to improve your teaching (Part One)." *Output*, Vol. 14, No. 3, 1994, p. 25.
5. Glen Bull, Gina Bull, Judy Thomas, and Judy Jordan. "Incorporating Imagery into Instruction." *Learning and Leading with Technology*, ISTE, March 2000, pp. 46–49.
6. F. D'Ignazio. "Welcome to the multimedia sandbox." *The Computing Teacher*, Vol. 17, No. 1, 1989, pp. 27–28.
7. L. Howles and C. Pettengill. "Designing an instructional multimedia presentation: A seven-step process." *Journal of Hypermedia and Multimedia Studies*, Vol. 3, No. 4, 1993, pp. 6–9. Eugene, Oregon: International Society for Technology in Education.
8. Judi Harris. "Virtual Vantage Points." *Learning and Leading with Technology*, ISTE, March 2001, pp. 14–17.
9. Glen Bull, Gina Bull, and Hollylynne Drier. "Exploring Data Warehouses." *Learning and Leading with Technology*, ISTE, May 1999, pp. 36–39.
10. Adapted from a learning activity developed by Liisa Jianopoulos, Faculty of Education, University of Ottawa, 1999.
11. Daniel T. Lake. "An Online Formula for Success." *Learning and Leading with Technology*, ISTE, March 2001, pp. 18–21.

12. Jeffrey Branzburg. "Talking to Parents Online." *Technology and Learning*, April 2001, p. 53.
13. S. Fletcher. "Using a database in an elementary school." *Computers in Education*, April 1988, p. 10.
14. Keith Jean, http://www.palm.com/community/stories/brobbins.html, May 2001.
15. B. Morgan (ed.). "101 things you want to know about educational technology." *Electronic Learning*, Vol. 10, No. 7, 1991, p. 25.
16. B. Tracy. As cited in "Raw material in information age is knowledge" by Janis Foord Kirk in *The Toronto Star*, November 20, 1993, p. G7.
17. Ibid.

General Bibliography

Furger, R. (1998). *Does Jane Compute?* Warner Books, New York, N.Y.

Giagnocavo, G. et al. (1997). *Internet Driver's License.* Classroom Connect, Lancaster, Pennsylvania.

Grabe, M., and C. Grabe. (1998). *Integrating Technology for Meaningful Learning, 2nd Ed.* Houghton Mifflin Co., Boston, Massachusetts.

Green, M. G. (1990). *Great Workshops: The Complete Do-It-Yourself Inservice Workshop Guide.* Tom Snyder Productions, Inc., Watertown, Massachusetts.

Hancock, J.(ed.) (1999). *Teaching Literacy Using Information Technology.* Australian Literacy Educators' Association, Adelaide, South Australia.

Heide, A., and L. Stilborne. (1999). *The Teacher's Complete and Easy Guide to the Internet, 2nd Ed.* Trifolium Books Inc., Toronto.

Lengel, J. C., and D. Kendall. (1995). *Kids, Computers, & Homework.* Random House Inc., New York, N.Y.

McKenzie, Jamieson A. (1999). *How Teachers Learn Technology Best.* FNO Press Inc., Bellingham, Washington.

McKenzie, Jamieson A. (1993). *Power Learning in the Classroom.* Corwin Press Inc.

McKenzie, Jamieson A. (2000). *Questioning, Research and the Information Literate School.* FNO Press Inc., Bellingham, Washington.

Roerden, L.P. (1997). *Net Lessons: Web-Based Projects For Your Classroom.* Songline Studios, Inc. and O'Reilly & Associates, Inc. Sebastopol, California.

Tapscott, D. (1998). *Growing Up Digital: The Rise of the Net Generation.* McGraw Hill, New York.

Willis, J., E. Stephens, and K. Matthew. (1996). *Technology, Reading, and Language Arts.* Allyn and Bacon, Needham Heights, Massachusetts

SAMPLE TECHNOLOGY -INTEGRATED LEARNING EXPERIENCE PLANS

Teacher candidates in the Faculty of Education, University of Ottawa, during the 1999–2000 school year created these sample learning experience plans. They are at four levels of difficulty, from primary to senior students.

Sample Primary Learning Experience Plan

Activity Title:	How Do We Get From Here to There?
Author:	Brian G. Yee, Faculty of Education, University of Ottawa, 1999
Grade:	One
Subject & Strand:	Language Arts: Writing and Reading; The Arts: Visual Arts

Expectations:

Language Arts:

- To organize information so that writing conveys a clear message.
- To develop word uses and build vocabulary.
- To print legibly.
- To respond to familiar or predictable language patterns.

Visual Arts:
- To produce two- and three-dimensional works of art that communicate ideas (thoughts, feelings, experiences) for specific purposes.
- Use the elements of design (color, line, shape, form, space, and texture), in ways appropriate for this grade when producing and responding to works of art.

IT component:
The students will be using graphics (paint/draw programs and word processing).

Recommended software: Kid Pix and/or Kid Pix Companion

IT Expectations:
Students will compose, revise and edit text:
- create original text using word-processing software, communicate and demonstrate understanding of forms and techniques.

Students will communicate through multimedia:
- create visual images by using such tools as paint and draw programs for particular audiences and purposes.

Students will navigate and create hyperlink resources:
- navigate within a document, CD-ROM, or other software program that contains links.

Students will use technology to investigate and/or solve problems:
- use technology to support and present conclusions.

Prerequisite IT skills:
- Familiarity using the mouse
- Familiarity with the keyboard
- Introduction to the components of Kid Pix

Description/demonstration of learning:
Using Kid Pix software, the students will write in the provided template. They may choose to illustrate their sentence with a graphic provided within the Kid Pix program to create their own picture. Each template will be saved to a student folder and printed, to be incorporated into a "big book" for the classroom library.

Approximate time required:
This activity will take approximately 40 minutes during the scheduled classroom writing time for two students to complete the activity. Due to computer scheduling, this activity may require two weeks for the whole class to complete the assignment.

Student grouping:
Due to limited computer access, students will be grouped in pairs and rotate through this activity as part of the scheduled writing time.

Activity Plan:
Preparation:
1. Create a template with a drawn picture or stamp. Print this template to have as an example for the class.
2. Have Kid Pix open with a new document. Ensure that the "small kid" mode is on in order to limit student access to other programs.

Motivation:
- The teacher will read a story to the class (see Resource list for suggested titles).

Context:
The teacher and class will sing the song "The Wheels on the Bus." Some leading questions may be asked at this time:
- How do we get to school?
- Does everyone come to school in the same way?

Instructional Process:
1. Introduce the sentence that the students will be writing as pocket chart activity for the whole class.
2. Read the sentence aloud.
3. Have the students read the sentence as a group chorus.
4. Develop a list with the students of the various ways that people get to school. Make word cards to add to the pocket chart and read these aloud with the class.
5. Introduce the students to Kid Pix. Demonstrate how the program can be used for drawing pictures and writing. Show the students the collection of stamps that are also available for making/decorating their pictures.
6. Develop some class rules pertaining to this activity (e.g., Limit the number of stamps that students use with each of their pictures).

Big Book Activity:
1. Have the students mount their graphics and text onto large colored construction paper.
2. Have the individual sheets laminated and then bound together.

Extensions/differentiation:

Suggested follow-up activities:
- Develop a "big book" from the collected writing and illustrations of the students.
- Provide a whole-group reading activity.
- Use this lesson as a lead into a unit called "Transportation and Technology."
- Develop a bar graph with the students of the type of transportation used from the information obtained in the writing activity.

Modifications for exceptional students:

Students with visual impairment:
1. Use Helvetica or Ariel font styles with a minimum of 36-point font.
2. Have another student work as a buddy to provide additional auditory cues if required.

Students with a physical impairment:
1. Use an inverted mouse or joystick mouse to assist the student in moving to various links in the software program.

Students with an intellectual impairment:
1. Provide the student with a prepared template of the sentence to be written.
2. Provide the student with assistance to complete the sentence if required.
3. Provide a choice for the student to work on the computer or provide the student with a hard copy of the template that can then be completed at their desk.

Resources:
- Davies, Charlotte, and Andrea Pinnington (eds.). *My First Look at Things That Go.* New York: Random House, 1991.
- Crews, Donald. *Freight Trains.* New York: Greenwillow Books, 1978.
- Nayer, Judy. *Wheels.* New York: Scholastic, 1994.
- Pienkowski, Jan. *Trucks.* New York: Dutton Children's Books, 1997.
- Young, Caroline. *The Usborne Book of Diggers and Cranes.* London: Usborne Publishing, 1991.

Sample Junior Learning Experience Plan

Activity Title:	Grade Six Daily
Author:	Tracey Vansickle, Faculty of Education, University of Ottawa, 1999
Grade:	6
Subject & Strands:	Language: Writing and Reading

Expectations:

Writing

Students will:
- communicate ideas and information for a variety of purposes (to inform, persuade, explain) and to specific audiences.
- use writing for various purposes and in a range of contexts, including school work (e.g., to develop and clarify ideas, to express thoughts and opinions).
- produce pieces of writing using a variety of forms (e.g., newspaper articles, lyrics, summaries of information), techniques, and resources... and materials from other media.
- use a variety of sentence types (e.g., questions, statements) and sentence structures (e.g., complex sentences) appropriate for their purposes.
- produce media texts using writing and materials from other media.
- revise and edit their work in collaboration with others, seeking and evaluating feedback, and focusing on content, organization, and appropriateness of vocabulary for audience.
- proofread and correct their final drafts, focusing on grammar, punctuation, spelling, and conventions of style.
- use and spell correctly the vocabulary appropriate for this grade level.
- use a variety of resources (e.g., computer spell check) to confirm spelling of common exceptions to spelling patterns.
- accurately use appropriate organizers (e.g., table of contents, index).
- integrate media materials (e.g., computer graphics) into their writing to enhance their message.

Reading

Students will:
- explain their interpretation of a written work, supporting it with evidence from the work and from their knowledge and experience.
- summarize and explain the main ideas in information materials, and cite details that support the main ideas.
- make judgments and draw conclusions about ideas in written materials on the basis of evidence.
- identify a writer's perspective or character's motivation.

IT component:

This project will require the use of a desktop publishing package, as well as word processing and graphics and/or clip art. The students will have the option of also using a scanner; one or more activities may be adapted to include computer use (such as electronic conferencing for editing or story generation) if the students and teachers are highly computer-literate.

Recommended Software:

Desktop publishing: Microsoft Publisher
Alternatives:

- The Children's Writing and Publishing Centre, Learning Company (Windows, Mac CD-ROM) — more limited features than Microsoft Publisher, but also easier for novices to use;
- The (Student) Writing Centre, Learning Company (Mac, Windows) (also more limited);
- PageMaker, Adobe (Mac, Windows); and
- Storybook Weaver Deluxe, MECC (Mac, Windows CD-ROM), which can be used for students without the prerequisite IT skills, although it is intended for primary students.

Graphics/illustrations for insertion into desktop publishing: Kid Pix; the students may, in addition, use a scanner for their own art work
Alternatives:

- CorelDRAW, Corel (Mac (older versions only), Windows)
- MacDraw II, Claris (Mac)
- MsPaint, Microsoft (comes with Windows 95 and 98)
- Corel PHOTO-PAINT, Corel (Mac [older versions only], Windows)

Word processing for insertion into desktop publishing : ClarisWorks
Alternatives:

- Microsoft Word, Microsoft (Mac, Windows)
- WordPerfect, Corel (Mac, Windows)
- Microsoft Works, Microsoft (Mac, Windows)

IT expectations:

Using word processing, students will:

- enter, delete, cut, copy, and paste text.
- manipulate the layout of a document using the toolbar menu.
- adjust the format of a document (text size, font, styles, text word-wrap).
- use spell check to proof a document; begin to use a thesaurus to modify text content.

Using clip art and/or paint and draw tools, students will:

- combine a graphic with a descriptive word, sentence, and paragraph.
- access, capture, and manipulate clip art and/or select and use paint and draw tools, and export the graphics to another program.

Using desktop publishing, students will:

- publish a document including words and graphics using a desktop publishing program such as MS Publisher.

Prerequisite IT skills:

Skills introduced, developed, or mastered in grades one through five, including adherence to appropriate computer etiquette; a strong ability to use the operating system of a computer and a school/classroom network (LAN); good file management capabilities; solid formal keyboarding skills; basic word-processing skills (such as entering text, using insertion point, cursor, backspace and delete, cut, copy, paste, adjusting format, and manipulating layout); experience using clip art and/or painting and drawing programs; some familiarity with desktop publishing.

Description/demonstration of learning:
Students will produce a newspaper containing the following:

- *page 1* — appropriate headings and captions; major (fictional or non-fictional) news articles with graphics or illustrations by each student in the group; and an index or table of contents for the document.
- *page 2* — an editorial page, with one editorial and one letter to the editor (on different issues) produced by each student; the students may include editorial cartoons, if desired.
- *page 3* — students' choice, can be mixed content: illustrated advertisements (commercial or public service), cartoons, reporting on technology or business, sports, etc. — at least one submission from each child.
- *pages 4 and 5* — literary pages with one poem, one book review or author's interview (author can be local or from class, but they must have "published" a book), and one short story or section of a (serialized) novella from each student. At least one illustration should accompany each of the latter.

Obviously, more pages may be added should the volume of documents necessitate this.

Approximate time required: Including preparatory work, this activity would be spaced across the entire school year, using approximately half the language time slots. The first seven months should focus on the combined literature studies (initial group discussion, individually reading and analyzing, and then imitating, collaborative editing, and finalizing) of the styles of writing above (approximately one per month). Approximately two months would then be dedicated to the group work required to prepare the summary newspapers.

Student Grouping: Students will do the initial writing and all revisions (research and draft[s] through to finished product) individually, except for the involvement and collaboration of other students in editing or content comments or suggestions, and a "conference" with the teacher. Students will then work in groups of three or four to produce the final group products (the newspapers).

Activity Plan:

Preparatory work: Following an introductory review of the meanings of fiction and non-fiction, discuss, then have the children identify, analyze, study, and recreate through their own writing features, elements, and characteristics of the following: media texts (advertisement: commercial, public service/informational, educational [health, reading, etc.]); short stories; fables, folk tales, myths and legends; novels, including book reviews; biographies; poetry and lyrics; articles and interviews (newspaper and magazine); editorials (including letters to the editor and cartooning). Set minimum and maximum length requirements.

Conduct several hands-on preparatory IT sessions on
- reviewing the creation of graphics; and
- accessing, capturing, manipulating, and exporting to desktop publishing clip art and graphics which have been created using paint and draw tools.

Procedure:

1. Each student selects what s/he considers to be one of the best — and most suitable for the nature of this exercise — examples of his/her own work from each of the writing genres above, and word processes them using ClarisWorks or other suitable software. Each student must contribute the specific documents outlined in the description of learning, above.

2. Using Kid Pix (or equivalent) drawing and painting tools and/or clip art, students create diagrams and illustrations to accompany their front-page articles, advertisements, and poems or short stories or novellas. They may, in addition, scan their own art into the computer.

3. Divide the students into small groups (three or four).

4. Each group plans or brainstorms (on paper or on the computer) their news-paper layout and determines which child has overall "editorial" responsibility for each of the pages. The group agrees on standard formatting such as titling conventions, number of columns, font, etc.

5. The children's documents are considered to be rough drafts. Each submission must be reviewed by at least two other members of the group, who will provide editorial comment on content, structure, and mechanics (spelling, grammar, punctuation, paragraphing, etc.). Provide the children with an editing checklist. Students must use both spell check and the thesaurus tool. This collaborative editing may be done orally using a hard copy, or on the computer, via electronic conferencing. If there is no consensus, the author retains final say.

6. The group drafts suggestions for appropriate headings and captions to accompany articles and editorials.

7. Each student "editor" is responsible for page layout and formatting, inserting headings and captions, and the insertion of the other students' text and graphics into his or her page. S/he will also do a thorough proofreading once the page is compiled.

8. Once the draft newspaper is complete, each group "conferences" with the teacher for a final review of the document.

9. Once all changes have been incorporated, the newspaper is printed in final form, and copies are provided to classmates and the library.

Extensions/differentiation:

- Children could conduct (supervised) "Meet the Author" chat room sessions on the school intranet, or with other schools, to discuss their poetry and short stories or novellas. Similarly, the students could hold live "Meet the Author" sessions accompanied by poetry or short story readings.

- The class could create a general or literary Web site where they could display not only the products of this activity, but also their other writings.

- Children could use multimedia (such as Hyperstudio) to create electronic books, wherein the author provides the voice for his or her own stories; these could be linked to the Web site.

- The exercise could be expanded to publishing books (either of individual students, or collections) or a literary magazine. A school-wide (desktop) publishing center could be established.

- Several classes could participate in a debate based upon issues raised in the student "editorials," using real-time electronic conferencing.

- Some groups could conduct research on the history of newspapers via the Internet or computer-based encyclopaedias, and then prepare and present a slide show presentation (using a program such as Powerpoint or Corel Presentations) to this class and others. Again, this could be linked to the Web site.

Learning Disabilities: More basic desktop publishing packages such as Storybook Weaver Deluxe can be used, and the requirement to export graphics can be dropped.

Visually Impaired: Use of a "talking" computer program (voice recognition and playback software) such as ViaVoice (IBM) would allow such a student to do the same work as the other children, with the exception of the illustrations. This type of software allows hands-free correction and editing, and has the ability to proofread out loud.

Sample Intermediate Learning Experience Plan

Activity Title:	Do Vampires Really Exist?
Author:	Melinda Spanglett, Faculty of Education, University of Ottawa, 1999
Grade:	7
Subject & Strand:	Math

Expectations:

Number Sense and Numeration — Overall Expectation
- Understand and explain that exponents represent repeated multiplication.

Number Sense and Numeration — Specific Expectation
- Generate multiples and factors of given numbers.
- Understand that repeated multiplication can be represented as exponents.
- Patterning and Algebra — Overall Expectation
- Identify, extend, create, and discuss patterns using whole numbers.
- Apply and discuss patterning strategies in problem-solving situations.

Patterning and Algebra — Specific Expectation
- Extend a pattern, complete a table, and write words to explain the pattern.
- Recognize patterns and use them to make predictions.
- Present solutions to patterning problems and explain the thinking behind the solution process.

Data Management and Probability — Overall Expectation
- Use computer applications to examine and interpret data in a variety of ways.

Data Management and Probability — Specific Expectation
- Identify and describe trends in graphs, using informal language to identify growth, clustering, and simple attributes.
- Display data on bar graphs, pictographs, and circle graphs, with and without the help of technology.

IT component: Spreadsheets and Internet browsers

Recommended software:
Microsoft Excel 97/98, Microsoft Internet Explorer 4.0

IT expectations:

Overall Expectations
- The learner will demonstrate knowledge and skills in the use of computer and other technologies.
- The learner will use a variety of technologies to access, analyze, interpret, synthesize, apply, and communicate information.

Specific Expectations
- Enter and edit data into a prepared spreadsheet to test simple "what if" statements.
- Create, modify, and use spreadsheets to solve problems related to content areas.
- Choose charts, tables, or graphs to best represent data.

Prerequisite IT skills:
Basic familiarity with Microsoft Excel 97/98, including creating simple formulas and using Chart features, ability to multiply numbers by 2 (through 100).

Description/demonstration of learning:
Students will identify and extend a number pattern into very large values, create and interpret a graph, and compare a math model with real-world statistics.

Approximate time required: 1 class period

Student grouping: Partners/Pairs

Activity Plan:
1. Launch Excel and set up a new worksheet with headings and formatting like the example at the top of page 250. (Hint: Double-click on the top of the vertical line between columns to fit column widths to your headings.) Enter no data yet.
2. Using Internet Explorer, go to http://www.census.gov/cgi-bin/ipc/popclockw and add it to your Favorites list.

3. Gather your class together, and ask what students know about vampires from movies, books, and TV shows. Kids will probably report such facts as vampires only come out at night, they sleep in coffins, they can turn into bats, they live forever, they drink blood to survive, and you become a vampire if you are bitten by one.

4. Tell students that they can now use mathematics to prove once and for all whether vampires really exist.

5. Write the assumptions below on the board. Be sure students understand them for the sake of the model.

ASSUMPTIONS

- One vampire does exist.
- That vampire must suck one person's blood each week to survive.
- Once a vampire bites a person, he or she becomes a vampire.

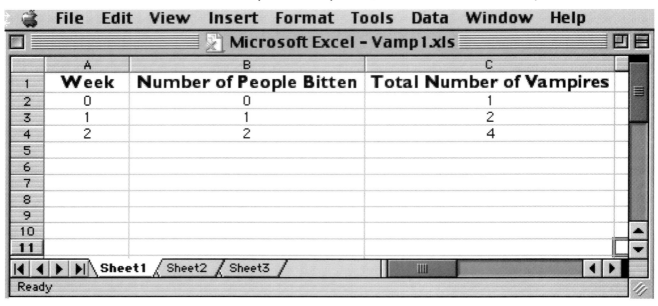

Week	Number of People Bitten	Total Number of Vampires
0	0	1
1	1	2
2	2	4

6. On your worksheet, type in the statistics for Week 0 as shown above. With your class, type in statistics for Week 1 (1 person bitten, 2 vampires at large) and Week 2 (2 more people bitten, 4 vamps on the prowl). Tell the students they will be responsible for filling in the rest.

7. Save the worksheet, divide your class into pairs, and have each pair work with a copy of the worksheet plus a photocopy of the Student Activity.

Student Activity: Description

Is math powerful enough to keep vampires away? Find out as you and your partner finish building the spreadsheet model your teacher started. What you discover may be shocking!

Step 1 — Bites Per Week

What to Do: Using the Excel worksheet your class started, work with your partner to fill in statistics through Week 8, using the following basic steps.

1. If there were 4 vampires at the end of Week 2, how many people would get bitten in Week 3? (4) And how many vampires would that make in total? (8)

2. How many people would those vampires bite in Week 4, creating how many more of their kind?

3. You get the idea now. Carry it through to the end of Week 8. How many bloodsuckers do you end up with? (256)

Step 2 — Graph Those Vamps!
What to Do:

1. Select your data in Column C, go to Insert, and choose Chart. Using Chart Wizard, select a type of chart that shows data over time. Click Finish.
2. Move your chart to the right side of your worksheet, so you can look at it side-by-side with your data. Create a graph to get a vivid picture of the vampire population boom.
3. What kind of trend does your chart show? Where might the pattern go from here?
4. Print your data sheet and your chart to have on hand for the next step.

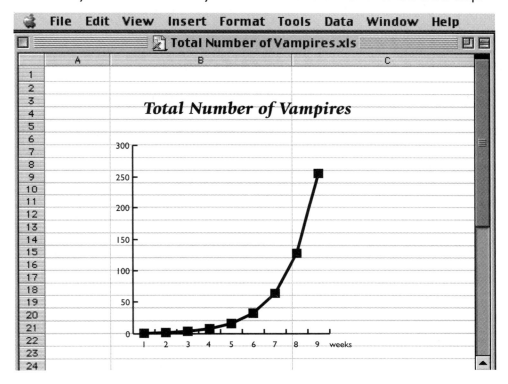

Step 3 — Formula, Bloody Formula
What to Do: Now you're going to get the computer to count seven more months' worth of vampires for you — in mere minutes!

1. Look again at your statistics through Week 8. In math terms, what is the relationship between vampires at the end of one week and the number of people bitten the next?
2. Here's another way of looking at it: What pattern do you see from week to week in the number of people bitten? What about the week-to-week vampire numbers?
3. With your partner, create a formula for Columns B and C in Week 9 (that's cell B11 and C11, respectively) that will extend the pattern of Weeks 0-8.
4. Implement your formula, and check to be sure that the pattern continues.
5. Now you can use Excel's AutoFill feature to complete your worksheet. For Column A, highlight cells A9 and A10, point to the "handle" in the lower right corner of A10, and drag it through A37.

6. Now fill in Column B by using AutoFill to drag the formula through week 35 (cell B37). Fill Column C by dragging the formula in C10 down through C37.

7. Format your vampire statistics by selecting Columns B and C, going to Format, choosing Cells, and selecting Numbers on the list. Type in 0 decimal places, and select Use 1000 Separator. Save your work.

8. How many vamps are there at the end of Week 35? If your formulas are correct, you should show 34,359,738,368. Say that number out loud: 34 billion, 359 million, 738 thousand, 368. That's a lot of living dead!

Step 4 — Vampire Reality Check

What to Do: So how does your vampire census match up against the actual world population? Here's how to find out. Check your worldwide vampire census against the real thing.

1. Launch Internet Explorer, and go to http://www.census.gov/cgi-bin/ipc/popclockw, the U.S. Census Bureau's World POP Clock. (Your teacher may have already added it to Favorites in Explorer.) This gives an up-to-the-second projected count of the world's human population, based on actual numbers plus estimated births and deaths.

2. What number is showing in bold type? It should be about six billion, give or take a few million. Select this number, go back to your Excel worksheet, and paste it into cell C38.

3. In cell D38, type in the label People on Earth.

4. Save and print your sheet.

5. Reconvene as a class to discuss your findings. According to your mathematical model, how many of the world's people are actually vampires? (Every single one of them — and then some!) At which point in your chart did the entire population of Planet Earth become vampirized? (Between Weeks 32 and 33.) Could this possibly be true? Congratulations! You have just constructed what mathematicians call a "proof by contradiction."

Sample Senior Learning Experience Plan

Activity Title:	Painting Portraits: Old Techniques and New Technology
Author:	Donna Ceci-Ward, Faculty of Education, University of Ottawa, 1999
Grade:	10
Subject & Strands:	Visual Arts: Theory, Creation, and Analysis

Expectations:

Theory:
Students will describe the steps of the design process in the creation of a self-portrait. They will explain how they incorporated qualities of artworks studied and mentioned in this lesson.

Creation: Students will produce a self-portrait meeting specific objectives, namely a representation of visual language used by an artist of their choice, studied previously for this lesson. They will use various strategies in creating these portraits and various forms of research. Students will make creative choices about their portraits that reflect the art of the historical period studied.

Analysis: Students will apply critical analysis to their portraits and the artwork studied. They will explain the significant expressive qualities of their portraits with reference to the categories of their chosen historic period.

IT component:
Students will use research from the Internet and CD-ROMs that provide information and aid in their understanding of the historic period of their choice, within the parameters set by the teacher (e.g., late nineteenth to early twentieth century). Recommended sites are listed at the end of this lesson. Students will also be using a paint program to draw their contour drawings on the computer and fill them in with colour to analyze formal composition and use of colour. Finally, in groups, they will combine their research and portraits to produce a word-processing document (or desk-top publishing presentation) that will be put together as a class.

Recommended software:
- CD-ROMs (e.g., Grolier's Encylopedia, Encarta, Art Gallery)
- Corel PhotoPaint 8 (or Adobe Illustrator 8)
- MSPaint or the Paint format in ClarisWorks or any simple paint program.
- Word-processing software (e.g., Word Perfect, ClarisWorks, MSWorks)

IT expectations:
Students will
- use current technologies both as research tools and as creative media.
- research from various sources using computer technology.
- use tools, materials, processes, and technologies safely and appropriately.
- demonstrate the ability to use an increasing range of tools, materials, processes, and technologies in producing works of fine art.

Prerequisite IT skills:
Students will have some familiarity with accessing the Internet. The teacher will guide them to the appropriate site and have specific tasks and questions for them to complete. For the MSPaint program basic computer skills are required. Some word-processing skills will be required to complete a document that will combine their portraits and research. As this will be a group endeavor, it is sufficient that each group has a student competent in this skill.

Demonstration of learning:
Students will use CD-ROMs and the Internet to find sources that will help them develop their visual images and to research historical works of art, pinpointing a specific artist and identifying certain elements they can incorporate into their own portrait. Finally, working in small groups, students will combine their efforts to produce a newsletter or booklet using word-processing or publishing software that will demonstrate their understanding of the particular style of the work of art that they have chosen to study and how it relates to their portrait (identifying elements of color, line, form, mood, expression, etc.).

Approximate time required:
This activity will take approximately seven (75-minute) lessons depending on the skill of the students with computer technology and the availability of computers.
- one class to research the historic period or artist from that period (with homework assignment).

- two classes to complete contour drawings by hand and on the computer.
- two classes to color in their computer drawings and print them out. (Teacher gives a short demo preferably with an example.)
- two or three classes to gather the information in groups, copy their paint portraits onto a word-processing document, write up the information (research should be done) for each portrait and print and save document.

Student grouping:

Initially, students will be working individually since these are personal expressions of their unique identity. Students will be paired in the lab to complete the first step using the paint program. Groups of two will be allowed for research on the Internet and CD-ROMs. Students will work in groups of four to complete two pages on a word-processing document and each group will collaborate to combine their efforts to complete the final document as a class project. Students are encouraged to help each other in the computer lab.

Activity Plan:

Prior to this lesson, the teacher will introduce, using a slide presentation, four movements in 19- and early 20th-century art. Discussion of styles and techniques and the power of expression in each movement, highlighting certain artists, is suggested. Students should have an understanding of the principles and elements of design. Before this lesson students will be asked to bring in or draw three or four objects that have meaning to them. Explain that they will be creating self-portraits, which is an artwork that "shows" the person who created it.

1. Students will be asked to choose one artist from the period discussed. They will research and report using the following criteria (one to two pages):
   - What is the artist's background?
   - Identify the artist's technique and philosophy.
   - Analyze a work of the artist; include reference to principles and elements of design.
   - What are your own feelings about the artist's work and what would you like to express in your own portrait?

2. Students will draw self-portraits using mirrors. Using a contour line, they will trace the outside and inside lines of their faces. Encourage them to use the whole page and as many lines as they can to describe their face. They should only look briefly at the page when drawing.

3. Using the objects that they have chosen to represent them, ask them to draw them on a separate piece of paper using contour lines.
4. In the computer lab, using a paint program, have the students draw their portrait from their contour line drawings and include the objects that they drew separately. They will have a line drawing of themselves on the screen with the objects arranged in an order that best represents their chosen style. The students will be asked to think about the elements of this style because it will be important for the next step.
5. Using a paint program, the students will now fill in their drawings with the colors that best reflect the style they have chosen. (For example, a reflection of Gauguin may be a portrait with clear, bright colors, but they will not be required to imitate the artist's style exactly). The teacher will guide and facilitate the progress of each student. Each student will save his/her work on a disk.

6. Back in class have the students write two or three sentences on how they feel about the style of their chosen artist and what they have expressed in their own self-portrait.

7. In groups of four, the students will create two pages on a word-processed document with their portraits from the paint program and their written descriptions of their artist and their portrait (two per page). Save and print. The entire class will compile these pages and create a title page. All pages can be combined into one booklet or displayed separately.

Extensions/differentiation:

An extension of this lesson would be to input the students' faces directly into the computer using a scanner or digital camera. The saved images are put into a folder. The students research and find a portrait that has meaning to them and these are also scanned and put into a separate folder. The students superimpose their faces over the scanned reproductions using a paint program and blend one into another using the eyedropper tool. Or they can manipulate the color on their digitized photos to create an expressive color portrait. Completed images are mounted next to their word-processing documents and displayed.

Another extension would be to use the images that the students create and compile a stack in Hyperstudio where each student makes a card with their portrait and an explanation of colors or style used. (This may accompany music if desired.)

For exceptional students, the portrait lesson can be extended to the creation of a collage type of image of their self-portrait using a variety of images and/or materials. Using advanced software they can combine images with photos and perhaps sound or turn it into a video presentation.

Resources:

ArtTeacher Connection Homepage:
http://www.inficad.com/arted/pages/portech.html

Bryant, Mary Helen. *Integrating Technology into the Curriculum.* Westminster, California: Teacher Created Materials, Inc., 1996.

Tillander, Michelle. "To Compute or not to Compute." *Arts and Activities,* November, 1996, pp. 16–19.

Pintura: Art Detective: An interactive art history site that informs and tests students' knowledge in a fun and mysterious way!
http://www.eduweb.com/pintura/a4.html

Inside Art: Takes a look at certain works of art, contains learning modules.
http://www.eduweb.com/adventure.html

Art History Resources on the Web
http://witcombe.sbc.edu/ARTHlinks.html

National Portrait Gallery, Washington D.C.
http://www.npg.si.edu/

Sanford's — A Lifetime of Colour: Teacher resources and techniques, lessons, portrait analysis, etc.
http://www.sanford-artedventures.com/
http://www.sanford-artedventures.com/create/tech_wrong_portrait3.html

The Metropolitan Museum of Art
http://www.metmuseum.org/htmlfile/education/portrait.html

Ontario Public District School Board Writing Partnership Course Profile, Visual Arts: Phase 1 Working Document, page xv.

SAMPLE ACCEPTABLE USE POLICY (AUP)

An AUP does not have to be a long, complicated document. It may simply state your educational goals, your school rules, and the consequences of breaking them. This sample comes from Holy Redeemer Catholic School, an elementary school in Kanata, Ontario.

Internet Use Agreement

Internet access is now available to all Junior level students at Holy Redeemer Catholic School. We are very pleased to offer this tool as a valuable resource to both students and teachers for the purpose of conducting research. Students will now have ready access to thousands of libraries and databases.

All Junior level students will receive Internet inservicing which focuses on safety issues as well as how to navigate the Internet to search for information for school-based projects. While we acknowledge that we cannot control the vast amount of information which is available on the Internet, every effort has been taken toward providing for online safety. The Holy Redeemer web site contains a *Resource Center* which includes *links* (or Internet web sites) which are based on classroom curriculum. Each of those links has been previewed for suitable use by students. When it is necessary to search for a particular topic, we will be making use of *Yahooligans*, a search engine specifically developed for students. We invite students and parents to read the "Conditions of Internet Use" section below. Both student and parent signatures are required for students to access the Internet.

Internet Terms and Conditions

1. Students are responsible for their own behavior on school computers. General school rules for behavior in keeping with the Holy Redeemer **Behavior Code** apply.

2. The Internet is provided for students to conduct research. Access to the Internet is granted to students who agree to conduct themselves in a responsible manner. Access is a privilege. Inappropriate use or behavior on the part of an individual will result in **cancellation** of Internet **privileges** for the **remainder** of the **year**.

Inappropriate Use or Behavior Consists Of:
- intentionally damaging computers
- attempting to download printing from the Internet without teacher permission
- consistently not attending to teacher instructions
- attempting to access inappropriate sites

(Please detach and return the bottom portion.)

STUDENT SECTION

I have read the Holy Redeemer Internet Use Agreement. I agree to follow the rules contained in this document. I understand that if I violate any of these rules, I will lose my Internet privileges for the remainder of the school year, and I may face other disciplinary measures.

Student's Name (please print) _____ Grade _____

Student's Signature _____ Date _____

PARENT OR GUARDIAN SECTION

As the parent or legal guardian of the student signing above, I have read the Internet Use Agreement and grant permission for my son or daughter to access the Internet. I understand that Internet access is designed for educational purposes. I also understand that Holy Redeemer cannot be held responsible for sites that are deemed as inappropriate but that Holy Redeemer staff have taken every precaution within their power to provide for online safety. I understand that my son or daughter will be held responsible for violations.

Parent Name (please print) _____ Date _____

Parent Signature _____

Commonly Asked Questions About Rubrics

Q. Should a rubric be created for every task?
A. No, rubrics are one form of assessment and like all other assessment strategies are appropriate for some tasks and not others. Rubrics that assess the skills involved in writing are very useful for both student and teacher; however, for other tasks such as multiplying numbers, more traditional marking schemes may be more appropriate.

Q. Will the use of rubrics lead to greater reliability in assessment?
A. Yes, rubrics will bring about greater reliability in assessment because the rubric clearly defines the assessment criteria for teacher, students, and parents. Having a clearly defined criteria will lead to a common understanding of the nature of high-quality performance. It defines what quality work looks like.

Q. Are there different types of rubrics?
A. All rubrics are based on specific criteria and levels of performance. The nature of the task will dictate if the rubric is more specific or comprehensive. A rubric could be used for a specific task such as letter writing and look at the parts of the business letter, its layout, language choice, and organization. The descriptors in this rubric would be very detailed. A rubric for a culminating performance task would provide feedback on the demonstration of a number of skills and therefore would be more comprehensive in nature.

For additional information on the use of rubrics, consult the following Web sites.

Automating Authentic Assessment with Rubrics from Florida's Brevard County Schools — one district's plan for implementing technology, the Newton Message Pad and rubrics. This site focuses on the rubric, making recommendations for its construction. It also looks at computerized assessment. http://stone.web.brevard.k12.fl.us/html/comprubric.html

A consortium called CLASS: Center on Learning Assessment and School Structure headed by Grant Wiggins. It features a bulletin board forum on the use of rubrics titled Ask Dr. Rubric. http://www.classnj.org/

Commonly Asked Questions About Assessment and Evaluation

Q. How do I incorporate both process and product in the assessment?

A. It is possible to incorporate both product and process in assessment. A variety of templates that include checklists, charts, and/or rubrics can focus attention on the desired skills and knowledge that are process and/or product based.

Q. How do I know if I my program is balanced in the area of assessment?

A A balanced assessment program has a variety of assessment methods. It will include assessment of product, process, and performance. It will include opportunities for self-, peer, and teacher assessment. A balanced program ensures that all steps have been taken to see if the student has attained the desired outcomes of the task.

Q. When would I use self-assessment?

A. Self-assessment can be used any time. Students will require training and guidance in assessing their work. The availability of assessment tools such as the rubric makes the task easier by specifying exactly the desired characteristics. Be sure that the questions required in self-assessment are in keeping with the maturity level of the students.

Q. How do I encourage the fair assessment by the student's peers?

A. Students will require practice in the assessment of one another's work. Products will be easiest for them to assess and the presence of clearly defined criteria will focus attention on the quality of the product. Discussion of given exemplars is also beneficial in the assessment of their peer's work.

Q. There are times when I want a number of students to produce a group product. How do I make the assessment fair to all members of the group?

A. The first step is to make sure that the expectations are clear to all group members. The development of joint rubrics and the discussion that revolves around the development will help to clarify the expectations. The teacher could make self- and peer assessment a part of the procedure and this will give the students a sense of ownership. Predetermined tasks ensure that all students contribute to the task. In addition, teacher observation of the group at work can encourage all members to "pull their own weight."

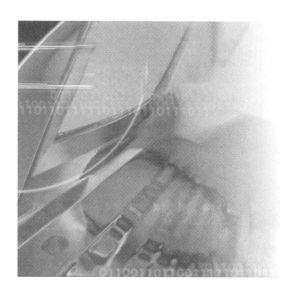

INDEX